STATE TRADING IN INTERNATIONAL MARKETS

State trading is most frequently associated with exports and imports of the COMECON countries. However, state trading by the developing and industrialized countries accounts for an even more significant portion of international trade than that generated by the COMECON countries. This 'western' state trading is seen to be gaining in importance and it is surprising that so little has been written by economists and others on the subject.

This book on state trading in developing and industrialized countries is a collection of papers dealing with some of the essential problems of state trading from the perspective of international commodity markets, international trade theory, economic development and international trade order. Such a diversity of aspects, which had to be necessarily considered in order to assess state trading, called for a multi-disciplinary team of scholars. This team, therefore, enables the study to take stock of the thinking on state trading and to attempt policy recommendations taking into account not only economic but managerial, legal and political aspects as well.

The study identifies, first, the essential mechanics of state trading in developing and industrialized countries, examines considerations motivating the maintenance of state trading operations, and assesses their importance by country and by commodity groups.

A special effort is made to unify economic analysis with institutional interactions (government contracts, plan targets, managerial constraints, political pressures, etc.). In a wider perspective, an assessment can be made as to whether specific state-trading techniques are first-, second- or third-best devices to achieve a given set of external and/or internal objectives.

The analysis of state trading in international commodity markets concludes with an assessment of the advantages and disadvantages of state trading for producer and consumer countries. Particular attention is paid to state trading as a means of assuring developing countries access to foreign markets in a number of commodities, given the structural adjustment problems that exist in the major developed countries.

M. M. Kostecki, the editor, is Associate Professor of Economics at the Ecole des Hautes Etudes Commerciales (HEC), University of Montreal. His previous appointment was in the field of operations research and mathematical economics at the University of Zurich. He holds an MA in economics from the Central School of Planning and Statistics in Warsaw and obtained his doctorate from the Graduate Institute of International Studies, University of Geneva.

He is the author of *East-West Trade and the GATT System* and has contributed articles to major journals of international economics and commercial policy.

State Trading in International Markets

Theory and Practice of Industrialized and Developing Countries

Edited by
M. M. Kostecki

St. Martin's Press   New York

ISBN 0–312–75693–3

Library of Congress Cataloging in Publication Data

Main entry under title:

State trading in international markets.

    Bibliography: p. 192
    Includes index.
    1. Commercial policy — Congresses. I. Kostecki, M. M.
HF1410.5.S7   1981   382′.3   81–2417
ISBN 0–312–75693–3   AACR2

Contents

The Contributors

Ivan Bernier
Professor of Law
Law Faculty
Laval University
Quebec

Jean-Emile Denis
Associate Professor of Business Administration
Ecole des Hautes Etudes Commerciales de Montréal
University of Montreal

Robert H. Floyd
Senior Economist
IMF
Washington

M. M. Kostecki
Associate Professor of Economics
Ecoles des Hautes Etudes Commerciales (HEC)
University of Montreal

Walter C. Labys
Professor of Economics
College of Mineral and Energy Resources
West Virginia University
Morgantown

P. J. Lloyd
Professor of Economics
Department of Economics
The Australian National University
Canberra

Harriet Matejka
Associate Professor of Economics
Graduate Institute of International Studies
University of Geneva

Alex F. McCalla
Professor of Agricultural Economics
University of California
Davis

Klaus Netter
Senior Economic Affairs Officer
UNCTAD
Geneva

Øystein Noreng
Professor of Business Administration
Oslo Institute of Business Administration

Frieder Roessler
Senior Officer
GATT Secretariat
Geneva

Andrew Schmitz
Professor of Agricultural and Resource Economics
University of California
Berkeley

Klaus Stegemann
Associate Professor of Economics
Department of Economics
Queen's University
Kingston

Raymond Vernon
Herbert F. Johnson Professor of International Business Management
Graduate School of Business Administration
Harvard University

List of Tables

List of Figures

Abbreviations

CIF	Cost insurance freight
COMECON (CMEA)	Council of Mutual Economic Assistance
EEC	European Economic Community
EFTA	European Free Trade Association
FOB	Free on board
GATT	General Agreement on Tariffs and Trade
IBRD	International Bank for Reconstruction and Development
IMF	International Monetary Fund
ITC	International Tin Council
ITO	International Trade Organization
ITC	International Trade Commission
MFN	Most-favoured nation treatment
MMC	Multinational Mining Companies
OECD	Organization for Economic Cooperation and Development
OEEC	Organization for European Economic Cooperation
OPEC	Oganization of Petroleum Exporting Countries
PMB	Public Marketing Board
STO	State Trading Organization
UNCTAD	United Nations Conference on Trade and Development

Acknowledgements

This book is a collaborative work, an outgrowth of much interchanging of perspectives and findings among the editor, those who have contributed some of the other chapters, and a number of additional scholars who gave so generously of their advice.

We are all very grateful for the inspiration we received from W. M. Corden of the Australian National University and from Raymond Vernon of Harvard University, who encouraged us to initiate this research project.

A major portion of these papers was presented at a conference held at the Ecole des Hautes Etudes Commerciales (HEC) of the University of Montreal in April 1979.

We would also like to thank the HEC, the Ford Foundation and the Social Sciences and Humanities Research Council of Canada for their financial support.

We are especially indebted to the Centre for International Business Studies at the HEC; its director, André Poirier; and its administrator, Sylvia Toledano, who lent so much assistance in organizing this endeavour.

Finally, I would like to thank Bonnie Darves-Bornoz and Sybil Denis, who edited a major portion of the manuscript; and Violet Jackson, who typed the entire text.

None of the persons mentioned above can be held accountable for any of the opinions and facts set forth in this study. That responsibility belongs to the authors, and to myself.

M. M. KOSTECKI

Introduction

Raymond Vernon

Some thirty years ago, the governments representing the principal trading countries of that period were assembled in Havana to frame a charter for a global trade organization. Although the period was one of anxieties and uncertainties, the emphasis at the time was on building anew, on avoiding the errors and conflicts of the past. It was a time, therefore, that lent itself to hope, yet a period that could easily lead to error and to illusion.

As far as the leading countries of that period were concerned, the hope of the majority was to achieve an open trading system, in which barriers to trade would be low and in which those that existed would be applied without discrimination against any particular source or market. This view was not universal, any more than it is universal today; then, as now, there were governments that had misgivings about the desirability of such a system, on the grounds that it might produce a distribution of income and power – both within countries and between countries – which was socially undesirable. Despite such misgivings, however, the goal of the open trading system prevailed, and with it went the related assumption that the markets in the system would be created mainly by commercial buyers and sellers, each constrained by its costs and each striving for a profit.

The governments that were drafting and negotiating this new world order of course were aware – indeed, acutely aware – of the fact that much of the world's trade was being conducted on a different basis. Governments were deeply involved in international trade in numerous ways, including the imposition of discriminatory tariffs and quotas, the payment of subsidies, and the conduct of state trading. But tariffs and quotas, it was supposed, could be brought down to tolerable levels and applied on a non-discriminatory basis; subsidies could be held in

1

check; state traders could conceivably agree to act as if they were commercial traders, buying and selling in the same way as a profit-maximizing firm.

Some of the hopes of those negotiators of thirty years ago, as it turned out, came remarkably close to realization. Tariffs and quotas were greatly reduced, at least in trade in manufactured goods among the advanced industrialized countries, and a beginning was made on the control of subsidies. But the early hopes for some sort of agreement on the practices of state-trading firms went nowhere. In the light of thirty years' subsequent experience, the approach that was devised at the time for dealing with state-trading enterprises now appears unrealistic.

Perhaps the first major challenge to the hopes of those that would have reduced state trading to an ordinary commercial activity came from the agricultural programmes of the advanced industrialized states. Governments in many of these countries had developed programmes for stabilizing and supplementing the income of their farmers, and had created state-trading agencies to carry out some part of those programmes. These state traders in agricultural products usually exercised control over competing imports, acted as discriminating monopolists in the export of products, and drew on the support of the public treasury whenever their costs exceeded their revenues. Operating under an explicit mandate from their governments, these agencies as a rule had no great difficulty in resisting the application of the general trade principles to their situations.

The advanced industrialized countries were the source of a second challenge as well. Government procurement practices have rarely been altogether free of discrimination in favour of domestic interests; and until very recently, the agreements of governments have done little to alter that basic condition. Accordingly, wherever state-owned enterprises existed, they could be expected to tilt their purchases and sales in favour of national interests. This tendency was particularly apparent whenever the transactions were associated with high technology or with the national defence.

Yet another major challenge came from the developing countries. These countries, of course, saw many things in the new trade rules that seemed out of keeping with their stage of development. In particular, any undertaking to restrain their state-trading enterprises seemed especially inappropriate to their circumstances.

There were various reasons why the developing countries resisted any limitations on the powers of their state-trading firms. For one thing, many developing countries had considerable misgivings about the general efficacy and superiority of a market economy, and many were prepared to experiment with the extensive use of controls. Many developing countries – emulating some of the more industrialized countries – established state-trading entities to perform some of the taxing and subsidizing and price-stabilizing functions that would otherwise have been assigned to the government ministries. Finally, even those countries that were prepared eventually to assign an important role to open markets and market prices in their national economies commonly had the feeling that a period of state trading might be needed before indigenous enterprises were in a position to be exposed to foreign competitors. In the meantime, governments had no desire to hamper their young enterprises with any agreed restraints.

Still another source of challenge came from the socialist centrally-directed economies. Some of these, in the interests of maintaining control, preferred to conduct their trade in balanced bilateral deals with their trading partners; in such cases, it was fruitless to require state-trading entities to choose their sources and markets on a non-discriminatory commercial basis. Moreover, practically all of these countries conducted their foreign trade through channels that insulated their internal price structure from the structure of world prices. In cases of this sort, efforts to constrain state traders by analogizing their trading mark-ups to tariffs had no operational meaning.

In the thirty years since this first abortive attempt to include state-trading firms in the rules of an international trading system, the international transactions conducted by such firms have expanded considerably. As the various articles in this volume demonstrate, state-trading enterprises are now to be found operating out of many countries in many different commodities. Moreover, as governments have expanded the number and variety of their enterprises in manufacturing, mining, and services, the international trade conducted by such firms has grown commensurately. The result is that, in some products, including wheat, copper, oil, and aircraft, state-owned enterprises are today a major factor in international markets.

The growth of such trade raises new questions about the adequacy of the existing rules of the game. Questions of this sort have been appearing for other reasons as well. Ironically, the very success of governments in promoting large increases in world trade over the past thirty years has been partly responsible for the new uncertainties. Some governments dare not open their economies any further, for fear of imposing unacceptable burdens of adjustment inside the economy; but at the same time, most governments are loath to pull back for fear of losing foreign markets and adding to domestic costs. Practically all governments recognize that if international trade is to continue to widen the opportunities and reduce the costs of trading countries, the rules will have to accommodate more complex principles than have heretofore governed. Accordingly, governments seem to be edging into an era which will see a major reconsideration of the rules of the trading game.

In devising a new set of rules to govern the behaviour of state-trading enterprises, there is no flinching from one overwhelming fact. These enterprises are characteristically engaged in the kind of activities that straddle the line between domestic policies and foreign policies. The taxing function and the trading function for instance are often interrelated; efforts to redistribute national income through the internal price system also have their direct impact on international trade. The intertwining of sensitive domestic issues with foreign policy issues poses an especially difficult challenge for devising an acceptable set of international institutions and rules of the game.

To deal with this challenge effectively, the international community will have to know much more than it presently knows about motivations, behaviour, and consequences of the operations of state-trading enterprises. Moreover, much of what is available is easily subject to misinterpretation. Because such enterprises are commonly used by governments to dispense subsidies to some target group inside the national economy, the meaning of reported losses has not always been easy to interpret. Because others are tax collectors for their governments, the meaning of reported profits has sometimes been just as obscure. The fact that governments often use such enterprises in the execution of bilateral trade deals, or in programmes of domestic protection, has tended to confuse the trade policies of the governments with the predilections of the enterprises themselves. On the other hand, the fact that ambitious managers of state enterprises have sometimes struck off for themselves on highly independent entrepreneurial adventures has led some observers to believe that state traders if left to themselves would be indistinguishable from private traders.

When governments eventually turn to the problem of devising new rules of the game for state enterprises, their general positions will inevitably be affected by the way in which they look upon economic systems in the large, that is, by their economic ideology. The challenge will be to try to find a *modus vivendi* that accommodates a number of distinctively different ideologies, so that nations can continue to benefit from some of the undisputed advantages of international exchange and so that those benefits can be equitably shared. To achieve that result will require at least two things: an extraordinary measure of mutual tolerance on the part of the negotiators; and an understanding in depth of the characteristics and consequences of the operations of state-trading firms. No single volume of essays will provide that understanding, but this volume represents a strong beginning.

1 State Trading by the Advanced and Developing Countries: the Background

M. M. Kostecki [1]

DEFINITION

State trading occurs when a government or a government-backed agency determines the essential terms (including prices or quantities) on which exports and imports have to take place. This definition emphasizes the role of government control, since it is, primarily, this direct control that makes state traders behave differently from private ones. And it is this distinctive behaviour which is at the heart of the 'problem of state trading'.

Under private trading, imports and exports take place on terms defined by private exporters and importers. The state authorities who collect duties impose quantitative restrictions, etc., are distinct from the traders themselves. More or less competitive private traders compare domestic with foreign prices, and either refrain from or engage in foreign-trade activities. Governments interfere with these activities basically through instruments of trade control which either affect price relations (tariffs, subsidies) or impose direct limits on quantities traded (quotas, licences). Within that framework, the private traders determine the baskets of traded goods, their prices, direction of trade and the logistic terms of transactions. A trader's freedom to choose, guided by the profit motive, is either limited or non-existent under state trading.

State trading has also been defined in the literature in terms other than the state-control factor. These generally include:

6

(a) public property;
(b) public management;
(c) public grant of exclusive rights; or
(d) most typical functions for which state trading has been main-
    tained.

Let us briefly discuss these criteria for defining state trading and explain why they are not appropriate for the needs of this study.

The first temptation is to define state trading by relying on public ownership as its distinctive characteristic. State trading would then mean the exports and imports of trading units wholly or mainly owned by the state. Although this definition might be convenient for sampling purposes, it has the basic drawback of not saying anything about state trading's objective functions and constraints, which this study attempts to examine.

State trading could also be defined as foreign trade conducted under public management, the latter including both the activities of government bureaucrats, as well as those of state-appointed and -controlled executives. The distinction between private and public management certainly may be a relevant criterion in identifying specific behaviour patterns in the foreign-trade business. Public management may be justifiably labelled less profit-oriented, more influenced by political environment, more bureaucratic and more responsive both to its various publics (e.g. trade unions) and to the pressure of informal government instructions. This definition could thus be useful to those concerned with the managerial characteristics of state trading. Even though this managerial dimension (of some concern below) may be a supplementary one, it is, none the less, far from sufficient if the essential mechanics of state trading as an instrument of state control and its international implications are to be clarified.

Some authors have attempted to define state trading by emphasizing the state monopoly aspect of the foreign trade enterprise.[2] Here, state trading signifies foreign trade conducted by trading units enjoying the exclusive and state-enforced right to trade in a given range of products. Although monopoly may be a typical aspect of state trading, it assuredly is not a necessary one. Indeed, many state-trading enterprises that have to compete with private business or public units can be used as instruments of trade control. Moreover, as will be shown below, the monopoly dimension is often implicit in many forms of state trading, as defined on the basis of the state-control criterion, and need not be spelled out in the definition.

Any effort to define state trading in terms of the functions it performs will also meet with important objections. State trading is one among many methods of government intervention in foreign trade. Consequently, the objectives for which it is pursued are not necessarily distinct from those aimed at by trade control measures over private trading.

The definition based on the criterion of direct government control thus provides the best starting point for our discussions. It is convenient for analysing the role of state trading in international commodity markets and dealing with state trading in the context of international trade theory. The government control element is also a central issue of several other chapters in this volume. The cases which necessitate specific analytical needs or sampling requirements call for a slightly different definition, and are explicitly indicated below.

TAXONOMY OF STATE-TRADING ARRANGEMENTS

In characterizing state-trading arrangements for the purpose of economic analysis, three aspects appear to be particularly important:

- (*a*) specific operational criteria imposed on state traders;
- (*b*) existence of central instructions directly determining the terms of foreign-trade transactions; and
- (*c*) maintenance, by the state, of a foreign-trade monopoly on a particular product.

Operational criteria (C). Private traders, presumably, are profit maximizers. Although the maximization of aggregate profit also characterizes a large number of state traders, some other operational criteria are frequently imposed on them. Governments may force the state traders to work on fixed profit margins (including a zero margin). They may also instruct them to maximize unitary export receipts or to minimize unitary import spendings, etc. The possibility that state traders' pricing rules will differ from those characteristic of private traders is, thus, an important economic point (Lloyd, Chapter 6, and Stegemann, Chapter 8 in this volume).

Central directives (D). Under state trading, the directives from the government (or a government-backed agency) may take the form of a particular quantity rule, compulsory pricing or other instructions referring to, for example, so-called logistic terms of transactions. Under state trading, direct instructions are, thus, another means of setting up the terms on which imports and exports must take place. Central directives may determine the level of trade, direction of trade, export prices, etc. and so implement policies of protection and discrimination. The use of these methods of government control peculiar to state trading creates important problems in international trade, a point which is extensively discussed in several chapters below.

Monopoly (M). State-trading units frequently benefit from the exclusive right, granted to them by the state, to import and export a given range of products. The monopoly element may be a necessary companion to government action which fixes a pricing rule or issues central directives (if the latter are to become effective instruments of a country's commercial policy). The monopoly privilege may enable the state-trading unit to exploit monopolistic or oligopolistic positions in the domestic market. Occasionally, it helps the state to establish a price-making power or to improve its bargaining position in the international market. The existence of the state monopoly in foreign trade is also, therefore, an intrinsic issue, since it may result in a higher degree of protection and discrimination or achieve better terms of trade than would be attainable, *ceteris paribus*, in its absence.

State-trading arrangements may feature the inclusion of one of the elements described above or a combination of two or three elements. Depending on the nature of these state-imposed characteristics, seven types of state-trading arrangement can be formally distinguished: *CDM*, *CD*, *CM*, *DM*, *C*, *D*, and *M*.

All of these types may be recognized among the state-trading arrangements maintained by the industrialized and developing countries.

State-trading institutions may be classified in three large categories, according to the type of foreign-trade function performed:

(a) trading agencies;
(b) regulatory agencies; and
(c) mixed agencies.

Trading agencies comprise a large variety of operational government departments, foreign-trade enterprises, public producing and trading enterprises, and statutory marketing boards operating in international markets. Units fully integrated into the government administration might be placed at one end of the spectrum. In Japan, for example, the distribution monopoly for the opium required for scientific and medical purposes is operated by a department of the Ministry of Health and Welfare. Similarly, the National Import and Export Office of Laos carries the responsibility for trading in items essential to the survival of poor segments of the population and constitutes an integral part of the Department of National Economy.

At the other end of the spectrum might be placed units clearly distinct from the government itself, but obviously sustained by government compulsory power. Thanks to government backing, numerous statutory marketing boards are able to run foreign-trade monopolies in particular agricultural products, and their operation is directly controlled by state authorities. Governments are frequently major subscribers to the capital stocks of producing or distributive enterprises with foreign-trade activities, interfering with those activities through the C, D or M link. Note, however, that the nationalization of such enterprises does not necessarily lead to a sufficient degree of government control which would make them state traders in the sense defined above.[3]

Finally, a large number of state-trading organizations are operated by the advanced and developing countries. These strongly resemble the foreign-trade institutions typical of the centrally-planned economies. The State Trading Corporation of India and the State Fishing Equipment Corporation in Norway provide examples of the most frequent form of such organizations – state-trading corporations registered as limited liability companies. Foreign-trade enterprises, such as the Indonesian Bhaktis, and many of the Egyptian or Syrian state-trading units, representative of the developing countries, closely follow the same pattern.

Regulatory agencies. One finds a large variety of regulatory state-trading institutions specifically involved in international commodity trading. Governments often prefer to dictate the terms on which foreign-trade transactions take place, leaving the execution of particular export and import deals to private traders. As a result, private traders most frequently act as agents of the government or of a government-backed entity and assume responsibilities for the operational part of trading. The functioning of regulatory agencies may be reduced to any of the three types of government inputs defined above (C, D, M). A good example of this type of agency is the Federal Wheat Administration in Switzerland, which holds the import monopoly on bread-flour for the Swiss market. A large number of the regulatory marketing boards in the present and former British Dominion could be classified under this heading (see Kostecki, Chapter 2 and McCalla and Schmitz Chapter 3 in this volume). Finally, an increasing number of regulatory offices guide commercialization of exports in some essential raw materials (e.g. oil, coal, metals) and determine the 'terms' of transactions for trade handled essentially by private traders.

Mixed agencies. In many instances, it is difficult to classify state-trading arrangements as either trading or regulatory agencies. This is often due as much to the diversity of the agency's function as to the variety among the commodities traded. More frequently, the difficulty hinges upon the fact that the responsibility for executing foreign-trade deals is equally shared by the agency in question and private traders. It is a fact that the channelling of international trade flows frequently involves state traders, multinational companies, or other private intermediaries. In the conduct of foreign trade, the state and private hands are, for the most part, so closely clasped that it is impossible to tell which is which. The list of agricultural state-trading arrangements included in the GATT sample shows that a major portion of them falls into the category of mixed agencies.

IMPORTANCE OF STATE TRADING BY INDUSTRIALIZED AND DEVELOPING COUNTRIES

The quantitative importance of international state trading generated by the industrialized and developing countries is difficult to measure for two reasons. First, it is impossible to collect a representative sample of such trading which is acceptable to all. The phenomenon lacks a clear-cut definition and its complexity makes it an elusive object of observation. Any attempt to compose such a sample would require examination not only of individual state-trading institutions, but also of individual commodity arrangements or even foreign-trade deals. The systematization of state trading would also imply a significant margin of arbitrary evaluation to decide whether any specific form of government control effectively allows government to set the essential terms of transactions.

Secondly, it is difficult to acquire the relevant statistics necessary, since internationally available sources refer to countries and/or commodities rather than to specific traders or trade deals. Nevertheless, the data available do emphasize the significance of state trading in the international trade of the industrialized and developing countries.

State trading is a particularly important occurrence in the international trade of agricultural products. Professors McCalla and Schmitz report that, in the four-year period, 1973 to 1977, more than 95 per cent of world wheat trade involved state traders as exporters, importers or both (Chapter 3). The estimation made in the preceding chapter for Western trade in all agricultural products shows that, in the mid-seventies, at least 27–8 per cent of OECD agricultural exports and imports were conducted under state-trading arrangements (Chapter 2).

State trading is also common in the international trade of mineral resources. The number of state traders in the international metal markets (especially, copper, tin and bauxite), increased during the last decade. Professor Walter Labys shows that the present share of such markets supplied under state-trading arrangements varied from 21–31 per cent, with the buyer's share being somewhat lower (Chapter 4).

A considerable expansion of state trading took place in the case of oil, especially in the wake of the OPEC policies of the early seventies and the concomitant moves in advanced countries to assure adequate access to oil supplies. It is very likely that, during the coming years, the role of multinational oil companies will be further restricted and the power of state traders expanded.

Strong elements of state trading (though present in somewhat less clearly defined terms) exist in the international steel trade. Note that the situation is quite different among the exporters of iron ore, probably because this sector is not plagued by the serious adjustment problems of steel which led to strong government intervention.

In the international trade of the industrial products of advanced market economies, the role of state trading seems to be considerably limited. However, even there, special attention should be paid to exports of industrial products handled under bilateral aid agreements. Indeed, government power in determining the terms on which such flows take place has been increasing. Note, for example, the various arrangements which have arisen from the ambitious plans of the Lomé Convention for industrial cooperation between EEC and Third-World countries.

State-trading arrangements, both for trade in commodities and manufactured goods, play a particularly important role in the foreign trade systems of developing countries (Netter, Chapter 10 in this volume). Several developing countries (e.g. Algeria, Iraq) are now utilizing quasi-state-trading foreign-trade systems. Many others rely heavily on state trading to channel exports of primary products, to administer foreign aid and, in some cases, to promote exports of manufactured products.[4]

It can be reasonably estimated that not less than 10–15 per cent of the international trade of developed and developing countries (not including government procurements) is susceptible to classification as state trading in the sense of our definition.[5] The amount of 'western' state trading in international markets is thus quantitatively four to six times greater than the exports and imports generated by the centrally-planned economies when dealing with partners outside the COMECON area.

State trading by the industrialized and developing countries is likely to gain importance during the next decade. That trend will probably be the outcome of the following factors:

— governments' desire to control extraction and exports of some raw materials;
— necessity to assure stable access to supplies of some resource goods by long-term inter-governmental contracts (e.g. oil);
— governments' desire to boost exports while managing troubled domestic industries or engaging in industrial cooperation with Third-World countries;
— growing pressure from farmers lobbying in some developing countries (e.g. Canada) to redistribute wealth and employment for their benefit.[6]

Even so, there is no reason to predict any significant proliferation of state trading, assuming, of course, that the major advanced and developing countries do not make substantial alterations in their nationalization policies.

STATE TRADING VERSUS TAXES AND SUBSIDIES

International trade theory. State trading, as defined here, is one method of government control among many, and can therefore be evaluated under the economic assignment theory. State-trading techniques can then be compared with other better known intervention measures and the problem of their equivalence or non-equivalence for the chosen market situations considered.

Peter Lloyd chooses to examine the question of that equivalence by comparing a state-trading monopoly's specific, government-imposed pricing rules with a set of *ad valorem* taxes-subsidies levied on competitive private traders (Chapter 6). Another approach to the problems of equivalence, not developed extensively in this volume, might be to make a comparison between taxes-subsidies or quotas and government-imposed quantitative foreign trade targets. Harriet Matejka looks at state trading as an object and/or instrument of trade control (using a slightly different definition) compatible with the requirements of the first-best trade intervention (Chapter 7). Both argue that the equivalence between state trading and other government intervention measures may be proven for the market solutions they have considered. They also specify some special economic conditions under which that equivalence does not hold, but these reservations are of little help in explaining the extent of state trading. From the trade theory point of view, state trading appears, essentially, to be a method of government intervention alternative to the imposing of taxes and subsidies on competitive traders. The reason why governments so frequently prefer state trading to these latter measures of trade control is difficult to explain within the realm of trade theory.

More than a quarter of a century ago, Professor Jacob Viner anticipated this problem and asked whether there could be any relevant general theory of international trade in a world of state trading and central planning.[7] In order to give a positive answer to that question, an effort must be made to find a broader approach to the theoretical issues of international trade. Nowhere has the need for political economic analysis of trade barriers been so great as in the case of state trading.

Political choice. The choice of government intervention instruments, as well as policies implemented through them, may be elucidated by looking at government decision-making. Governments, when formulating their economic policies, are not so much guided by economic rationality as by a desire to maximize political support and minimize political opposition.[8] Accordingly, in choosing between state trading and taxes-subsidies, government is not so much influenced by the desire to maximize economic efficiency and national welfare as by the desire to preserve a favourable balance of political forces.

A strong explicatory element in such an approach has already been elucidated by efforts to deal with the tariff structure of some developed countries.[9] As far as state trading is concerned, the necessity for such an approach is clearly confirmed by the findings of this volume.

Indeed, state trading is frequently preferred to taxes-subsidies schemes for redistributing income among different groups because it is more covert and, as such, less likely to give rise to political protest.

The issue of political rivalry ensuing from a conflict of producer and consumer interests, as related to particular state trading arrangements, could also be analysed from the perspective of the economics of information. State trading tends to be more complex, and the evaluation of its real economic costs and benefits for individual interest groups more difficult to ascertain. In terms of analytical framework and the statistical evidence required, a taxes-subsidies scheme is more explicit. While this situation may be advantageous to producers, whose interests are strongly concentrated; it is a hindrance to consumers, whose interests tend to be dispersed.

The concentrated interest of a few is likely to give rise to stronger and more effective political action than the dispersed interests of a large number of people (consumers). Consequently, producers will be better motivated to invest in information, since the marginal cost of doing so will be below the expected marginal return for a greater investment than in the case of consumers. For this reason, one might affirm *a priori* that state trading arrangements are usually more prone to favour producers at consumers' expense than the more transparent policies implemented under an explicit taxes-subsidies system.

Procedural choice. The question of equivalence between measures of government intervention might also be viewed from the angle of the procedural model of choice. Government decisions regarding levels of protection and discrimination are usually subjected to different procedural requirements, depending on the instruments chosen for their implementation. The introduction of a new treasury-financed subsidy system, attempting to satisfy strong producer-lobby demands, may meet with more rigid procedures and stronger parliamentary scrutiny than the equivalent policy under a state-trading arrangement. Modifications of tax levels are quite likely to fall within the competence of rival institutions (e.g. Ministry of Industry and Commerce versus Ministry of Consumer Affairs); decisions may be, thus, time-consuming and difficult to reach. The choice of some procedural channels over others may also affect the decision's outcome. Unfortunately, in many cases, the rationale of government economic decisions is better understood by examining the procedures involved than their economic effects.[10] Some government-set target levels, may, thus, prove to be impractical because of the framework of procedural choice.

In many cases examined in the following chapters, it is clear that state trading offers greater flexibility than the taxes-subsidies, when the former's simpler procedural requirements for policy modification are taken into consideration. In economic perspective, that flexibility probably provides the most important, if not an unique advantage of state trading over other instruments of trade control.

The more complex a given procedural framework, the less likely it is that decision-makers will be motivated by economic rationality in their choices. This 'rationality' aspect might also lead some to prefer state-trading techniques to taxes-subsidies as a means of implementing first-best trade policies.

INTERNATIONAL CONSTRAINTS

Governments are inclined to use state trading as a means to circumvent their international obligations in respect to other measures of government intervention. While internationally recognized norms impose limits on government use of tariffs, quotas, subsidies, etc., governments are incomparably freer to control trade through the use of state-trading techniques.

This state of affairs testifies that existing international arrangements fail to scrutinize state-trading operations. The international effort to deal with state trading, as undertaken by the GATT, aims to make state traders behave as private competitive traders. To fulfil such an objective is wishful thinking. The findings of this study clearly show that, as a rule, state traders exist precisely to behave in a manner different from private traders. Consequently, to require that governments give lip-service contradictory to that basic truth (as the GATT does) is not a very successful way of dealing with the problem; new solutions have to be sought after (Bernier, Chapter 12 in this volume). A number of alternative techniques for achieving trade liberalization under state trading are examined in this volume (Roessler, Chapter 13). It seems that the international effort to control state trading should concentrate more on the arrangements through which governments direct specific trade operations than on the trading enterprises that impart them.

Moreover, state-trading techniques are frequently more consistent with the basic logic of international commodity agreements (based on price and quantity commitments) than the traditional approach to international trade cooperation, which is based on the progressive removal of trade barriers and assumes the existence of competitive private traders. In the latter case, the international effort could be better spent regulating international trade results than on setting codes of conduct for government intervention.

STATE TRADING IN INTERNATIONAL MARKETS

The presence of state traders in international markets has not been without consequence; the results vary considerably in type and intensity. The effect on market structure provides the most conclusive evidence. In many commodity markets, state trading accounts for a significant share of world imports and exports. This market share is probably best translated into the language of international price-making power in the case of the OPEC cartel (Noreng, Chapter 5 in this volume). The cartel comprises both state-owned and private exporters; it relies, however, on central pricing and central control of exported quantities and, as such, requires the use of state-trading techniques by all participating exporters.

Some find it reasonable to suggest that state trading provides the only realistic means of establishing an effective commodity cartel in international markets. The problem is considered particularly in reference to wheat (Chapter 3), although it seems doubtful that the OPEC success could be repeated by 'green power' policy.

State traders are often considered to be oligopolists in the international markets of some agricultural products, and in the regional markets of several mineral commodities. However, the evaluation of the role that particular state traders play in those markets brings the contributors of this volume to rather mixed conclusions. Certainly, this does not confirm the common belief that the expansion of state trading necessarily results in diminished competition in international markets. In many cases, state-trading arrangements have been introduced solely to check monopolistic trends in a given market. In others, traders reacted in retaliatory fashion and effectively prevented state-trading agencies from taking the lead in influencing price formation. Cases have been cited, however, in which the use of a state-trading agency brought significant improvement of bargaining power in foreign markets.[11]

Another issue which poses a question is that of the role of state traders operating outside the interpretative framework of 'perfect' competition, in respect to international price instabilities. Although the empirical evidence does not seem to be conclusive, a long list of arguments is advanced to support the hypothesis that state-trading arrangements may be expected to contribute more to price stability than private traders (Chapter 2 and 3).

Finally, state trading in foreign markets is often linked to unfair trade practices such as dumping or market disruption. Both the empirical evidence available and the theoretical considerations (e.g. see: Stegemann, Chapter 8 in this volume) seem to confirm that assumption. Governments do show a natural tendency to risk unfair commercial behaviour in foreign markets in order to reduce the social pain of domestic unemployment or excess capacities. It is suggested that state trading frequently provides the best way to deal with such problems (Stegemann, Chapter 8 in this volume).

STATE TRADING AND ECONOMIC DEVELOPMENT

State trading is often considered to be a convenient way of implementing the objectives of economic development – particularly for countries desiring to experiment with the extensive use of the public sector and central planning. Because of their position, developing countries are commonly led to employ state-trading arrangements to perform functions attributed elsewhere to fiscal systems (Floyd, Chapter 9 in this volume).[13]

A particularly important aspect of state trading in the developing countries is its employment to bring about geographical diversification and modification in the commodity structure of exports. It is suggested that state-trading organizations might be successfully used to promote economic cooperation among the developing countries since it offers, at least in the view of some authors, a particularly suitable way of initiating trade in that sphere (Netter, Chapter 10 in this volume).

Developing countries often maintain state-trading arrangements in order to facilitate their trade relations with the socialist countries and to conduct trade under aid agreements with the developed market economies. As far as the last point is concerned, there seems to be a contradiction, at least in political terms, in that western aid to the developing countries encourages the expansion of state trading. Indeed, if one is to believe the official political doctrine of some aid-giving countries, this aid is intended, among other things, to safeguard the 'liberal element' in the Third World. Expansion of state trading clearly contradicts that objective.

One of the important functions of the public sector in developing countries is to initiate entrepreneurship and to give new impetus to industrial activities. The export marketing functions of state traders are a case in point. In reality, industrialization of the developing countries relies upon access to foreign markets where the newly produced industrial goods can be sold. State traders may have an especially important task to perform here: to establish the link between domestic producers and foreign buyers. They may widen commercial contacts and open new commercial channels of distribution with more success than fledgling private enterprises could on their own initiative.

A typical problem of state traders (and not only in the developing countries) is their lack of efficiency. The findings concerning the performance of some agricultural marketing boards in Africa (Denis, Chapter 11 in this volume) suggest that the export prices obtained by these boards were lower than prices for comparable commodities traded by private firms.

Similarly, the import price paid by some of the state-trading organisations of developing countries for wheat and other food products tends to be higher than the average international price. Many authors emphasize, as well, the difficulty of maintaining commercial standards of efficiency, particularly for state traders operating as monopolies, i.e. fearing no competition from private traders. Mismanagement, poor organization, and corruption are prevalent in some state-trading organizations in the developing countries. However, any critical judgement of this unsatisfactory situation should be placed in the context of pre-state-trading realities, such as the disregard of foreign trading companies for the host country's interest and the political cost of foreign economic domination.

POLITICS AND TRADE

State trading is, in many respects, a political issue. First, its acceptability or non-acceptability is strongly determined by the type of political philosophy prevailing in the controlling group. It tends to be more easily acceptable to those believing in socialism and central planning rather than to those trusting to private ownership and free markets. In some developing countries (e.g. Syria and Tanzania) the creation of state-trading enterprises has been favoured by the desire to further socialist ideas, whereas in other countries (e.g. US), it has met with strong opposition from those who champion the principles of liberal economy.

One of the most important political motives behind the establishment of state trading in several developing countries (e.g. Kenya, Uganda, Indonesia) was the desire to limit the dominant role of foreign enterprises in their countries' foreign-trade systems. In other cases, it was brought about by the need to limit the politically undesirable dependence on multinational enterprises, or the desire to increase the participation of nationals in entrepreneurship related to foreign trade. Often political gain from establishment of state trading resulted in considerable economic cost, at least in the short run. Nationalization, as a rule (with the exception perhaps of some raw materials), deprives the state-owned enterprises in the Third World of favourable financing, experienced management and marketing facilities abroad.

Expansion of state trading may have some important implications for the larger system of international relations. The post-war multinational trade order has been based on what is frequently referred to as a two-track system – with trade issues travelling their own paths and not interfering with traffic elsewhere.[14] The growing importance of state traders in international markets threatens to end this two-track system. State trading can easily lead to politics through trade and trade through politics. This creates a danger going far beyond the rise of protectionism, as implemented through traditional trade-control measures. This constitutes a challenge for all those trading nations that are more influential in their capacity as traders than as political powers.

NOTES AND REFERENCES

1. The author is grateful to Frieder Roessler for his comments on a draft of this chapter.
2. For a brief review of different definitions of state trading suggested in the literature, we also refer you to Chapter 6 by Peter Lloyd in this volume.
3. The fragility of any clear-cut and formalistic definition of state trading is well illustrated by state trading in steel. Indeed, in a world where governments control outputs, look for export contracts, provide financial backing and run or closely supervise a complicated system of quasi-state trading arrangements providing for 'voluntary' export restrictions, foreign suppliers' market shares,

etc. the private and public foreign-trade businesses are totally enmeshed. In that context, where should the 'government guidance' of Japan's steel exports be placed? How is the line to be drawn between private trading and state trading, when the government hand is omnipresent in the managerial decision-making of so many industries, which, if left alone, would most probably collapse?

4. M. M. Kostecki, 'State Trading in Industrialized and Developing Countries', *Journal of World Trade Law*, vol. 12, no. 3 (May/June 1978) p. 201.

5. Modern governments frequently buy goods abroad for their own consumption (national defence, public administration). The purchasing of foreign goods, destined not for resale but for government consumption, is usually termed government procurement.

6. M. M. Kostecki, 'International Implications of State Trading by the Advanced Countries', in Yair Aharoni and Raymond Vernon (eds), *Public Enterprises in the Mixed Economies* (Boston: Harvard Business School, 1979).

7. Jacob Viner, *International Economics* (Glencoe, Illinois: The Free Press, 1951) p. 16.

8. This section is influenced by Anthony Downs, *An Economic Theory of Democracy* (New York: Harper & Row, 1957).

9. See: Richard Caves, 'Economic Models of Political Choice: Canada's Tariff Structure', *Canadian Journal of Economics*, no. 9 (1976) p. 278–300. G. K. Helleiner, 'The Political Economy of Canada's Tariff Structure: An Alternative Model', *Canadian Journal of Economics*, no. 2 (1977) pp. 318–26.

10. For a general review of different forms of so-called bounded rationality, see: James G. March, 'Bound Rationality, Ambiguity, and the Engineerng of Choice', *The Bell Journal of Economics*, vol. 9, no. 2 (Autumn 1978), pp. 587–608.

11. Bargaining power signifies the trader's ability to influence the terms of particular foreign trade deals in his favour.

12. G. K. Helleiner, 'The Fiscal Role of the Marketing Boards in Nigerian Economic Development, 1947–1961', *Economic Journal*, vol. LXXIV, no. 295 (September 1964).

13. Dharam P. Ghai, *Current Problems of Economic Integration; State Trading and Regional Economic Integration Among Developing Countries* (New York: United Nations, 1973), p. 11.

14. Richard Cooper, 'Trade Policy is Foreign Policy', *Foreign Policy*, no. 9 (Winter 1972–3), pp. 19–21.

2 State Trading in Agricultural Products by the Advanced Countries

M. M. Kostecki[1]

(1) THE NATURE OF AGRICULTURAL STATE TRADING

For the purposes of analysis referring to agricultural trade, state trading may be broadly defined as exporting and importing on government-defined terms of transaction. This includes central pricing, establishment of export and import quantity targets, determination of quality standards and central directives concerning the logistics of international trade transactions.

This chapter will discuss the regulatory and trading activities of a large variety of government or government-backed agencies, such as state-trading enterprises, statutory export marketing boards or government departments.[2] The Food Agency of Japan, the Western Australian Egg Marketing Board or the Canadian Dairy Commission illustrate the diversity involved.

The purpose of this chapter is to evaluate the advantages and disadvantages of maintaining state trading in agricultural products and to explore the important implications that these arrangements may have for the large system of international agricultural trade among the advanced countries. In that context, it will be important to start by summarizing the major distinctive features of the agricultural state trading concerned.

CENTRALLY DETERMINED TERMS OF TRANSACTIONS

Whether or not the actual handling of agricultural exports and imports is conducted by private traders a state-trading government can considerably limit the trader's freedom of choice by directly fixing the terms on which agricultural foreign trade takes place. Agricultural state trading tends to be organically linked with domestic agricultural policy. On the organizational level, this is reflected by the fact that agencies determining the terms of foreign-trade transactions also usually have the power to regulate domestic output, to set producer and consumer prices, and to guide the domestic marketing system.

In agricultural state trading, export prices, quantities and other centrally fixed parameters affecting foreign trade are likely to become instruments of a country's commercial policy. These instruments may present an important advantage over the traditional trade-control measures such as tariffs, variable levies, subsidies, quotas, etc. Traditional trade-control measures may induce traders to engage in one type of foreign-trade business, or it may impede engagement in another kind. By contrast, state-trading techniques may oblige traders to engage in a particular foreign-trade business and to conduct it on specific terms.

State-trading techniques are frequently concealed, while traditional trade-control measures are publicly known. This creates an important difficulty for the international regulation of state trading. State-trading techniques also tend to be more rigid and more efficient than traditional trade control in assuring that agricultural foreign-trade flows take place in conformity with more general domestic and external policy objectives. Under state trading, central instructions may be area-, country- or even transaction-specific – a degree of intervention rarely feasible in the case of traditional control.

Another important aspect of state-trading techniques, as distinguished from traditional trade control, is their flexibility. Instructions are more adaptable to new external conditions or government objectives. The modifications are subject to less complex procedures and are rarely the object of international regulations.

Finally, state trading most frequently entails a more highly centralized decision-making process. Under state trading, decision-makers may be more easily indentified. They are fewer and their negotiating competence is likely to affect a larger volume of trade flows than in a system composed of numerous private traders.

In global terms, then, state-trading techniques may implement policies of protection and discrimination, resulting in sudden and unpredictable changes in export and import flows. Their use may create problems somewhat different from those attributable to traditional trade-control measures. Some of the problems created by such techniques in the international trade of agricultural products will be discussed below.

FOREIGN-TRADE MONOPOLY

More often than not, foreign-trade monopoly will be an integral feature of agricultural arrangements relying on state-trading techniques.[3] Foreign-trade monopoly signifies that the exclusive right to export and import a given range of products is granted to a state-trading agency, even though that right may be subsequently delegated to individual traders who act as executors of central instructions. The existence of the state foreign-trade monopoly is a very effective means of separating domestic from foreign markets, for particular agricultural goods. In a monopoly, there is no automatic link between domestic and foreign prices; there is a guarantee that decisions on export and import prices, quantities traded and other terms of transactions will either remain with government authorities or with managers of state-trading units.

From the organizational point of view, two types of state-trading monopolies for agricultural products may be distinguished. The most common case is that of a single trading firm directly involved in the foreign-trade business.[4] The second type of state monopoly is based on target contracting. A regulatory state agency fixes prices and/or trade quantities, determines timing of shipments, etc. The execution of foreign-trade operations, however, is confined to private trading firms.[5]

SPECIAL PRIVILEGES

Agricultural state-trading units usually benefit from important privileges granted by the state, in respect to both their domestic- and foreign-trade operations. On the domestic level, a frequent privilege involves the open use of an agency's monopoly power, even when similar practices might be forbidden or considerably restricted in private firms. An agency which fixes domestic-producer prices (and/or output), consumer prices, and which runs a foreign-trade monopoly may gain important profits in one market and use them to subsidize sales in other markets. The most frequent type of arrangement is one in which the self-financing export subsidy is based on price discrimination against domestic consumers (see section 5).

A large variety of linking schemes is used in the agricultural state trading of advanced countries. In some cases, for example, the export expansion objective is assured through a quantity-linking scheme. This arrangement obliges users of a domestically produced commodity to export a given percentage of domestic purchases.[6] In other instances (e.g. liquor monopolies), imports receive substantial mark-ups and higher prices are paid to less-efficient domestic producers. We shall attempt, below, to explain some reasons why agricultural state trading by the advanced countries tends to rely on these producer-biased schemes.

The state traders of agricultural products frequently enjoy many other important subsidy-equivalent privileges. First of all, a large portion of the cost of storage, transportation equipment, etc., is either assured directly by the government or financed through governmental credit on terms that no private financing institution would grant to private traders. Public agricultural agencies can usually count on the large financial reserves necessary to overcome poor international market conditions or to undertake a large-scale marketing effort.

Secondly, agricultural state-trading agencies tend to enjoy tariff and tax exemptions, lower transportation and insurance rates, and other privileges, abolishing competition from foreign or domestic private traders.

(2) SOME QUANTITATIVE ESTIMATES

The difficulties encountered in measuring the quantitative importance of state trading in Western trade have already been briefly sketched (Chapter 1).

The objective of this section is, thus, to give the reader some sense of the importance of state trading in western agricultural trade. In spite of its deficiencies, the GATT sample offers a good starting point;[7] it gives some idea of the importance of advanced countries' agricultural state trading (internationally recognized as such). The commodity-country matrix of that sample is presented in Appendix 1.

Agricultural state trading accounts for a major part of the GATT sample dealing with advanced countries. Note that the relatively significant role of state trading in Western agricultural trade stands in contrast to the very small share of public ownership in the agricultural production sector of advanced countries. The sample indicates that state trading is almost a rule for the agricultural exports of South Africa, which operates twenty-two export marketing boards. It is also prevalent in New Zealand (eight boards), Australia (seven boards) and Canada.

In the United States, where the free-enterprise philosophy is much more prominent than in Canada, the private marketing of grain for both domestic and export use has been preferred to state trading.[8] Consequently, no US state trading in grain is included in the GATT sample. Some doubts may arise about the non-existence of US state trading in grain in the context of the US-USSR Grain Supply Agreement, which considerably limits the freedom of US private exporters to determine the terms of transactions with the Soviet Union. State trading in farm products is also important in Austria, Finland, Japan and Norway.

State trading accounts for a particularly large share of Western exporting of sugar and butter, grain trading, and importing of alcoholic beverages, tobacco and silk.

The agricultural state trading included in our sample accounts for about 28 per cent of agricultural exports and about 27 per cent of agricultural imports by the advanced countries.

The figures indicated possibly tend to underestimate the importance of the phenomenon. Not all government-backed boards are included in the above sample (e.g. Egg Marketing Board in Canada). There are many provincial statutory boards (e.g. in Australia, Canada and the US), some of which could be considered state-trading arrangements, according to the definition adopted in this paper.[9] Finally, some governments clearly understate the public disposition and imperative powers of some marketing boards and attempt to present them exclusively as producer 'self-help' organizations.[10]

However, even on the basis of our incomplete sample, the following conclusion may be reached. The advanced countries' state-trading systems for agricultural products generate a much larger share of trade in Western markets than the state-trading systems of the COMECON countries do for all accountable goods.

(3) HISTORICAL PRELIMINARIES

Agricultural state trading has a surprisingly long history. The existence of a state monopoly of corn in ancient Rome (A.D. 189) 'supported by the riches and power of the minister' has been reported in Gibbon's *Decline and Fall of the Roman Empire*. (The monopoly met with great popular discontent, since it was considered to be the immediate cause of famine.) Historical examples of some similar arrangements can be found in the medieval cities of Northern Italy or among the colonial trading corporations.

Requests for a central role of government entrepreneurship in the marketing of grain became quite frequent from the thirteenth century onwards. Although Necker prudently preferred tight state control to state entrepreneurship in trade of grain, writers like Galliani (1770) and Desaubiers called for state trading. Durkheim believes that these requests were precursory to what was later referred to as 'socialisme', i.e. an ideology that tends to grant to the state a central role in economic activities.[11]

A new issue of agricultural state trading is that of farm producers trying to secure government assistance to ease their economic plight. Indeed, state trading in its modern form was mostly initiated when times were bad and when emergency regulations were required.

Several government-backed marketing boards were established after the First World War, when overproduction created problems in the agricultural sectors of some advanced countries. During the mid-1920s a new form of government intervention in agricultural trade, namely governmental marketing boards, emerged in the Southern British Dominions.[12]

State-trading agencies became even more widespread during the 1930s, when depressed conditions in the agricultural sector of many developed economies required a 'new protectionisme'.[13]

The pattern of state involvement with domestic and export marketing and the degree of government entrepreneurship in foreign trade varied considerably. These aspects may be briefly summarized as follows:

(i) In some countries (e.g. Denmark, Sweden, Ireland, producer self-help organizations were successful enough in taking care of the most serious of their problems. Governments encouraged cooperative movements and created commodity cartels which, combined with rigid foreign-trade control, protected the farm population from the frustration of the 1930s. No imperative power was required to assure the loyalty necessary for the successful operation of those self-help producer organizations; nor was it necessary to turn them into marketing boards of a public nature. This partially explains the absence of agricultural state trading in these countries even today.

(ii) The cooperative movement was unable to successfully maintain centralized export marketing in the present and former British Dominions, which traditionally generated an important share of the world's agricultural exports. This was at least partly due to the lack of loyalty among the large group of widely dispersed farm producers, who would also have made quite divergent demands on the operations of a central marketing arrangement. Government involvement in establishing such schemes through creation of public or semi-public agencies, equipped with imperative powers, was thus a necessity (see also, sections 6 and 7 below). This resulted in the creation of many statutory marketing boards in Australia, Canada, New Zealand, Rhodesia, South Africa and even Great Britain. These boards were mostly producer-controlled legalized monopolies, given exclusive power to conduct foreign trade and to control output. They were allowed to acquire the farm production and to set consumer and producer prices.[14]

(iii) State trading – in variable degrees and patterns – was also introduced in the 1930s by some European countries. The National Socialist governments of Germany and Italy conducted their foreign-trade operations in all important agricultural products through state-trading enterprises. State trading in agricultural was also maintained in France and several countries of Central Europe.

State trading lost its battle in the United States during the 1920s. The commitment of the US Congress to the philosophy of economic liberalism resulted in a refusal of the so-called McNarry-Haugen bills (1924–8) which provided, among other things, for the establishment of a government export corporation.[15]

After the Second World War, the return to private trade channels in agricultural trade was not immediate. For years, the UK continued bulk purchases as part of its policy to safeguard its population's food supplies. Most countries of continental Europe followed the same pattern until the late 1940s.

State trading in agriculture was partly eliminated in the United Kingdom and some European countries when scarcities disappeared. Nevertheless, it remained a permanent featue of commercial policies, affecting an important share of the farm trade of developed market economies.

(4) DOMESTIC PRICE STABILIZATION AND STATE TRADING

The foreign-trade strategies of state traders are frequently, paradoxically enough, of secondary importance, and spring from domestic imperatives such as price stabilization, farmers' revenue, rural employment, continuity of food supply, desire for national self-sufficiency, etc. As Professor Warley puts it:

> Agricultural trade policy is a classic instance of national sector problems being exported to other countries.[16]

This is clearly illustrated by state-trading arrangements that support domestic price stabilization and by the linking schemes discussed below.

Governments are much more concerned with securing domestic price stability than price stability outside their borders. Since little can be done about the inelastic domestic demands facing fluctuating domestic production, prices are usually stabilized by making the supply function more elastic.[17] This can be accomplished, to some extent, by an appropriate storage policy when goods are storable. However, even in the case of storable goods, adjustments are most frequently made through foreign trade, and a flexible management of exports and imports is necessary.

Although governments may choose from a number of instruments to regulate foreign trade and to promote domestic price stabilization, state-trading techniques are extensively used. This is essentially the case for the state trading in rice by the Food Agency of Japan (see below), or in butter and skim milk by the Canadian Dairy Commission.

The economics of a state-trading arrangement maintained to stabilize domestic prices might be briefly summarized as follows:

> A central public agency, aiming to ensure its country's self-sufficiency in a given product and to achieve domestic price stabilization, fixes a domestic target price. Under the self-sufficiency assumption, the target price should ideally be equal to the closed economy market price. However, in order to provide farmers with stable income and to influence production decisions, the target price must be fixed *ex ante*, whereas the equilibrium market price is known only *ex post*. Disparities between the centrally fixed target

price and the equilibrium market price are, thus, very likely to appear, and corresponding adjustment through state trading is required. Consequently, the agency is granted foreign-trade monopoly rights to handle the resulting sporadic shortages and surpluses and to effectively separate domestic from foreign prices.

The figures which illustrate state-trading operations in rice by Japan's Food Agency (see Table 2.1) are a good example.

The domestic producer price of rice in Japan is clearly above the world market price. This means that the Food Agency of Japan will suffer losses when exporting accidental surpluses and will make excess gains when importing accidental shortages. In the early 1970s, the agency's exporting was extensive for a country claiming a policy of self-sufficiency in rice. However, some of Japan's rice exportation took place in response to strong requests from developing countries who were short of food.[18] The Japanese rice was exported on concessional terms for an amount not only below the domestic price, but inexpensive for the foreign buyers as well.[19]

The primary characteristic of a state-trading agency that operates in international markets mainly to achieve domestic price stabilization is likely to be its weak international bargaining power. The agency's international offer (demand) curve will tend to be perfectly inelastic, with the agency trying to market surpluses (or buying to cover domestic shortages) at almost any price. A system of budgetary transfer, equivalent to export subsidies or import taxes, may be required in order to correct the inconsistencies caused in an agency's accounting by differences between domestic and international prices.

Efforts to increase the elasticity of an agency's offer curve in the international sale of agricultural surpluses may stimulate a so-called 'non-commercial' demand. Many state-trading agencies habitually drain off a certain portion of their surpluses through various food-aid programmes to the developing countries. They may also sell some portion to centrally-planned economies willing to buy in larger quantities at prices lower than those set in an open international market.[20] The existence of this so-called non-commercial demand results in a considerable politicization of international trade in agricultural products. It leads to more politics through trade and trade through politics, greater market segmentation and increased market rigidity resulting from bilateral purchasing agreements, bilateral aid arrangements, etc.

Considering the impact that state trading may be said to have on

TABLE 2.1

Domestic output and state trading of rice
in Japan (1971–6)

Year	Domestic output (1000 tons m)	Import (1000 tons m)	Export (1000 tons m)	Foreign trade production ratio‡ (%)	Domestic producer price† (US $/ton)	Export price* (US $/ton)
1971	10 887	13	912	8.5	433	129
1972	11 897	3	183	1.6	496	148
1973	12 149	25	540	4.7	613	299
1974	12 292	63	309	3.0	756	542
1975	13 165	36	11	0.4	858	364
1976	11 772	22	0.2	0.2	933	255

* Export prices are those of Thailand (standard government quality, FOB Bangkok).
† Domestic producer prices for Japan refer to a crop year, other data to calendar year.
‡ The foreign trade production ratio is calculated according to the following formula: Imports + Exports/Domestic Output · 100%.

Sources: GATT Doc. L/4140/Add. 8 (July 1975), p. 3; FAO, *Trade Yearbook 1975*, vol. 29 (Rome: 1971) pp. 134–6, and *Yearbook 1976*, vol. 30, (Rome: 1977) p. 115; 'The Oriental Economist', *Japan Economic Yearbook 1975/76* (Tokyo: Nihombashi, August 1975) p. 214, and *Yearbook 1977/78*, August 1977, p. 222; FAO, *Bulletin Mensuel Economie et Statistique Agricoles*, vol. 24, no. 2 (February 1975) p. 40, vol. 25, no. 9 (September 1976) pp. 46 and 48, and vol. 26, no. 9 (September 1977) pp. 49 and 51; FAO Doc. OCP: RI-78/6 (December 1977) p. 3.

international price instability, one is brought to somewhat mixed conclusions. In some respects, it may be argued that state trading to stabilize domestic prices is likely to increase policy-induced instabilities in the open markets for international products. This risk is especially high when unexpected shortages or surpluses appear simultaneously in several importing, producing, or consuming countries. However, what difference does it make whether the instability caused by policies of a specific country are the result of state trading or of private trading. Professor D. Gale Johnson and others have contended, for example, that the principal destabilizing element in the world grain trade has been the internal policy of the European Economic Community and its variable levy system, not the operations of Canadian' and Australian state marketing boards.[21] Even when the duopoly, tripoly or buyer's model of pricing in wheat markets is alternatively assumed, it becomes quite irrelevant whether a particular domestic policy is implemented with or without the help of state trading.

On the other hand, one could propose two reasons why state trading could exercise a stabilizing effect on international agricultural markets. First, it can be reasonably assumed that a country maintaining a central state agency will find it easier to assess the supplies of various agricultural products and to conclude long-term arrangements with importers.[22] Such arrangements may be expected to increase the regularity of agricultural trade flows and market stability. Secondly, as Professors McCalla and Schmitz argue in Chapter 3, private traders maximizing short-term profits may be interested in volume and price fluctuations; state traders are much more concerned with absolute price levels. The character of the market intermediary – private trader or state trader – may, thus, have some repercussions on international price stability.

Among the foreign trade arrangements used to promote domestic price stabilization, state-trading schemes represent only one set of means. Similar results are frequently obtained by imposing various systems of levies, quotas, subsidies and other forms of trade control on private agricultural traders. If state trading is more often used than traditional trade control measures to assure domestic price stability, other reasons must be accountable: state trading's greater flexibility, its less transparent quasi-taxing dimension, its bargaining capacity, etc. These, along with some other aspects of agricultural state trading, will be discussed below.

(5) LINKING SCHEMES

The agencies managing a country's domestic supply schemes for a particular range of agricultural products usually enjoy a state-trading monopoly. Since it is able to determine domestic price and output and to separate the domestic from the foreign market, the agency may implement discriminating monopoly policies to optimize profit for domestic farm producers. Commenting on the Australian marketing boards in the early sixties, Professor Lewis noted:

> The chief instrument of agricultural marketing policy in Australia is the home consumption price system under which supplies of export products are diverted to overseas markets in order to raise domestic prices above export parity.[23]

The basic economics of a linking scheme relying on state trading and monopolistic exploitation of the home market are briefly discussed below. In Figure 2.1, *D* is the domestic- and *WW'* the foreign-demand curve. The foreign-demand curve, being perfectly elastic, depicts both

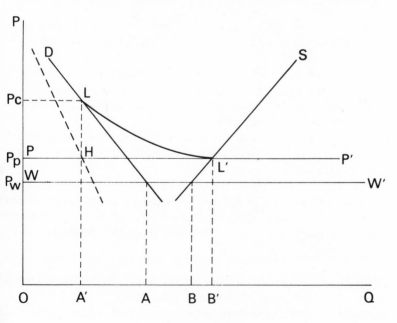

FIGURE 2.1
State trading and linking scheme

the marginal and average revenue curves for the foreign market. S is the domestic producers' supply curve. It traces out the marginal cost of domestic production.

Assuming a free-trading situation, domestic production is OB, domestic consumption is OA and the quantity AB is exported at the world market price (P_w).

Now, a state-trading agency (e.g. a statutory marketing board) is established. The agency benefits from the foreign-trade monopoly in a given product, i.e. it has the executive right to export and import. It also sets both producer and consumer prices at home. The agency is assumed to aim at improving farm producers' returns.

The agency will tend to exploit its monopoly power when selling at home, paying the domestic farm producer the pooled weighted average price from sales in home and foreign markets. The LL' curve in Figure 2.1 may be referred to as the producer price schedule and it indicates, *ceteris paribus*, the relation between the level of domestic output and the price paid by the state-trading agency to domestic farm producers.

What are the effects of this scheme's operation?

(1) *Production effect*: since the agency introduces a production price (P_p) higher than the world market price (P_w) domestic production rises by BB'.[24]

(2) *Consumption effect*: domestic consumption falls by $A'A$ because of the agency's monopolistic practice. (The domestic marginal revenue equals the marginal cost of domestic production in point H). Consumption is now OA'.

(3) *Export or balance of payment effect*: agency's exports increase by the sum of the production and consumption effect $(A'A + BB')$. Export equals $A'B'$.

(4) *Redistribution effect*: the price to the domestic consumer has risen from P_w to P_c. The price to domestic producers has also risen from P_w to P_p. There is, thus, a redistribution of income from domestic consumers (monopoly gain) to domestic producers (implicit production subsidy).

There is no revenue effect, since the totality of the monopoly gain is spent on subsidization of domestic production. (Producer price is assumed to depend upon both the monopoly gain and the quantity of output.)

The simple partial equilibrium model, along the lines presented in

Figure 2.1, has been developed by Parish and used by Parish and Banks and Mauldon[25] to explain the operation of the linking scheme implemented under the state-trading for some dairy products in Australia. Similar state-trading arrangements have been put in use for a varying range of farm products by South Africa, New Zealand, Canada and some Western European countries.

The wheat-pricing policy of the Australian Wheat Board in the late 1960s and the early 1970s is a good example of a state-trading arrangement operating a linking scheme (see Table 2.2). During the period examined, the board's export prices were significantly below domestic consumer prices and the monopoly gain of the board was used to increase the revenues of domestic wheat producers.[26]

Although the international implications are of a somewhat different nature, it may be worth noting that an important discriminatory dimension also characterizes several import monopolies operating as domestic fiscal arrangements for alcoholic beverages and tobacco. The higher prices paid to domestic producers (as compared to foreign producers) certainly contradicts frequent government assertions that the monopoly has fiscal gain and health control as sole objectives. Note that, since domestic supplies normally tend to be less elastic than foreign supplies, the price paid to a domestic producer by a profit maximizing monopoly should even fall below the international market price. In reality, however, what prevails is the desire to support domestic producers, and the mark-up on imported products considerably exceeds that imposed on comparable domestic goods.[27]

Self-financing subsidy schemes, those mainly handling exports as well as those conducting imports of agricultural products, result in three price systems. The domestic producer price is above the world market price but lower than the domestic consumer price. Since a similar effect could have been obtained through the combined use of production subsidies, consumption tax and import tariff, one wonders why state trading is so frequently preferred to these other measures.[28]

First, even when a state-trading agency specifies domestic-price stabilization as its main objective, it has a natural tendency to fix the domestic target prices or export quantity targets too high. Since no one knows what the closed economy market price should be, the target price will be determined in the domestic bargaining process. The statutory marketing boards (and other state-trading arrangements concerned) are variously composed of producers, government representatives and/or consumers. Consumers, however, are rarely adequately represented in these institutions.[29] Even the presence of

TABLE 2.2

Wheat prices for export and home consumption practised
by the Australian Wheat Board ($ US/ton)

Crop year	Export price (FOB ports) P_e	Home consumption price (FOB ports) P_k	Difference between home consumption and export price $P_k - P_e$
1968/69	53.7	70.4	16.7
1969/70	54.4	61.7	7.3
1970/71	54.1	63.8	9.7
1971/72	58.5	71.4	12.9
1972/73	69.3	86.2	16.9

Sources: FAO, *National Grain Policies 1975* (Rome: FAO, 1976) p. 60; FAO, *Annuaire de la production 1976*, vol. 30, p. 281, and vol. 27, p. 327.

governmental appointees does not guarantee that the domestic consumers' interests will be seriously taken into account. Governments have their own objective function, not necessarily influenced by consumer interests. They can, for example, favour an agency's monopolistic pricing at home for balance of payment reasons, or in expectation of higher income (or reduction of loss) for the treasury.[30] In some cases, there is not sufficient parliamentary scrutiny over the operations of agricultural state-trading agencies. As a consequence, many of them pay little attention to government policy decisions on domestic consumer prices when making use of their monopoly power.[31] Campbell has also suggested that the important foreign-trade adjustments required to achieve domestic price stabilization frequently stemmed from the marketing boards' failure to control the relevant supplies.[32] Generally speaking, many state-trading agencies that were expected to stabilize domestic prices became, by mutation *de facto*, linking schemes subsidizing domestic farm production.

The use of state-trading arrangements to implement linking schemes in agriculture also has a more basic explanation.

The agricultural policies of the major advanced countries seem to conform to a more general hypothesis that the economic decisions of a rational democratic government are biased against consumers in favour of producers. As a rule, producers attempting to influence policies of concern to them are better organized and better informed than consumers. Consumers are less inclined to care about any particular policy, since every consumer is affected, in small ways, by a large number of issues.[33]

Governments usually prefer to satisfy farmers' demands for higher income through the establishment of a statutory marketing board or another type of central agency rather than a direct subsidy. In fact, the establishment of a government-backed, but producer-controlled, monopoly to maximize farmer revenue (through price discrimination via home consumption) puts no strain on the treasury; the subsidy does. Moreover, a linking scheme implemented under state trading is subjected to less public control and is less visible than an explicit subsidy. Finally, farm producers tend to put more trust in a state-trading arrangement (over which they have control) than in an explicit subsidy subject to periodic parliamentary approvals. Indeed, many state-trading arrangements – once established – continue to exist, even when the reasons justifying their maintenance have disappeared.

This simple analysis of the export linking scheme may also be applied to numerous import arrangements.

Indeed, state-trading agencies in countries that protect domestic producers, but are also impelled to import agricultural goods, frequently link their tariff equivalent import profit to a domestic production subsidy. This is the case of several Western European countries and Japan, where state-trading arrangements are used for trade in grain and dairy products.

What international repercussions might result from state-trading arrangements operating along the principles discussed above?

First of all, these schemes will tend to expand exports above the free-trade level, as a result of contracted domestic consumption and increased domestic production. These policies add state-trading to the impressive armouries of instruments at a government's disposal for implementing export expansion and import substitution in agricultural trade.

In exports, where a linking scheme pushes the domestic price above the export price, the risk of dumping and market disruption is considerably increased. The terms of this type of state-trading operation suggest a total refusal to share the international responsibilities of agricultural trade. Consequently, the agricultural markets of many advanced countries tend to be highly protected and international policy clashes are a frequent occurrence.[34]

State trading appears, then, as one among many means through which trade policies are subordinated to domestic imperatives of revenue support and output expansion. It relies on the dangerous assumption that the basis of economic problem-solving is national, an assumption which contradicts the principle of post-war international economic relations as outlined in Cordell-Hull's vision.

If this is ever to be brought about through international action founded on a commonly accepted code of behaviour, not trade results, it is obvious that any effective international agreement on state trading in agricultural goods should be backed by a corresponding agreement which would coordinate domestic agricultural policies.

What is, however, indigenous to state trading, and not to private trading, is government's control of state traders by specific instructions, rather than by rules with more general applicability.[35] International cooperation with respect to state trading should, thus, rely on agreements based on trade effects, rather than on trade policy regulations. Agricultural state trading, with its centrally-determined terms of foreign-trade transactions, corresponds more logically to commodity agreements based on quantity and price commitments than to the traditional GATT approach (and that of several regional groupings), which support the progressive removal of trade barriers and the virtues of competitive private trading.

(6) MONOPOLY AND BARGAINING POWER OF STATE TRADERS

Many of the advanced countries' agricultural state-trading agencies presumably have some degree of price-making power in international markets. Although it is not appropriate to measure the degree of an agency's price-making power in market allotment, the latter may certainly indicate the importance of the monopoly problem in international agricultural trade.

Several examples of agricultural state-trading arrangements, accounting for a significant share of world exports or imports, are included in Appendix 2. The international price-making power of agricultural state traders is particularly evident in the case of public agencies trading in grain. (On this point, also see following chapter.)

Many of the marketing boards in Australia, South Africa, New Zealand and Canada seem to have significant control over particular regional markets. In several cases, some degree of price-making power, even in international markets, is a likely possibility.[36]

Is there any reason to believe that state trading might serve better than tariffs to exploit a country's price-making power in foreign markets? Primarily, the use of international price-making power usually requires some restriction in the level of trade. A country which exploits monopoly power should equalize marginal export revenue and marginal export cost; any failure to do so will imply a loss to the country in question. Assigning the exploitation of a country's monopoly power to a single export firm, rather than a tariff ministry, may be based on the realistic assumption that a trade manager will be a better choice for the job than a government employee. This statement is not so much based on mistrust of civil servants' abilities as on the following observations:

(1) Managers of a STO will probably have much greater flexibility in responding to new market conditions than the tariff ministry. Usually, a government's freedom to regulate tariffs is limited by international tariff commitments. Moreover, tariff changes are apt to call for more complex and time-consuming procedures than would modifications in an agency's business strategies.

(2) While export performance usually influences the remuneration of an agency's manager, no such link normally exists between the salary of a ministerial employee and tariff revenue. The average manager of a state-trading agency will, thus, tend to be better motivated in his job than the average civil servant.

(3) Finally, trade managers will tend to be more competent than ministerial employees in dealing with particular product markets. Bureaucrats usually specialize in a much larger range of problems than traders who conduct execution of specific commercial transactions.

Another important argument in favour of state trading in some agricultural products is closely related to the idea of international cartel arrangements. The issue is particularly timely and interesting, in the context of recent proposals to create an international cartel in wheat. As exhibited in the work of Alex McCalla and Andrew Schmitz (Chapter 3 in this volume), state-trading and/or export-marketing boards are clearly the only means by which one could effectively introduce a wheat cartel. When a country's grain export is conducted by a large number of private exporters (as is the case in the US) instead of a single-desk selling agency, it is possible for foreign buyers to deal secretively and simultaneously with different exporting companies.[37] A central agency is more likely to dispose of an efficient information system and, by dealing in larger volume, enjoy bargaining power. The advantage of a central state-trading agency over dispersed private trading is admirably illustrated by the USSR purchases of US grain in the 1973–6 period.[38] Recognition of this occurrence elicited the establishment of a quasi-state-trading arrangement in the form of a USSR-US Grain Supply Agreement.[39] However, the idea of a single-desk selling agency for the United States does not seem very suitable. First of all, in the light of recent research, it looks as if the effect of any export cartelization in international grain markets would be relatively minor, compared to the effect of similar action by major wheat importers. It has been suggested that the most wheat exporting nations could achieve by forming an export cartel would be to remove the buying power of importers.[40] It is also improbable that a US marketing board could operate as smoothly as the wheat boards in Canada or Australia. One practitioner of the international grain business has stated that a marketing board may operate efficiently only so long as the grain volume it handles does not become too large. Once the traded volume exceeds a certain maximal point, bureaucracy takes over and the situation gets out of hand. These observations seem quite relevant to the United States, since it exports much more grain than state traders in Canada and Australia. The task of marketing grain is also more complex in the US than in Canada.[41] Given these considerations, it is doubtful that state trading would be of any advantage to the US, even if it were politically acceptable (which is also not very probable). Consequently, the creation of a single-desk selling agency for export of US grain remains a subject for discussion rather than for action.

The use of state trading may be advantageous where market-splitting strategy is involved. Implementation of market-splitting strategies, through discriminatory tariffs (or even quotas), may appear more flagrantly incompatible with the government's international commitments on non-discrimination. Discrimination policies imple-mented under state trading are less visible to partner countries and are frequently preferred on those grounds. Moreover, a single-desk sell-ing agency can more easily channel exports in a way that permits it to equalize returns from different price markets or outlets. First of all, discriminatory export pricing can be more easily implemented under centralized marketing than by a larger number of exporters. Secondly, centralized export marketing by a public agency, combined with appropriate government action, has frequently been effective in introducing 'trade resistance', restraining the foreign markets discriminated against from diverting trade from the agency in question.

One frequent example of increased 'trade resistance' is that which results from bilateral trade agreements or government-to-government contract sales. Establishment of long-term contracts on market share not only eliminates competition among domestic exporters, but also often enables the state traders to acquire some degree of price-making power in the foreign markets concerned.

Governments of some advanced countries particularly concerned with assuring access to adequate food supplies (e.g. Japan and the UK before its accession to the EEC), also favour long-term contract arrangements for reasons of stability. The fact that premium prices are sometimes paid when trade takes place under long-term contracts may be justified by Professor Hick's logic: 'it may be worthwhile to sacri-fice some efficiency in order to acquire greater security.'[42] Another way of introducing 'trade resistance' is through differentiation in transportation rates among areas or countries. Here, government action, combined with that of a state-trading agency, could be a particularly effective way of assuring that the country's shipments of agricultural exports take place in conformity with optimal marketing strategy.

There are numerous examples of market-splitting strategies implemented by agricultural state traders. The Australian State Egg Board and the Australian Meat Board, for example, have sole authority to choose the destination of exports concerned, clearly using their power to implement discriminatory export pricing. Price discrimination among sugar importers is also maintained by the Queensland Sugar Board of Australia. In the early seventies, prices on a total of about 1 200 000 tonnes per annum were established under conditions of long-term contracts negotiated by the board with Japan, New Zealand, and several other countries. Only the remaining export sales of the board were based on the world market price.

It was in this same spirit that market share arrangements and average historical prices were adopted, as exemplified in the case of butter exports by New Zealand *vis-à-vis* the UK. The 1972–7 export prices were based on the average CIF returns obtained by the board in the UK market during the 1962–72 period. Butter export quantities (about 60 per cent of the board's butter exports) were also specified and included in the UK's Treaty of Accession to the EEC. The destination price system is also employed by most state agencies trading in grains.[43]

In several important cases, it is clear that state trading was introduced either to re-establish a balance of bargaining power with other countries' monopolies or to counteract the excessive market power exerted by overseas owned processing firms, organized conference shipping lines and private importers.[44] Sadan has suggested, looking at the dairy boards' experience, that collective bargaining would have been obviously advantageous in the case of collective freight contracts with shipping interests.[45]

It is impossible to ascertain which country benefits most from establishment of a state monopoly, without knowing the partner agencies' relative bargaining strength. The agency's bargaining strength depends on its access to alternative markets. International farm product markets are frequently segmented; this is due to the existence of long-term bilateral arrangements, variations in freight rates, rigidity of marketing channels, etc. Alternative markets tend to be more easily available to state-trading agencies handling large quantities since they are more likely to rely on multiple sources of supply or demand than smaller traders. The agency's bargaining strength will also be influenced by the relative importance of given exports and imports for its country. Cutting back in exports which are an important source of the country's export revenue would be quite harmful. When export revenue accounts for an important share of producers' income, the state-trading agency tends slightly to undercut world prices, for fear that large quantities of domestic output might not be sold.[46] This is an important issue for many state-trading agencies. Exports generate about 30–45 per cent of farmers' annual cash income in Canada. For Australia and New Zealand, the share of exports in total domestic production varies from 98 per cent (wool) to 15 per cent (lamb). In the case of New Zealand, agricultural exports provide about 85 per cent of that country's export revenue and balance-of-payment considerations are frequently evoked to justify maintaining state trading for a wide range of agricultural products.

The agency's bargaining power will also depend on the country's capacity to transfer earning from one industry to an alternative industry and on the period of time that has to elapse between inputs and outputs.[47] So, a state trader operating in a country where labour and other production factors may be easily transferred, will tend to have a stronger bargaining position than one in a country with a mono-culture. The bargaining power of an exporting agency will also tend to be stronger in the case of 'short crops' (e.g., wheat, vegetables) than in the case of 'long crops' (e.g., wood, rubber).

Bargaining power may thus serve as a valid argument for setting up a state-trading monopoly there where private traders, because of competition, are unable to take full advantage of a country's strength on the world market. However, the proliferation of state trading aimed at improving bargaining power introduces the danger that a countervailing form of state monopoly will be introduced in partner countries.

The use of monopoly power by a state agency in agricultural trade may have important international implications.

There is, first of all, a natural tendency for governments to use trade for political purposes when the country is in control of a significant share of the world market. The importance of state trading, particularly in grain and other commodities with strongly monopolistic market structures, presents the danger that a 'green power' may follow the 'politics through oil' pattern. This would lead, as stated above, to more politics through trade and trade through politics. It is doubtful whether that approach could be advantageous to the majority of advanced countries which are food-dependent.

Secondly, market-splitting strategies tend to result in institutional rigidities and bilateralism in the international agricultural markets.

The stability obtained through government-to-government arrangements, long-term contract sales, etc. may mean more instability in the open international market. When any of those arrangements is discontinued, sudden price fluctuations are likely to occur in the open market. Moreover, unexpected agricultural surpluses or shortages will probably first affect the prices and quantities traded in the open market before affecting those traded under long-term contracts.

(7) CENTRALIZED AGRICULTURAL MARKETING

Marketing is a particularly important issue in the trade of agricultural products and the desire to improve its functioning motivated creation of some agricultural state-trading agreements.

The first argument in favour of a central agency (or at least in favour of a central marketing scheme) is the fact that individual export marketing may result in important externalities. This is particularly true in the case of fruits, meat and dairy products, where the country of origin may be a significant distinctive feature for foreign buyers. If a private exporter of, say, Australian dairy products, undertook a successful publicity campaign in foreign markets, other Australian producers might also benefit from it without assuming any cost. A desire to avoid externalities in the export marketing of certain agricultural products led to establishment of export marketing boards in the former and present British Dominions.

A state-trading monopoly may also be the only practical institutional solution for assuring that reasonably large volumes of farm exports are handled under one administration. Important economies of scale are frequently achieved through this type of arrangement. (This may be of particular interest for those producer countries located at some distance from their markets.) However, solutions of this sort are profitable only if marketing costs account for a relatively important part of the CIF export price, and if the marketing system's performance has a decisive impact on the country's world market share. It may not be worthwhile to undertake publicity in foreign markets or establish representatives abroad unless exports are important enough.[48] Using centralized marketing to replace the sales efforts of individual exporters might lower the cost of export marketing since, among firms of the same country, these individual efforts tend to cancel each other out.[49]

Important economies of size might also accrue from the pooling of large export quantities, which is likely to lower the cost of shipment, port handling, brokerage, insurance, etc. Domestic buying and exporting by a single-desk selling arrangement facilitates the establishment of standard quality grades, permits regularity of shipments, and increases the reliability of performance. Better prices are available and more new buyers attracted.

The economic argument for central coordination of marketing activities through state trading may also draw on the basic logic of Coase's theory of the firm.[50]

The chain of operations from farm producers to foreign buyers is a pyramid. At the bottom, many farmers deliver their output to the purchasing station. In the middle, the exportable products are sorted, graded, processed, packed and transported to the port gate. At the summit, the exporter operates from the port gate up to the foreign market. For one reason or another, government entrepreneurship may be required at a specific level of that pyramid and later expanded in order to assure more efficiency through central coordination of different types of activities.

For example, government involvement with storage might be required to assure continuity of supplies to domestic consumers.

J. M. Keynes noted that 'the competitive system abhors the existence of stocks, with as strong a reflex as nature abhors a vacuum, because stocks yield a negative return in terms of themselves.'[51] Since individual enterprises and self-help producer organizations rarely concern themselves with maintaining socially desirable stock, government involvement is necessary. In some food-deficient countries, increasing government participation in storing farm products has been recently motivated by the disappearance of large cereal surpluses. Note that there is an increasing tendency in many developed market economies to employ quantitative planning techniques in managing a country's stocks. This, in turn, induces the quantitative planning of required foreign-trade flows and foreign-trade targets are introduced to assure consistency between stock policies and foreign trade of the products involved.[52]

Success in exporting agricultural products depends primarily on the marketing system's degree of excellence and the adequacy of infrastructures such as transportation, refrigeration, etc. This includes heavy investments which usually put too great a financial burden on domestic agricultural producers. Government entrepreneurship in some of these essential facilities (with large capital coming from government sources) occurs frequently in many developed market economies. Note that an overwhelming majority of state-trading agencies dealing with farm products are also involved in these types of activity. Sometimes, this is linked with the use of quantitative targets as instruments for managing the domestic marketing chain.

The state trader's role in coordinating domestic production, international marketing, and intermediary activities may be particularly important in the case of perishable goods. One must perceive agricultural marketing not just as an act of exporting and its concomitant activities, but as a succession of important phases from production to delivery to the foreign consumers. At some point in this process, state entrepreneurship may be required because investment is too heavy, or risks too high to attract private traders.[53]

Centralized marketing is, in some cases, a desirable arrangement which improves a country's terms of trade through its effect on non-price variables, such as improved grading, timing, product differentiation, or more skilful publicity. Government entrepreneurship in export marketing may be required for lack of private entrepreneurs willing to take the risks or financial burdens of such activities. This form of state trading is, in most cases, equivalent to an export subsidy, since preferential terms of financing, preferential transportation rates, etc. are involved.

Note that many of the marketing techniques escape international control. They may thus be used to implement protectionist and discriminatory policies and, as such, require special attention in international trade.

In addition, there is a growing government concern about access to food supplies and, correspondingly, with multinational companies which control the marketing of large shares of agricultural trade. That concern is likely to stimulate a future proliferation of agricultural state trading motivated by the marketing function.

(8) OPTIMAL MANAGEMENT RULE

Most of the objectives for which the state trading of agricultural products has been maintained by the developed market economies could be classified in one of the following categories:

   (i) domestic price stabilization;
  (ii) fair income to domestic farm producers;
 (iii) continuity in domestic food supply, at low and stable prices;
 (iv) increase in treasury revenue or decrease of treasury spending;

   (v) improvement of terms-of-trade;
  (vi) fostering agricultural exports;
 (vii) reduction in overhead cost of foreign trade operations;
(viii) fulfilment of international commitments.

The first four categories refer to domestic agricultural policies and the last four are of direct relevance to foreign trade.

State-trading agencies usually aim, simultaneously, at a number of objectives. The ranking of particular targets according to their relative importance varies among countries and products and over time. The agency's multiple objective function may be expressed in very general terms as follows:

$$\min x = \sum_i n_i^+ k_i^+ + \sum_i n_i^- k_i^- ,$$

where k_i^+ and k_i^- are respectively the deviation above and below the ith target level, and n_i^+ and n_i^- are weights attached to the target deviations.

The products of the weight adjustor (n) and the target deviation (n^+k^+ or n^-k^-) for the high-priority target should always be greater than the corresponding products for low-priority targets. The high-priority target will thus be better served by an agency than a low-priority target, under given associated constraints.

If domestic price stabilization is the priority, most heavy weights will be assigned to any deviation from the domestic target price. A state trader subjected to that type of target ranking will essentially behave as described in section 4 (Domestic Price Stabilization and State Trading), possibly at the expense of objectives (iv) and (v), as listed above. If income maximization for domestic farm products is the priority, it is possible that objectives (iii) and (iv) will suffer most, etc.

Particular objectives may thus be complementary, neutral or conflicting. For example, the price stabilization objective for the domestic market (i) will most probably conflict with the objective of maximizing the treasury revenue (iv) or with the desire to exploit a country's monopoly power in international trade (iv). Domestic price stabilization (i) may be a neutral objective when linked with the reduction in overhead cost of foreign-trade operations. The objective to assure fair income to domestic producers (ii) may be complementary to the external objective of improving terms-of-trade (v) or reducing the overhead cost of foreign-trade operations (vii).

The complexity of this set of objectives and the changes in rank of each item over time requires an efficient managerial system. The optimal management system will probably require an arrangement assigning all essential instruments for achieving this complex set of objectives to a single agency. From this point of view, some state-trading techniques may provide a first-best solution when compared with alternative methods, such as trade-control measures or other non-state-trading distortion devices. But the complexity of the objectives aimed at by many agricultural state traders makes it difficult to evaluate the international implications of their activities. Trade policies implemented under state trading arrangements are susceptible to frequent modification, depending on the external and internal variables that determine them. The importance of state trading in international agricultural trade could thus contribute to the instability and unpredictability of agricultural commodity markets.

(9) SHORTCOMINGS OF AGRICUTURAL STATE TRADING AND CONCLUDING REMARKS

In spite of its virtues enumerated above, agricultural state trading may have important disadvantages. Some of them will be considered below.

First of all, many cases may be cited where the existence of agricultural state trading may be better exemplified by the Schumpeterian 'trahison des clercs' than by any gain in efficiency. The existence of a state-trading monopoly may in fact have important adverse effects on so-called X-efficiency – efficiency within the agency itself.[54] The establishment of a state-trading monopoly eliminates the danger of competition from private traders; managerial motivations may therefore change, and mechanisms for upholding commercial standards of efficiency may become inoperative.[55] Moreover, efficiency loss is often to be blamed on an ill-conceived division of responsibilities between agency managers and government officials. If individual ministries maintain direct interference in the day-to-day management of state trading, there can be no distinction between policy and operational aspect, no clear division of competence and responsibility. The problem of efficiency may be further complicated by the lack of any clear-cut criteria for judging the agency's success (in the absence of the profit motive), and by the impossibility of comparing the state monopoly's performance with that of competing enterprises, since the latter are not allowed to operate. The most that can be done is to assess the success of the agency in achieving the objectives of the 'scheme'.[56]

Scepticism, concerning the X-efficiency of state agencies, is an important issue since it may nullify many of the advantages of state trading listed above.

Professor Warley has suggested that, in spite of the original expectations motivating the creation of many agricultural marketing boards, these boards have rarely achieved any significant gain from increased efficiency.[57] In addition, they have made no significant contribution to the improvement of performance in the marketing sector.[58] It has frequently been noted that better grading, more appropriate timing of shipments or economies of size, in respect to market information, may be achieved without recourse to state trading. In several cases of agricultural marketing in Australia, New Zealand and South Africa, agricultural boards were not allowed to engage in marketing activities abroad, since private firms were believed to be more efficient in performing that task.

One possible way of dealing with the problem of inefficiencies in the commercial activities of some central agencies would be to restrict the role of those agencies exclusively to regulatory functions.[59]

Another possible way of dealing with the X-efficiency problem would be to abandon the state-trading monopoly and to carry on state-trading in competition with private traders. This solution is very rarely used since a state monopoly is a condition *sine qua non* for attaining many of the non-marketing objectives of state traders.

Finally, it has been demonstrated that premiums can sometimes be obtained by direct decentralized negotiations with foreign buyers. State traders may, in fact, lack flexibility or tend to treat all foreign partners alike; this impedes improvement in a country's bargaining position in international markets.

The assessment of pros and cons for state trading in agriculture should be conducted on a case by case basis; for conditions may differ considerably between countries, commodities or over time, and, along with them, the advantages and disadvantages of maintaining particular state trading arrangements.

From a somewhat broader perspective, however, it could be claimed that the basic advantage of state trading over traditional trade-control instruments, as used in Western agricultural trade, is its flexibility. This flexibility derives from the fact that state trading requires less complex domestic procedures for policy modifications and is subject to less international scrutiny. Then too, in numerous cases, the complexity of government objectives calls for the assignation of all essential instruments for achieving them to a single agency. In that respect, the creation of a state-trading arrangement may be the only realistic solution to managerial requirements.

Another advantage of state trading may be demonstrated by making a distinction between what one could call political and economic efficiency. Although economic efficiency would favour solutions improving the well-being of some without worsening the well-being of others, political efficiency may favour arrangements improving the well-being of some without letting the others know that they are worse off. Indeed, the economics of state-trading arrangements are frequently less transparent to the general public than the taxes and subsidies obtained through efficient political lobbying. This is particularly true of government-sanctioned and producer-controlled marketing arrangements, such as the statutory marketing boards. Here, the choice of state trading over private trading is motivated by internal reasons.

Important, but less obvious, advantages of state trading in agricultural products are frequently cited in connection with export marketing and matters related to monopoly, international bargaining power, or fulfilment of international commitments on quantities and/or prices. In reference to the last point, state trading based on foreign-trade targets may be deemed necessary to enable governments to make bulk purchases and to engage in other government-to-government contracts determining traded volumes and prices. However, the advantages of these state-trading arrangements over private long-term contracts cannot be precisely weighed without further investigation. Similarly, any general appreciation of the advantage of agricultural state trading, in respect to foreign-trade marketing, international bargaining or monopoly power, will depend on the feasibility of other solutions, international market conditions, international politics, national traditions in public administration and a number of other factors.

NOTES AND REFERENCES

1. The auther is grateful to T. K. Warley and Andrew Schmitz for their comments on a draft of this chapter.
2. The basic sample considered in this paper is drawn from the state-trading agencies engaging in international trade of agricultural products, and reported

by the OECD member countries and South Africa to the General Agreement on Tariffs and Trade.

3. In about 90 per cent of agricultural state-trading arrangements listed in the GATT sample, foreign-trade monopoly is maintained.

4. This includes the trading agencies and, to some extent, the mixed agencies. In many cases, one is dealing with agricultural trade where both state-trading agencies and private traders are involved. For example, much of the wheat shipped by the Canadian Wheat Board also heavily involves the private grain trade from the United States. This is true not only in terms of shipping, but also in terms of outright purchases of grain by the United States from the Canadian Wheat Board.

5. This type of state-trading monopoly is that of the regulatory marketing boards in the present or former UK Dominions or the state trading practised by several Western European countries.

6. As, for example, it has been the case for South African maize. See: R. N. Britz, 'The Marketing of South African Maize', *South African Journal of Economics*, vol. 37 (September 1969), pp. 209–11.

7. The GATT inventory of agricultural state-trading agencies might be criticized for two main reasons. First, the definition of state trading on which it is based is not very clear (see, Yvan Bernier Chapter 12 in this volume). Secondly, it is far from complete, even if a somewhat more generous appreciation is allowed for the dubious cases.

8. Alex McCalla, Andrew Schmitz, 'Grain Marketing Systems: The Case of the United States vs. Canada', *American Journal of Agricultural Economics*, vol. 61, no. 2 (May 1979), pp. 199–212.

9. Professor Lewis A. Fischer, from McGill University, drew my attention to the fact that, among the 105 provincial marketing boards operating in Canada, several could be considered as generating state trading, if the definition of this paper is used.

10. See: B. A. Delagneau, 'Agricultural Co-operative Marketing within the Context of the EEC Competition Policy', *Journal of Agricultural Economics*, vol. XXVII, no. 1 (January 1976).

11. Emile Durkheim, *Le Socialisme* (Paris: Presses Universitaires de France, 1971), p. 182.

12. Leslie A. Wheeler, 'The New Agricultural Protectionism and its Effects on Trade Policy', in Robert L. Tontz (ed.) *Foreign Agricultural Trade, Selected Readings* (Ames: The Iowa State University Press, 1966), p. 324.

13. For a detailed account see: FAO, *Agricultural Protection: Domestic Policy and International Trade*, Doc. C73/LIM/9 (November 1973). Alex McCalla, 'Protectionism in International Agricultural Trade, 1850–1968', *Agricultural History*, no. 43, (July 1969) pp. 329–43.

14. For an analysis of the evolution and complex functions of those board see: J. C. Abbott, H. C. Creupelandt, *Agricultural Marketing Boards: Their Establishment and Operation*, FAO Marketing Guide, No. 5 (Rome: FAO, 1974), pp. xii–236.

15. J. N. Lewis, 'Organized Marketing of Agricultural Products' in Australia', *The Australian Journal of Agricultural Economics*, vol. 5, no. 1 (September 1961), p. 4.

16. T. K. Warley, 'Western Trade in Agricultural Products', in *International*

Economic Relations of the Western World 1959–1971 vol. 1, *Politics and Trade* (London: Oxford University Press for the Royal Institute of International Affairs, 1976), pp. 287–402.

17. D. Gale Johnson, 'World Agriculture, Commodity Policy, and Price Variability', *American Journal of Agricultural Economics* vol. 57, no. 5 (December 1975), p. 824.

18. GATT Doc. L/4140/Add. 8, July 1975, p. 3.

19. For more details on rice export from Japan by destination (1970–76), and some features of Japan's commercial policy with respect to rice see: FAO Doc. OCP: RI 78/6 (December 1977), p. 6.

20. Tim Josling, 'Government Price Policies and the Structure of International Agriculture Trade', *Journal of Agricultural Economics*, vol. XXVIII, no. 3 (September 1977), p. 269.

21. D. Gale Johnson, op. cit., p. 827. Colin Carter and Andrew Schmitz, 'Import Tariffs and Price Formation in the World Wheat Market', in *American Journal of Agricultural Economics*, vol. 61, no. 2 (May 1979).

22. On these grounds, it has been argued that US private grain companies are likely to contribute more to instabilities in world grain markets than the Canadian Wheat Board. See: Andrew Schmitz, Alex McCalla, 'The Canadian Wheat Board', in Sidney Hoss (ed.) *Agricultural Marketing Board – An International Perspective*, (Cambridge, Mass.: Ballinger Publishing Co., 1979), p. 97.

23. Lewis, op. cit., p. 1.

24. Note that the production effect, if allowed for, results in a loss for the country, since the cost of producing the additional 'BB' of output is higher than the revenue from selling that additional output abroad.

25. R. M. Parish, 'The Costs of Protecting the Dairying Industry', *The Economic Record*, vol. 38, no. 82 (June 1962), pp. 167–82. E. L. Banks, R. G. Mauldon, 'Effects of Pricing Decisions of a Statutory Marketing Board; A Case Study', *The Australian Journal of Agricultural Economics*, vol. 10, no. 1 (June 1966), pp. 1–13.

26. Due to important price increases in the international wheat market in 1973/74 and 1974/75, this situation changed.

27. For the case of the liquor monopoly of Ontario and Quebec in Canada see: Klaus Stegemann, *Canadian Non-Tariff Barriers to Trade* (Montreal: The Private Planning Association of Canada, 1973). Keith Acheson, 'Revenue vs. Protection: the Pricing of Wine by the Liquor Control Board of Ontario', in *Canadian Journal of Economics*, vol. X, no. 2 (May 1977), pp. 246–61.

28. For discussion of the question of equivalence of protection of exportables see: W. M. Corden, *The Theory of Protection* (Oxford: Clarendon Press, 1971), pp. 14–17.

29. Keith Campbell, 'The State Marketing Board – Relic or Prototype', *The Australian Journal of Agricultural Economics*, vol. 17, no. 3 (December 1973), p. 181.

30. It may also be important to note which government department supervises the agency in question. Government departments are frequently at odds. Some of them may favour egoist government interests (Treasury), others may be concerned with balance of payment equilibria or unemployment, still others may be consumer biased (Ministry of Consumer Affairs).

31. Ruth L. Cohen, 'Further Reflections on Agricultural Marketing', *Journal of Agricultural Economics*, vol. xiv, no. 4 (December 1961), p. 431.

32. Campbell, op. cit., p. 181.

33. For an excellent analysis of this problem see: Anthony Downs. *An Economic Theory of Democracy* (New York: Harper & Row, 1957), pp. 238–59.

34. For example, at the end of 1977, the New Zealand Dairy Board was stuck with 67 000 tons of unsold butter in the UK, in spite of the fact that New Zealand dairymen produce at about one-third of the EEC producer price. *The Wall Street Journal* (January 22, 1979), p. 1.

35. See the discussion of the contrast between the normative and the result-oriented approach by Frieder Roessler (Chapter 13 in this volume).

36. A certain degree of price-making power may also be assumed for a number of importing agricultural state traders in Japan and Western Europe.

37. Schmitz and McCalla, op. cit., p. 97.

38. Note, however, that the degree of concentration in private grain export in the US is relatively high. The five largest private exporters of US grain handle close to 90% of that country's grain exports.

39. For more details on the Agreement and the Soviet deals see: D. Gale Johnson, *The Soviet Impact on World Grain Trade* (Montreal: British North American Committee, 1977), pp. x–62.

40. See: Colin Carter, Andrew Schmitz, 'Import Tariffs and Price Formation in the World Wheat Market', in *American Journal of Agricultural Economics*, vol. 61, no. 3 (August 1979) pp. 517–22.

41. Alex McCalla, Andrew Schmitz, 'Grain Marketing Systems: The Case of the United States versus Canada', in *American Journal of Agricultural Economics*, vol. 61, no. 2 (May 1979).

42. J. R. Hicks, 'The Theory of Uncertainty and Profit', *Economica*, vol. 32 (May 1931), p. 173.

43. This system is sometimes required to compensate for important differences in freight rates. The freight rates faced by the Australian Wheat Board may well illustrate the case. In some important foreign markets, they tend to be considerably higher than those of the US or Canada. See: FAO, *Trade Yearbook* (1976), p. 23.

44. See: D. F. Campbell, 'Control of Agricultural Marketing in New Zealand', in M. J. Moriarty (ed.) *New Zealand Farm Production and Marketing*, (London: Oxford Univesity Press, 1963), p. 91. Michele Dawe Veeman, 'New Zealand Marketing Boards', in *Agricultural Marketing Boards – An International perspective* (Cambridge, Mass.: Ballinger, 1979) p. 230.

45. Ezra Sadan, 'Milk and Dairy Marketing Boards', in *Agricultural Marketing Boards – An International perspective,* p. 230.

46. The problem of export pricing versus a country's dependence on export revenue is discussed in practical terms in references to the Maize Board of South Africa by Britz, op. cit.

47. The issue is discussed by F. V. Meyer, 'Bulk Purchases', *Economica*, New Series, vol. XV, no. 57–60 (1948), pp. 51 and 54.

48. Several marketing boards operate offices abroad; e.g. the Dairy Board of New Zealand succeeded in developing new markets in Third-World countries partly due to operation of such offices and its capacity to adapt its production

to the somewhat different needs of that area.
49. See also a more general discussion of sales cost by Norman Buchanan, 'Advertising Expenditures: A Suggested Treatment', in *Journal of Political Economy*, vol. 50 (August 1942), pp. 556–7. Sadan maintains that one of the first signs of efficiency through coordinated export marketing is, however, the corresponding endeavour avoiding loss of space and time in the vessels contracted. Sadan, op. cit., p. 230.
50. R. H. Coase, 'The Nature of the Firm', *Economica*, New Series (1937), vol. IV, pp. 386–405.
51. J. M. Keynes, 'The Policy of Government Storage of Foodstuffs and Raw Materials', *Economic Journal*, vol. 48 (September 1938), pp. 449–66.
52. This is, for example, the case of the Norwegian Grain Corporation Statens Kornforretning which has to provide food security for a country that imports about 50 per cent of its grain requirements.
53. In the exporting of fruit, the export risk usually falls on the exporter, even when the fixed selling method is used. This may put a considerable burden on the exporter if the government does not assist him.
54. The concept of *X*-efficiency has been explicitly introduced by H. Leibenstein, 'Allocative Efficiency Versus '*X*-Efficiency', *American Economic Review*, vol. 56 (June 1966), pp. 392–415.
55. The case is discussed by J. C. Abbott, 'The Efficiency of Marketing Board Operations', in *The Marketing Board System* (February 1974), pp. 229–241.
56. See: L. H. Samuels, 'Aspects of Controlled Marketing in the Union', *South African Journal of Economics*, vol. 5, no. 1 (March 1947), p. 47.
57. R. K. Warley, 'The Future Role of Marketing Organizations', *Journal of Agricultural Economics*, vol. XV, no. 4 (December 1963), p. 555.
58. Campbell, op. cit., p. 183 and Lewis, op. cit., p. 1.
59. This pattern has been followed by some marketing boards in Australia, Canada, New Zealand and South Africa.

3 State Trading in Grain

Alex F. McCalla and Andrew Schmitz

INTRODUCTION

This chapter explores the role state trading plays in the international grain trade. Principal attention is paid to trade in temperate zone grains, namely wheat and coarse grains.[1] The only significantly traded grain excluded is rice.[2] The volume of grain trade has grown steadily over the post-war years. During the same period the proportion of trade in which state traders are involved as exporters, importers or both has increased. For example, in the four-year period 1973–7, more than 95 per cent of world wheat trade involved a state trader as an exporter, importer or both. Thus it is useful to examine in more detail the role that state traders play.

For purposes of this chapter we accept Kostecki's definition of state trading.[3] That is ' . . . exporting and importing on government defined terms of transaction'. It includes trading by government ministries or departments, government corporations, producer marketing boards granted government monopolies, and exclusively licensed trading companies. The terms of the transaction include the determination of at least price, quality and quantity parameters. Whether or not the actual trade (handling) is conducted by the private sector (a common occurrence in the grain market) is not important to market outcomes.

We begin the chapter with a brief discussion of the nature of the grain trade and terminology used therein to set the stage for our discussion. We then review the structure of international grain markets and the role of state trading. The next section discusses the interrelationships between state trading and domestic policy. The chapter then turns to structural and theoretical considerations of a mixed market including state traders. We conclude that any theoretical or empirical analysis must take both kinds of actors into account.

THE NATURE OF THE GRAIN TRADE

The grain trade is similar to any other form of international transaction and involves the production and collection of a product in dispersed locations in an exporting country and its movement to dispersed consumption points in the importing country. At some point between production and consumption a contractual transfer of ownership occurs. In the grain trade that contractual arrangement involves many factors including prices, quantity, quality, point of ownership transfer, terms of payment – when and in what currency, marine insurance, carrying charges, responsibility for unforeseen events, time period of delivery and means for settlement of disputes. The first three factors – price, quantity and quality – we call basic terms and conditions. The latter set of factors are called logistical factors. Given the variety of factors involved and the spatial distribution of trade, contractual arrangements in grain can have many forms. Table 3.1 outlines six basic contractual types which are common in the grain trade. The first three – FOB, FAS and FST require the exporter to deliver only to the exporting port. All other functions are provided by the importer either directly or through middlemen. The last three – C&F, CIF and DFD involve the exporter in movement of the grain to at least the importer port of entry. The most frequent forms of trade are FOB and CIF.

These factors are important for discussions of state trading for several reasons. First, state-trading exporters almost never become directly involved in the logistical terms of grain handling. The Canadian Wheat Board, for example, sells principally on an FOB basis leaving the importer to deal with the risks involved in shipping, freight, foreign exchange, etc. Similarly, state-trading importers typically buy on a CIF or DFD basis. This means that in contractual arrangements involving a state-trading exporter and state-trading importer, a middleman (usually a multinational grain firm) is always involved in at least the logistics of the trade. Secondly, a private trader buying grain from a state-trading exporter FOB without prior sales contract has a large range of contractual variables on which to negotiate with importers, private or state. Thus, in these cases considerable scope for price variation exists. Also in a trade with a significant number of state traders the role of any origin sales by private traders gives these traders considerable scope for inter-market arbitrage and price discrimination which a state trader may not have. Thirdly, the complexity of international grain markets, with the attendant risk,

TABLE 3.1

The taxonomy of the grain trade.
Exporter and importer responsibilities and point of contract (*)

Functions / Type of contract	(1) Production	(2) Transport to export point	(3) Loading	(4) Ocean transport	(5) Insurance	(6) Foreign exchange arrangements	(7) Unloading	(8) Transport to final destination	(9) Consumption
1. Free on Board (FOB) – in spout to boat (bulk)	Farmers	EX *	IMP	IMP	IMP	IMP	IMP	IMP	Domestic users
2. Free Along Side (FAS) – bags on wharf	Farmers	EX *	IMP	IMP	IMP	IMP	IMP	IMP	Domestic users
3. FST–FOB plus stowed and trimmed on boat	Farmers	EX	EX *	IMP	IMP	IMP	IMP	IMP	Domestic users
4. Cost and freight to importer dock (C&F)	Farmers	EX	EX	EX *	IMP	IMP	IMP	IMP	Domestic users
5. Cost, insurance and freight (CIF)	Farmers	EX	EX	EX	EX *	EX/IMP	IMP	IMP	Domestic users
6. Delivered to final destination (DFD)	Farmers	EX	EX	EX	EX	EX	EX	EX *	Domestic users

Note: An exporter or importer could contract with a third party (grain merchandiser) for any or all of functions 3, 4, 5, 6, 7, and 8. If these are fixed fee for service contracts, who does them will not alter the principal contractual factors of price, quantity and quality.

places a large premium on good information. Thus, a state-trading exporter which sells only FOB or a state-trading importer that buys only CIF may not have the access to information regarding market variables that an active middleman may have. We return to this point later in the paper. In terms of the international grain market a limited set of multinational firms do most of this business. It is estimated that four or five multinational exporters handle 90 per cent of US grain exports and 70 per cent of world grain exports.[4]

THE STRUCTURE OF INTERNATIONAL GRAIN TRADE AND THE ROLE OF STATE TRADING

The importance of state trading in international grain markets is a function of two principal factors – the structure of the grain trade and the number of national participants pursuing state trading. Each is considered in turn.

THE STRUCTURE OF INTERNATIONAL GRAIN TRADE

Tables 3.2 and 3.3 present weighted average origin-destination trade flows for major participants in international wheat and coarse grain markets for selected years between 1966 and 1976. Data in the intersections of exporter rows and importer columns show the actual flow and the relative importance of that flow to exporter and importer. Table 3.2 shows, for example, that in 1975–6 (weighted 1974–5 (1/4), 1976–1976 (1/2), 1976–7 (1/4)) the United States exported 29.3 million metric tons of wheat (45 per cent of world exports) of which 2.8 million metric tons (10 per cent of US exports) went to the EEC. In the same year the EEC imported 5.9 million metric tons (9 per cent of world imports), of which 2.8 million metric tons (47 per cent of the EECs imports) came from the US. Thus the ratio in the matrix cells indicates the relative importance of the bilateral trade flow to both exporter and importer.

The data in Table 3.2 show several things about the international wheat market. First, the proportion of total trade accounted for by the six largest exporters consistently exceeds 95 per cent. Within those six, the United States, Canada, and Australia account consistently for more than 75 per cent of exports, with the US share rising and the shares of Canada and Australia more variable and showing no discernible trend. The participation of Argentina, the EEC, and the USSR is even more variable. On the import side, concentration in terms of

TABLE 3.2

World trade in wheat:* sources and destinations weighted averages† for 1966–7, 1969–70, 1972–3 and 1975–6

Exporters \ Importers	Year	World Quantity mmt¶	Per cent of world exports	EEC‡ mmt	EEC‡ per cent	Japan mmt	Japan per cent	Peoples Republic of China mmt	Peoples Republic of China per cent	India mmt	India per cent	USSR mmt	USSR per cent	Arab Countries § mmt	Arab Countries § per cent	Brazil mmt	Brazil per cent	Per cent of exports bought by seven major importers
World	1966–7	55.4	100	8.0	(14)	4.0	(7)	5.2	(9)	6.6	(12)	4.0	(7)	6.1	(11)	2.5	(5)	66
	1969–70	49.0	100	8.2	(17)	4.5	(9)	4.3	(9)	2.8	(6)	0.7	(1)	6.0	(12)	2.1	(4)	58
	1972–3	62.5	100	6.2	(10)	5.4	(9)	4.9	(8)	1.9	(3)	9.9	(16)	7.9	(13)	2.6	(4)	62
	1975–6	64.4	100	5.9	(9)	5.7	(9)	3.3	(5)	5.4	(8)	7.0	(11)	11.2	(17)	3.0	(5)	64
United States of America	1966–7	20.9	[38]	2.4	(11)/[30]‖**	2.1	(10)/[53]	0	(0)/[0]	5.2	(25)/[79]	0	(0)/[0]	2.8	(13)/[46]	1.2	(6)/[48]	65
	1969–70	16.9	[34]	2.2	(13)/[27]	2.4	(14)/[53]	0	(0)/[0]	2.1	(12)/[75]	0	(0)/[0]	1.3	(8)/[22]	0.9	(5)/[43]	52
	1972–3	28.0	[45]	2.5	(9)/[40]	3.1	(11)/[57]	1.1	(4)/[22]	0.9	(9)/[47]	5.4	(19)/[55]	2.7	(10)/[34]	1.1	(4)/[42]	60
	1975–6	29.3	[45]	2.8	(10)/[47]	3.2	(11)/[56]	0.4	(1)/[12]	3.7	(13)/[69]	3.0	(10)/[43]	4.2	(14)/[38]	1.6	(5)/[53]	64
Canada	1966–7	13.3	[24]	3.4	(26)/[43]	1.4	(11)/[35]	2.1	(16)/[40]	1.0	(8)/[15]	3.0	(23)/[75]	0.1	(1)/[2]	0	(0)/[0]	83
	1969–70	9.6	[20]	2.8	(29)/[34]	1.1	(11)/[24]	2.0	(21)/[47]	0.5	(5)/[18]	0.7	(7)/[100]	0.6	(6)/[10]	0.1	(1)/[5]	81
	1972–3	14.2	[23]	2.4	(17)/[39]	1.5	(11)/[28]	3.3	(23)/[67]	0.5	(4)/[26]	3.2	(23)/[32]	0.6	(4)/[8]	0.5	(4)/[19]	85
	1975–6	12.1	[19]	2.3	(19)/[39]	1.4	(12)/[25]	1.7	(14)/[52]	0.4	(3)/[7]	2.0	(17)/[29]	0.8	(7)/[17]	0.8	(7)/[27]	78
Australia	1966–7	6.7	[12]	0.7	(10)/[9]	0.5	(7)/[13]	2.2	(33)/[42]	0.4	(6)/[6]	0.2	(3)/[5]	0.6	(9)/[10]	0.1	(1)/[4]	70
	1969–70	7.4	[15]	1.4	(19)/[17]	1.0	(14)/[22]	1.8	(24)/[42]	0.1	(1)/[4]	0	(0)/[0]	1.0	(14)/[17]	0	(0)/[0]	72
	1972–3	6.4	[10]	0.5	(8)/[18]	0.9	(14)/[17]	0.5	(8)/[10]	0.2	(3)/[1]	0.6	(9)/[6]	1.6	(25)/[20]	0	(0)/[0]	67
	1975–6	8.1	[13]	0.1	(1)/[2]	1.1	(14)/[19]	1.1	(14)/[33]	0.5	(6)/[9]	0.9	(11)/[13]	2.1	(26)/[19]	0	(0)/[0]	72
Argentina	1966–7	3.9	[7]	0.8	(21)/[10]	0.7	(18)/[13]	0.7	(18)/[13]	0	(0)/[0]	0.6	(15)/[15]	0	(0)/[0]	1.1	(28)/[44]	82
	1969–70	2.2	[4]	0.6	(27)/[7]	0	(0)/[0]	0	(0)/[0]	0.1	(2)/[4]	0	(0)/[0]	0	(0)/[0]	1.0	(45)/[48]	77
	1972–3	2.4	[4]	0.4	(17)/[6]	0.1	(4)/[2]	0	(0)/[0]	0.1	(4)/[5]	0	(0)/[0]	0.1	(4)/[4]	0.9	(38)/[35]	67
	1975–6	3.5	[5]	0.5	(14)/[8]	0	(0)/[0]	0.2	(6)/[6]	0.1	(3)/[2]	0.8	(23)/[11]	0.5	(14)/[4]	0.6	(17)/[20]	77
EEC	1966–7	4.1	[7]			0	(0)/[0]	0.2	(5)/[4]	0	(0)/[0]	0.1	(2)/[3]	1.4	(34)/[23]	0.1	(2)/[4]	44
	1969–70	4.8	[10]			0	(0)/[0]	0.5	(10)/[12]	0.1	(2)/[4]	0	(0)/[0]	2.1	(44)/[35]	0	(0)/[0]	56
	1972–3	5.2	[8]			0	(0)/[0]	0.1	(2)/[3]	0	(0)/[0]	0	(0)/[0]	2.3	(44)/[29]	0	(0)/[0]	52
	1975–6	6.6	[10]			0	(0)/[0]	0	(0)/[0]	0.7	(11)/[13]	0	(0)/[0]	3.4	(52)/[30]	0	(0)/[0]	64
USSR	1966–7	3.9	[7]	0.1	(3)/[1]	0	(0)/[0]	0	(0)/[0]	0	(0)/[0]			0.6	(15)/[10]	0	(0)/[0]	18
	1969–70	6.1	[12]	0.6	(10)/[7]	0	(0)/[0]	0	(0)/[0]	0	(0)/[0]			0.3	(5)/[5]	0.1	(2)/[5]	16
	1972–3	3.1	[5]	0.1	(3)/[2]	0	(0)/[0]	0	(0)/[0]	0	(0)/[0]			0.1	(3)/[1]	0	(0)/[0]	15
	1975–6	1.9	[3]	0	(1)/[8]	0	(0)/[0]	0	(0)/[0]	0.3	(9)/[16]			0	(0)/[0]	0	(0)/[0]	0
Per cent of imports supplied by six major exporters	1966–7		[95]		[93]		[100]		[100]		[100]		[98]		[90]		[100]	
	1969–70		[96]		[93]		[100]		[100]		[100]		[100]		[88]		[100]	
	1972–3		[95]		[95]		[100]		[100]		[100]		[97]		[94]		[96]	
	1975–6		[96]		[97]		[100]		[100]		[100]		[96]		[98]		[100]	

* Excludes Durum.
† Weight – year noted 50 per cent, year t−1 – 25 per cent, year t+1 – 25 per cent.
‡ Excludes intra-EC trade.
§ Near East (except Afghanistan, Cyprus, Israel and Turkey) and North Africa.

¶ mmt = million metric tons.
‖ Parentheses ( ) is the percentage of an exporters exports going to that destination.
** Square bracket [ ] is the percentage of an importers imports coming from that origin.

Source: International Wheat Council: *Review of World Wheat Situation* and *World Wheat Statistics* various issues.

importing countries and regions is less. The traditional European market is declining in relative importance. China, Brazil and Japan have held relatively constant shares, while the Arab countries are of rising importance. The participation of the USSR and India is highly variable largely as a function of their weather patterns. More than one-third of the wheat exports go to additional LDC countries not listed. The total LDC market is of rising importance, in some years accounting for 60 per cent total wheat imports.

Table 3.3 shows that for trade in coarse grains, six countries account for 80 to 90 per cent of total exports and one, the US, accounts in some years for more than 60 per cent of exports. Thus, there appears to be growing one-country dominance on the export side. On the import side, the largest importer is the EEC but its share of the market has declined from over 45 per cent to less than 30 per cent over the twelve-year period. The USSR, Western Europe outside the EEC, and Eastern Europe now account for over 30 per cent of imports. Japanese imports are increasing steadily in actual volume but the relative share is falling. Imports by Western Europe outside the EEC and Eastern Europe are also rising. The USSR participation in the market, as with wheat, is highly variable. In sum, the export side is dominated by the US and the import side to a lesser and declining extent by Japan and the EEC. In terms of trade flows the coarse grain market is more concentrated between fewer origins and destinations than is wheat trade.

ROLE OF STATE TRADERS

The importance of these structural changes becomes obvious when one considers the role that state trading plays for each of the major participants. In terms of major exporters, Canada, Australia and the USSR have been state traders since the interwar period; Argentina was a state trader until the mid-1970s but now relies more on the private trade although most facilities are still government controlled; the USA, EEC, and Thailand rely on private traders. Thus, on the export side the growing dominance of the US means that the relative importance of grain trade originating in state traders has declined. On the import side, the opposite is occurring. Traditional markets in Western Europe which rely on private traders have declined while the importance of the centrally-planned economies and the developing countries has increased. Given that centrally-planned economies, and virtually all developing countries, pursue state trading, the importance of state-trading importers has risen.

TABLE 3.3

World trade in coarse grains:† sources and destinations weighted averages‡ for 1966–7, 1969–70, 1972–3 and 1975–6

Exporters / Importers	Year	World quantity mmt§	Per cent of world exports	EEC§ mmt	EEC§ per cent	Japan mmt	Japan per cent	People's Republic of China mmt	PRC per cent	India mmt	India per cent	USSR§ mmt	USSR per cent	Western Europe outside the EEC¶ mmt	W. Europe per cent	Eastern Europe¶ mmt	E. Europe per cent	Canada mmt	Canada per cent	Per cent of exports bought by eight major importers
World	1966–7	39.4	100	18.7	(47)	7.2	(18)	*	(.1)	1.6	(4)	*	(.)	5.6	(14)	1.3	(3)	0.6	(2)	89
	1969–70	38.7	100	16.0	(41)	9.7	(25)	*		0.2	(1)	0.2	(1)	4.8	(12)	1.8	(5)	0.6	(2)	86
	1972–3	56.3	100	16.5	(29)	12.2	(22)	1.0	(2)	0.6	(1)	5.8	(10)	6.6	(12)	2.6	(5)	0.7	(1)	82
	1975–6	67.9	100	16.9	(25)	13.8	(20)	0.5	(1)	n.a.		7.8	(11)	8.3	(12)	6.7	(10)	n.a.		
United States	1966–7	21.9	[56]	10.5	(48)/[56]	4.5	(21)/[63]	0		1.6	(8)/[100]	*		1.9	(9)/[34]	0.9	(4)/[69]	0.6	(4)/[100]	93
	1969–70	18.3	[47]	7.5	(41)/[47]	5.9	(32)/[61]	0		0.1	(1)/[50]	4.0	(16)/[69]	1.3	(7)/[23]	0.8	(4)/[44]	0.6	(4)/[100]	90
	1972–3	34.2	[61]	10.7	(31)/[65]	7.7	(23)/[63]	0.9	(3)/[90]	0.4	(1)/[67]			3.3	(10)/[50]	0.9	(3)/[35]	0.7	(2)/[99]	84
	1975–6	44.4	[65]	n.a.		n.a.		n.a.		n.a.		n.a.		n.a.		n.a.		n.a.		
Canada	1966–7	1.3	[3]	0.6	(46)/[3]	0.3	(23)/[4]	0		0		0		0.1	(8)/[12]	*	(5)/[6]			77
	1969–70	2.0	[5]	1.1	(55)/[7]	0.4	(20)/[4]	0		0		0		*		0.1	(10)/[15]			80
	1972–3	4.1	[7]	1.4	(34)/[8]	0.9	(22)/[7]	*	(5)/[10]	0		0.5	(12)/[9]	0.1	(2)/[2]	0.4				80
	1975–6	4.3	[6]	n.a.		n.a.		n.a.		n.a.		n.a.		n.a.		n.a.				
Australia	1966–7	0.7	[2]	0.4	(57)/[2]	0.2	(29)/[3]	0		*		0		*		*		0		86
	1969–70	1.2	[3]	0.6	(50)/[4]	0.5	(42)/[5]	0		*		0		*		*		0		92
	1972–3	2.1	[4]	0.3	(14)/[2]	1.3	(62)/[11]	0.1	(5)/[2]	*		0.1	(5)/[2]	*		*		0		86
	1975–6	3.1	[5]	n.a.		n.a.		n.a.		n.a.		n.a.		n.a.		n.a.		n.a.		
Argentina	1966–7	5.3	[13]	4.0	(75)/[21]	0.2	(4)/[3]	*		0		*		1.0	(19)/[18]	*		0		99
	1969–70	6.6	[17]	3.7	(56)/[23]	1.3	(20)/[13]			0		0.1	(2)/[50]	1.1	(17)/[23]	*		0		94
	1972–3	5.9	[11]	3.1	(53)/[19]	0.6	(10)/[5]	2	(3)/[20]	0.2	(3)/[33]	0.2	(3)/[3]	1.1	(19)/[17]	0.1	(2)/[4]	0		93
	1975–6	7.2	[11]	n.a.		n.a.		n.a.		n.a.		n.a.		n.a.		n.a.		0		
EEC	1966–7	1.9	[5]			*		0		0		0		1.4	(74)/[23]	0.3	(16)/[23]	0		89
	1969–70	2.4	[6]			0.3	(13)/[3]	0		0		0.1	(4)/[50]	1.2	(50)/[25]	0.7	(29)/[39]	0		96
	1972–3	3.5	[6]					0		0		0.8	(23)/[14]	0.9	(26)/[14]	1.0	(29)/[38]	0		77
	1975–6	1.8	[3]	n.a.		n.a.		n.a.		n.a.		n.a.		0		n.a.		n.a.		
Thailand	1966–7	1.3	[3]	*		0.8	(62)/[11]	*		0		0		0		0		0		62
	1969–70	1.5	[4]	*		0.7	(47)/[7]	0.1		0		*		0		0		0		47
	1972–3	1.7	[3]	*		0.7	(41)/[6]	0.1	(6)/[10]	0				0		0		0		47
	1975–6	2.4	[4]	n.a.		n.a.		n.a.		n.a.		n.a.		0		0		n.a.		
Per cent of imports supplied by six major exporters	1966–7		[82]		[83]		[83]		[100]		[100]		[100]		[79]		[100]		[100]	
	1969–70		[83]		[81]		[94]		[100]		[50]		[100]		[75]		[89]		[100]	
	1972–3		[91]		[94]		[92]		[100]		[100]		[97]		[82]		[92]		[100]	
	1975–6		[93]																	

* = less than 50000 mt.
† Coarse grains include: maize (corn), barley, oats, rye and sorghum.
‡ Weights year listed 50 per cent, year t−1 − 25 per cent, year t+1 − 25 per cent.
§ Excludes intra-EEC trade.
¶ Excludes trade between centrally planned economies.
|_ mmt = million metric tons.
** Paentheses ( ) is the percentage of an exporters' exports exports going to that destination.
†† Square brackets [ ] is the percentage of an importers' imports coming from that origin.
n.a. = data not available – FAO – *World Grain Statistics* was discontinued in 1974.

Source: UNFAO: *World Grain Trade Statistics*, 1965/66 – 1973/74 and International Wheat Council, *Review of the World Wheat Situation*, 1974/75 – 1976/77.

Table 3.4 presents a more detailed matrix for wheat for the period 1973–7. Each intersection in the matrix shows the nature of the bilateral trading relationship (P–P – private to private, P–S – private to state, S–P – state to private and S–S – state to state) and the average trade flow over the period. It should be noted that the regional groupings are designated as state traders when the majority of the trade is conducted by state traders. Thus, the numbers in this table, and Table 3.5, may overstate the importance of state trading. We argue it is not a significant overstatement, given that the importance of non-state traders in Western Europe outside the EEC, Central America, South America, rest of Asia, Middle East and Sub-Sahara Africa are quite small relative to regional and world trade. A partial list of state-trading organizations is found in Appendix 3.

Table 3.5 presents a summary of state trading in wheat in the post-war period. Several things stand out. First, the proportion of wheat trade which involves only private traders is small and declining, involving about 5 per cent of the trade in 1973–7. The reciprocal of course is that 95 per cent of world trade in wheat involves a state trader on at least one side of the transaction. Secondly, state trader to state trader transactions account for about one-third of the trade and seem to be stable. Thirdly, the importance of state trading on the export side of the market is declining, reflecting (1) the rising importance of the US as an exporter and (2) the discontinuance of state trading by Argentina. Fourthly, the rise in importance of state-trading importers is substantial, reflecting the rising importance of centrally planned and LDC importers in the wheat market, most of whom pursue state trading.

Comparable data for coarse grains cannot be easily (if at all) generated. However, it can be postulated that the role of private traders is significantly greater for the following reasons:

(1) the US is a more important element in the market;

(2) Australia does not state trade in coarse grains, rather trade is controlled by producer marketing boards in each state;

(3) Japan imports only barley as a state trader, other coarse grains are imported by trading companies;

(4) the relative importance of LDCs is much smaller; and

(5) many countries (particularly in Western Europe outside the EEC) which state trade in food grains do not do so for coarse grains.

Partially offsetting these factors is the rising volume of coarse-grain exports to the USSR and Eastern Europe which do state trade. The

TABLE 3.4

World wheat trade matrix – trading relationships and actual trade – 1973-7 average
(000, metric tons)

	EEC	Western Europe outside EEC†	Eastern Europe	USSR	Central America	South America	Peoples Republic Of China	India	Japan	Rest of Asia	Middle East‡	North Africa§	Sub-Sahara Africa	Oceania	Total exports	Percent of world trade
Argentina¶	P*-P 435	P-S** 65	P-S 262	P-S 501	P-S 12	P-S 900	P-S 172	P-S 40	P-S 16	P-S 36	P-S 54	P-S 257	P-S 28	P-S –	2,778	4.4
Australia	S-P 60	S-S 13	S-S 6	S-S 592	S-S –	S-S 170	S-S 1,090	S-S 601	S-S 891	S-S 1,882	S-S 951	S-S 917	S-S 172	S-S 153	7,498	11.8
Canada	S-P 2,340	S-S 266	S-S 609	S-S 1,561	S-S 890	S-S 954	S-S 1,717	S-S 370	S-S 1,450	S-S 772	S-S 263	S-S 485	S-S 188	S-S –	11,865	18.7
EEC-9	–	P-S 254	P-S 174	P-S 1	P-S 122	P-S 60	P-S 52	P-S 444	P-S 1	P-S 1,050	P-S 714	P-S 2,341	P-S 776	P-S 28	6,017	9.4
U.S.A.	P-P 2,419	P-S 624	P-S 729	P-S 2,635	P-S 1,125	P-S 3,886	P-S 1,172	P-S 3,038	P-S 3,193	P-S 4,288	P-S 2,705	P-S 2,709	P-S 710	P-S 7	29,240	46.0
U.S.S.R.	S-P –	S-S –	S-S 1,788	–	S-S 144	S-S –	S-S –	S-S 259	S-S –	S-S 669	S-S –	S-S –	S-S –	S-S –	2,860	4.6
Total imports	5,254	1,222	3,568	5,290	2,293	5,970	4,203	4,752	5,551	8,697	4,687	6,709	1,874	188	60,258	
Percent world	8.3	1.9	5.6	8.3	3.6	9.4	6.6	7.5	8.7	13.7	7.4	10.6	2.9	0.3		95
Total world trade															63,500	100

Notes: *P = private trader
    **S = state trader
    † = other western Europe includes Austria, Finland(S), Greece, Iceland, Malta, Norway(S), Portugal(S), Spain(S), Sweden(S), Switzerland(S), Yugoslavia(S).
    ‡ = Middle East includes Afghanistan(S), Cyprus, Iran(S), Iraq(S), Israel(S), Jordan, Kuwait(S), Lebanon(S), Saudi Arabia(S), Syria(S), Turkey(S),
    United Arab Emirates, Yemen(S), Democratic Yemen(S).
    § = North Africa includes Algeria(S), Egypt(S), Libya(S), Morocco(S), Sudan(S), Tunisia(S).
    ¶ = Argentina vacillated between state and private trading over the period. As of 1979, private traders operate. Therefore, for this period Argentina is
    counted as a private trader.

Source: International Wheat Council *World Wheat Statistics*, various issues.

data in Table 3.3 suggest that in 1975–6 more than 85 per cent of world coarse-grain exports originated with private traders. Similarly, more than 60 per cent of coarse-grain imports were imported by private traders. More detail on specific bilateral trading relationships is unfortunately not available. Also, data on long-term trends is not available.

This review of wheat and feed-grain markets clearly shows differences in the importance of state trading in the two markets. State trading is of growing importance in the wheat market principally because of the increasing trade of LDCs and centrally planned economies. It is relatively less important in coarse-grain markets because

TABLE 3.5

State trading in wheat — percentage of volume of
principal exporters accounted for by state traders

	1953–7 per cent	1963–7 per cent	1973–7 per cent
1. Private exporters to private importers	10.7	5.9	4.4
2. Private exporters to state importers	33.3	51.2	56.6
3. State exporters to private importers	28.3	8.1	4.3
4. State exporters to state importers	27.7	34.8	34.7
Summary			
Exports by private traders (1 + 2)	44.0	57.1	61.0
Exports by state traders (3 + 4)	56.0	42.9	39.0
Imports by private traders (1 + 3)	39.0	14.0	8.7
Imports by state traders (2 + 4)	61.0	86.0	91.3
Volume of trade included above (000 m.t.)	23,475	49,891	60,385
Total world exports 000 m.t.	25,596	56,397	63,506

Sources: 1953–7 – UNFAO – World Grain Trade Statistics.
1963–7 and 1973–7 – International Wheat Council, *Review of the World Wheat Situation*, various issues.

coarse grains are primarily imported by rich countries as livestock feed and these countries are less inclined to state trade in a feed input.

This section of the chapter has shown the apparent rising importance of state trading in grain and has also shown that the relative importance of state trading changes with changing market structure. It sets the stage for asking economically more interesting questions. The next two sections of the paper explore the relationship of state trading and domestic policies and some further structural and theoretical considerations.

STATE TRADING AND DOMESTIC POLICY

One hypothesis that could be stated is that state trading by a nation in temperate zone agriculture products is generally an element of domestic policy rather than an explicit international trade policy. This is not to say that once state trading is established countries may not attempt to exercise market power. Rather it says that the principal motivation for establishing state trading was domestic.

There are at least four plausible domestic reasons why nations might state trade in grains. First, most developed nations pursue domestic agricultural prices and incomes policies which involve price, and often supply management. These policies require elements which regulate the quantities and prices of traded goods so that the international market does not negate domestic objectives. State trading is one, but not the only, possible means. Secondly, an increasing number of developing and centrally-planned countries operate extensive subsidized urban food distribution programmes where retail prices are significantly below producer and/or world prices. State trading is again one means available to prevent events in the international market from disrupting domestic programmes. Thirdly, the form of economic organization may be such that state trading is the only compatible form of international interface. For example, a centrally-planned economy with public ownership of production and/or distribution systems, may find private international trade incompatible with domestic organization. Fourthly, nations may seek to manage trade for foreign exchange reasons and/or to allow intercommodity and insectoral trade-offs in commercial policy. To the extent that the agricultural production sector and the domestic food distribution system are elements in overall economic security and stability policies, state trading offers a centralized vehicle for trade management.

Most, if not all, of current state trading in grain can be explained by one or more of these domestic reasons. Canada got into state trading in grain as a result of the collapse of the prairie-grain marketing system and the resultant economic distress of prairie farmers. Dominant concerns with market equity led to a collective system of grain marketing which required state trading of exports.[5] The Australian Wheat Board also was established as an integral element of domestic agricultural stabilization policy. The USSR, China and Eastern Europe all state trade for the principal reason that the role of the state in domestic agriculture and agricultural policy is large. In addition, consistency with domestic food subsidy programmes and overall economic objectives regarding trade balances and foreign exchange constraints also play a role. Most Western European countries outside of the EEC state trade as integral parts of domestic agricultural price and income stabilization programmes. Japan state trades both because import skimming profits finance domestic farm programmes and because state or licensed trading is consistent with overall trading objectives. Virtually all developing countries in Asia, Africa, Latin and Central America state trade as a by-product of pursuing domestic food subsidy programmes whose management is crucial to domestic political stability.

However, we must be careful not to overdraw the case. All nations pursue domestic policies for one or more of the reasons outlined. Yet, all do not pursue state trading. Thus, a dominant domestic objective is a necessary, but not sufficient, condition for state trading. Several major traders do not state trade. The United States has domestic objectives similar to Canada and Australia but has used different policy means to implement them. The US has pursued complicated and expensive farm programmes which have involved domestic price support and supply control. Accompanying these have been trade policies which have involved quantitative trade restrictions and at times subsidized exports. The problems of an exporting nation which seeks to differentiate domestic prices from international prices are inherently difficult when this is attempted in conjunction with a market economy, as the US has discovered. The task for an importer is much easier. Internal prices can be easily managed by manipulation of import quantities and prices. The EEC, by use of the variable levy, has effectively supported internal farm prices by absolutely isolating domestic prices from international fluctuations. However, as a result of domestic output expansion, the EEC is moving rapidly towards a net export position in grains. It has already reached that point in wheat. How the EEC will seek to manage foreign trade as an exporter will be interesting.

The fact that state trading originates for domestic reasons does not mean that once in place international objectives do not emerge. The Canadian Wheat Board, for example, states as one of its objectives maximization of producer returns. As Bieri and Schmitz[6] have shown, this leads to different behaviour than if the Board behaved as a competitor or a private trader. Thus, the Canadian Board, and likely also the Australian Board, have clear international goals considered necessary to accomplish domestic objectives. Similarly, state-trading importers have international objectives. The Japanese are interested in getting a specific quantity of imports at as low a price as possible so as to maximize skimming profits. However, for Japan the objective is probably modified by the need for a reliable and consistent supply of grain. Carter and Schmitz[7] have argued that Japan (and the EEC) may be pursuing an optimum tariff policy. For most other state-trading importers the international objective appears to be to minimize the costs of importing necessary supplies either because of domestic production shortfalls or expanding domestic food distribution programmes. Thus, their demands are going to be variable and conditioned by foreign-exchange availability.

The desire to exercise market power through supply management and price control is likely present in all state traders. The actual exercise of that power is conditioned by many factors including relative size, capacity to hold stocks, elasticity of demand and supply functions and consistency with domestic objectives.

The pattern that seems clear in international grain markets is that we have a mixed market where state traders, private multinational grain firms and domestic government policies interact in the market. Each of these groups has different objectives in terms of goals and time horizon and different means to influence outcomes. It is likely that private traders seek to maximize short-term profits. Therefore, they may be much more interested in volume and price fluctuations than they are in the absolute level of price. These objectives are antithetical to state-trading importers and exporters alike.

STRUCTURAL AND THEORETIC CONSIDERATIONS

This section reviews past attempts to deal with actual grain market structures and then attempts to develop further theoretical approaches which take into account market structure considerations.

PAST ATTEMPTS

Frequently it is assumed that all actors in international grain markets behave as perfect competitors, allowing the application of spatial or non-spatial competitive price equilibrium models. Based on the discussion above, of the actual structure of grain markets and the differing objectives and sizes of major traders, this approach is at least open to question. The opposite extreme would be to assume a world of state traders dealing with each other in covert bilateral negotiations. This is a world of bilateral monopolies where price outcomes using conventional theory are indeterminate. The actual outcome would reflect the actual market power of the monopsonist *vis-à-vis* the monopolist. An 'equilibrium' world price would not exist. This clearly seems counter to the reality of a world trading price. Thus, neither extreme approach seems feasible.

McCalla[8], in a recent paper, attempts to list all possible bilateral combinations involving importers, exporters, and multinational grain firms. He also includes government policy in both exporting and importing countries. The paper appears to have structural reality but does not present a model of multilateral price formation. However, the approach may give some interesting partial insights. For example, if a state-trading exporter faced the EEC in a bilateral trade negotiation, it seems theoretically possible for the state trader to raise its price to threshold price levels because the EEC has given away market power by the use of the variable levy.[9] But the real problem is how does bilateralism become transformed into multilateral price formation.

Several writers have attempted to view the price formation issue in the international wheat market in terms of oligopoly theory. These models have implicitly assumed that the three large exporters are state traders because each approach considers the trading country as a single decision making unit. McCalla[10] postulated a cooperative duopoly with price leadership by one of the duopolists (Canada) and a fringe of competitive followers. Taplin[11] applied a combination of the market share and the kinked demand curve solution to the market with Canada functioning as a monopolist to set price, with the US following. In a more recent work, Alaouze, Watson and Sturgess[12] postulate a triopoly model with Canada as a revenue maximizing price leader. All of these models achieve deterministic price solutions on the basis of simplistic pricing rules which imply implicit if not explicit collusion and passive behaviour by the largest exporter, the United

States. The previously noted paper by Carter and Schmitz[13] presents a competing approach to price formation which contains essentially no structural parameters.

None of these approaches gives a satisfactory answer to the question of the influence of state trading on world grain price formation under current market conditions. They do, however, give us some notions of the complexity of real international markets which involve public and private intermediaries as well as domestically-oriented agricultural and food policies.

TRADE THEORY AND STATE TRADING

Much of the standard pure theory of trade deals only with producers, consumers, and government as, for example, in the Ohlin theory of international trade. The trading sector (i.e., the marketing intermediary who buys from producers and sells to consumers) is not explicitly included. This is a serious neglect in the theory because, as already indicated, several different kinds of intermediaries are involved in linking producers and consumers. Some models have recently been developed (e.g., Bieri and Schmitz[14] and Just, Schmitz, and Zilberman[15]) where, in addition to consumers, producers and government, marketing firms are introduced. These firms are of different types each pursuing different objectives. For example, a producer marketing board (PMB) may seek to maximize producer returns while a private firm has as one of its objectives the maximization of returns to shareholders. However, while these models point out that the outcomes may be different depending on whether or not marketing is done by state trading or by the private sector, they are limited in that both types of market intermediaries are not included in a single model. The previous sections point out that, in grains, the international market is made up of *both* private and government traders. This issue is discussed in a later section.

In standard theory, the government plays the role of establishing optimal tariff policies and the like which are first best for a single country providing its trading partner does not retaliate. As Johnson[16] has clearly demonstrated, many types of tariffs can be introduced, depending on the specified goal (e.g., self-sufficiency, defence, or maximum government revenue). This has direct bearing on the recent discussions about the possibility of forming a wheat cartel among the major exporters (United States, Canada, and Australia). In theory, a wheat cartel could be implemented by the imposition of an optimal export tax. Apart from problems of retaliation and the like, there is the further problem of the institutional framework needed to carry out the export-tax solution. Canada and Australia have the needed institutions because marketing is done through state-trading marketing boards. This type of institutional arrangement fits the standard theory. However, for the United States, it is quite different because grain is marketed largely through the private sector. How would the US set a joint optimal export tax along with the governments in Canada and Australia? In addition, there may well be a conflict in goals between the government and the private marketing sector. As an example, it is well known that the cartel arrangement in wheat is supported by the Canadian Wheat Board, but not by the private grain firms in the United States. Marketing boards, in order to maximize producer returns, should engage, at least in the short-run, in supply-restrictive policies and hence reduce the volume of exports. Private grain exporters, on the other hand – because of their control of shipping facilities and other components in the marketing channel – tend to promote export volumes since the larger the volume shipped the greater are their returns.

One other point which the pure theory of trade emphasizes is that goods exchange for goods, and equilibrium is determined where the offer curves intersect. In state trading in wheat, for example, it is likely easier for the country to negotiate wheat prices with respect to the other goods they export and import rather than only with respect to wheat. However, when the private sector does the trading, it is primarily interested in only the goods it handles. This issue may take on more light by an example. It has been suggested that a wheat cartel could cause Japan to go to Brazil for additional grain supplies, and hence cartels may be ineffective in raising producer returns. However, the question by producers has been then why not let the Japanese sell all their cars to Brazil? It seems that the notion of the 'terms of trade' in the pure theory context only has meaning if governments negotiate prices and volumes on an aggregate basis rather than having the private sector negotiate trade on a commodity-by-commodity basis.

PRICE FORMATION AND STABILITY

In the standard theory of trade, there are not 'future markets'. In wheat and feedgrains, there currently are active futures markets, especially in the United States. Some have argued that the existence of grain futures ensures competition, provides a price discovery mechanism, and allows people to shift risks onto those who are willing to assume them. Interestingly, if prices and quantities were negotiated on a government-to-government basis, such a market likely could not function. Also, if long-term agreements were made on prices and volumes, instability would be greatly reduced. Unlike marketing boards and/or governments, the private grain-trading sector has been reluctant to enter into long-term wheat agreements.

One could debate at length the merits of future markets and the issue as to who loses and who gains from these transactions. In such a debate one should recognize that many products are traded internationally where no futures markets exist (e.g., rice and oranges). Also, the role of information is very important when debating this issue. Relative to the private grain trade in the United States, grain producers have very little information on international markets which may explain why most farmers do not use futures markets. This can provide an added advantage for the private marketing sector to widen the gap between prices at the producer and consumer levels. On the other hand, a board set up to maximize producer returns would use superior information to enhance producer returns rather than behaving as a pure middleman.

Apart from long-term agreements, the issue of price stability is important insofar as stocks are used to 'manufacture' price instability. As Bieri and Schmitz[17] point out, marketing boards in optimally allocating stocks attempt to create price stability at both the producer and consumer levels whereas the private sector may use stocks to manufacture price instability at the producer level. Thus, state trading through optimal stock management can lead to different results about price instability than the trading and holding of stocks by the private sector.

One can take the above model one step further and apply it to a world where governments deal with private traders. As an example, a great deal of instability in the world wheat market is due to the buying policy of the Soviet Union. Could at least part of this be reduced by more state trading on the part of the United States? Is the Soviet Union intentionally 'manufacturing' price instability at the expense of wheat exporting countries? It is certainly to their advantage to create expectations that prices will stay strong, thus increasing wheat production, and then go 'dead' in the market and create a surplus situation among exporters creating once again a buyers' market. Such instability, while generally costly to producers, is likely beneficial to both private marketing firms and importers.

INTERACTION OF PRIVATE TRADERS AND STATE TRADING

As shown previously, international grain markets involve both state and private traders. However, most theoretical models have not included both. The following is a theoretical attempt to do so. In a market in which different market intermediaries are involved, questions arise regarding how prices are determined, as well as their level, if one firm pursues an objective different from other firms in the market. In the grain-marketing case, one can easily defend the hypothesis that the objectives of the Canadian and Australian Wheat Boards are different than for the private trade. Among the objectives of the boards is the maximization of producer returns whereas, for the private trade, one of their main objectives is to maximize profits and returns to shareholders. As will be demonstrated in a non-competitive environment, the outcomes for a PMB maximizing producer returns are quite different than for the private sector maximizing returns to shareholders.

Consider a market where only a PMB exists as a marketing intermediary. In Figure 3.1, *D* is the foreign demand schedule and *S* is the foreign supply curve. Assume that 'normal marketing costs' are

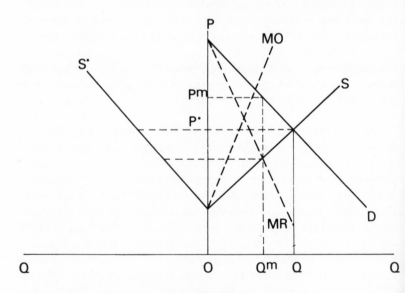

FIGURE 3.1
Marketing boards and private traders

already included in *S* – the simplest of all possible models. With competition, the free-trade price is P^*, and OQ of the product is exported. At the extreme, the board can improve the welfare position of producers by behaving as a monopolist. The board will charge P^m to foreign consumers and restrict sales from OQ to OQ^m (note that the loss in economic rent from monopoly pricing is less than the area which is equivalent to the optimal export tax).

The solution for a private trader can also be represented in Figure 3.1. Clearly, the outcome is different than for a board arrangement since, in the former case, the surplus was extracted from consumers and now is extracted from both producers and consumers. The private sector will equate the marginal outlay curve, *MO*, to *S* with *MR* to arrive at the optimal pricing solution. Note that the price difference between what producers receive and what consumers pay goes to the private marketing firm unlike that in the board case.

Clearly, *both* the private traders and PMBs operate in the same international market. Thus, it is interesting to hypothesize how prices are determined in a market where different marketing institutions exist pursuing different objectives. One model is presented in Figure 3.2. Suppose that S^* represents the supply schedule for the exporting country whose marketing is carried out by a board arrangement. *S* is

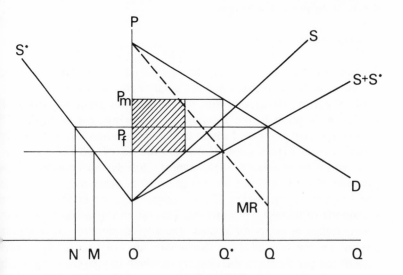

FIGURE 3.2
A market with both a board and the private trade participating

the supply in the country whose exports are sold by the private trade. The foreign demand is represented by D. With competition, the free-trade price is P_f. Suppose now that the marketing board acts as a price leader by equating the sum of S^* and S with MR. Exports are reduced from OQ to OQ^*. Accordingly, production in each country is reduced and how the PMB distributes the benefits will influence future supply

Note that, in the country where the board exists, while production is reduced from ON to OM, prices for producers increase from P_f to P_m, resulting in the net welfare gain. If, as has to be the case in this model, the private sector also charges P_m, the real producer prices will depend on the degree of monopoly power exercised by the private sector. At one extreme, the cross-hatched area would be given to producers, with the result that only normal profits would be made by the private sector. On the other hand, the private trade would keep the area in the form of excess profits. Thus, it is interesting that, even though the board and the private sector priced the same on the demand side, a wide discrepancy can exist between producer prices in both countries.

The above model would also hold if the private sector acted as a price leader or there was some form of private collusion in the market place. The important point is that one cannot argue that competition always prevails when marketing institutions from different countries set identical prices for buyers.

MULTINATIONAL FIRMS

A striking difference between the operations of the PMBs and the private grain trader is that some of the latter companies are of a multinational nature. Because of this, they do not buy grain only from US producers in order to meet export commitments; for example, US companies have purchased wheat from the Canadian Wheat Board in order to meet export sales. However, the boards do not buy from other countries in other to make export sales. To our knowledge, for example, Canada has not bought grain from other nations to meet their export commitments. Their export sales are confined to the magnitude of domestic production. This raises a question about producer welfare at any point in time. The large companies, by shopping around for the best deal for themselves, do not necessarily always benefit the producers in the country in which the parent company is located.

Also, what are the implications for pricing? Consider Figure 3.3

where S^* is the supply in the country where the board does the marketing. The competitive price is P^c. However, due to the multinational nature of the private sector, it can use both S and S^* to meet the foreign demand provided the board will sell to the private sector. This seems unrealistic since the board will market directly to foreign buyers at least part of the crop produced. Thus, it is more realistic to think of S^* as an excess supply curve. If this is true, the private sector could price at P^* and reap excess profits on the production from both countries. The extent to which this is possible depends on how knowledgeable the board is with respect to current and future marketing conditions. Clearly, the returns to the private sector from gathering information are very high since they can use the information not only to capture quasi-rents on S but also rents on S^*. Also, because of their involvement in all market sectors, their unit costs of information are likely lower.[18]

The models to date have concentrated on basic price and quantity dimensions of the grain trade. However, possibilities also exist for private firms, particularly the multinationals, to profit from being involved in the logistical elements of trade mentioned earlier. Some

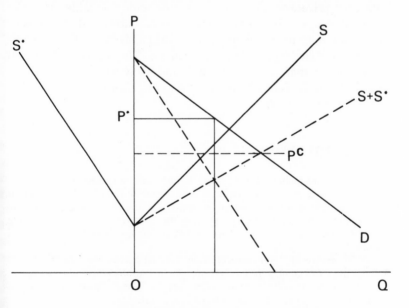

FIGURE 3.3
Multinational marketing firms

private firms own facilities in several countries, are involved in ocean transport and deal extensively in foreign exchange, thus providing additional possibilities for gain that are not available to single-nation state traders.

CONCLUDING COMMENTS

This chapter has presented a brief discussion of the role of state trading in major food and feed grains. We have shown that the market involves private and public traders and that the role of state trading is increasing at least in wheat. Our discussion has attempted to integrate both by attaching specific objectives to each sector. As we point out, often the objectives of a marketing board or a government can be in conflict with those of the private trade. Perhaps this explains why, for example, the notion of a wheat cartel has received mixed reactions, or why the USSR seems to have gotten the upper hand in the Russian grain transaction. In order to provide an understanding of such issues, this paper stresses that models have to be built which explicitly deal with both private-trading firms and state traders in addition to the standard analysis where only consumers, producers and government are considered – the latter only playing the passive role of implementing trade policies such as tariffs and quotas. The reality of the world grain trade is that state traders are, and likely will continue to be, heavily involved. Thus a better understanding of their role is central to analysing world markets.

NOTES AND REFERENCES

1. Coarse grains include maize (corn), barley, oats, sorghum and rye.
2. The structure of the rice market is quite different than for other grains in that (1) a very small percentage of rice production is traded and (2) the principal exporters (with the exception of the United States) are developing countries. Oilseeds (soybeans) are excluded because state trading plays a small role.
3. M. M. Kostecki, 'Agricultural State Trading by the Developed Market Economies', *Les cahiers du CETAI*, no. 78–05 (Août 1978).
4. John Freivalds, *Grain Trade: The Key to World Power and Human Survival* (New York: Stein and Day, 1976), p. 116.
5. See Andrew Schmitz and Alex McCalla, 'The Canadian Wheat Board' in S. Hoos (ed.), *Agricultural Marketing Boards – An International Perspective* (Cambridge, Massachusetts: Ballinger Publishing Company, 1979), pp. 79–99.

6. J. Bieri and A. Schmitz, 'Market Intermediaries and Price Instability: Some Welfare Implications', *American Journal of Agricultural Economics*, vol. 56, no. 2 (May 1974), pp. 280–5.

7. Colin Carter and Andrew Schmitz, 'Import Tariffs and Price Formation in the World Wheat Markets', *American Journal of Agricultural Economics*, vol. 61, no. 3 (August 1979) pp. 517–22; the original article on an optimum tariff is S. Enke, 'The Monopsony Case for Tariffs', *Quarterly Journal of Economics*, vol. 58 (February 1944), pp. 229–45.

8. A. F. McCalla, 'Strategies in International Agricultural Marketing: Public vs. Private Sector', in Jimmy S. Hillman and A. Schmitz (eds.), *International Trade and Agriculture: Theory and Policy* (Boulder, Colorado: Westview Press, 1979), pp. 209–38.

9. T. Josling, 'Government Price Policies and the Structure of International Agricultural Trade', *Journal of Agricultural Economics*, vol. XXVIII, no. 3 (September 1977), p. 266.

10. A. F. McCalla, 'A Duopoly Model of World Wheat Pricing', *Journal of Farm Economics*, vol. 48, no. 3, part 1 (August 1966), pp. 711–27.

11. J. H. Taplin, 'Demand in the World Wheat Market and the Export Policies of the United States, Canada, and Australia', Ph.D. Thesis, Cornell University, 1969.

12. Chris M. Alaouze, A. S. Watson, and N. H. Sturgess, 'Oligopoly Pricing in the World Wheat Market', *American Journal of Agricultural Economics*, vol. 60, no. 2 (May 1978), pp. 173–85.

13. Carter and Schmitz, op. cit.

14. Bieri and Schmitz, op. cit.

15. R. E. Just, A. Schmitz, and D. Zilberman, 'Price Controls and Optimal Export Policies Under Alternative Market Structure', *American Economic Review*, vol. 69, no. 4 (September 1979) pp. 706–14.

16. Harry G. Johnson, *Aspects of the Theory of Tariffs* (Cambridge: Harvard University Press, 1972).

17. Bieri and Schmitz. op. cit.

18. Other aspects of the role of information as it relates to private vs. state trading are discussed in Alex F. McCalla and Andrew Schmitz, 'Grain Marketing Systems: The Case of the United States versus Canada', *American Journal of Agricultural Economics*, vol. 61, no. 2 (May 1979), pp. 199–212.

4 The Role of State Trading in Mineral Commodity Markets

Walter C. Labys

The purpose of this paper is to examine the role played by state-trading organization (STOs) in the evolution of international minerals markets. Of particular interest are the implications regarding commodity market structure, market power and price formation. These implications are analysed here through a framework previously developed by the author.[1] After a brief description of the framework, the paper addresses its application to state-trading activity in four minerals of major importance to industrialized as well as to developing economies: copper, tin, bauxite, and iron ore.

FRAMEWORK FOR ANALYSING PRICE FORMATION

As an initial step to discussing the framework, it is necessary to define state-trading organizations in a way useful for mineral-market analysis. According to Kostecki,[2] state trading normally implies that imports and exports take place in terms of transactions which have been determined by governments. In some cases, the governments maintain export/import enterprises – state-trading organizations (STOs). In others, governments use central directives to determine the terms of contractual arrangements, even if the execution of those arrangements is left to private traders.

In mineral markets, state trading is practically the exclusive form of exchange activity in COMECON countries. State trading is also gaining prominence in developing countries, following an increase in the nationalization of mineral firms. Finally, forms of state trading have appeared in industrialized market economies, where it serves to assure control and to improve bargaining in the procurement of mineral raw materials.

The framework proposed to analyse the impact of state trading concentrates on the major factors which are thought to influence mineral price formation: market conditions, market structure and their implications.[3] The components of that framework are further illustrated on p. 294, below. *Market conditions* refers to the determinants underlying mineral supply and demand flows.[4] Supply is affected by economic, geologic, technologic and institutional determinants; other important considerations are investment and supply costs, and their respective fluctuations. Demand determinants include economic, technologic and quality or taste factors. In addition, the demand structure must be defined according to the level of demand: primary, intermediate or final demand.

Mineral market structure pertains to market organization and power, while organization refers to the configuration of the actors in the market. The latter are normally grouped according to their functions, such as sellers (producers, local processors, government and private intermediaries, and possibly multinational firms); and buyers (intermediaries, processors, and wholesale-retail distribution industries). Power refers to the quantities in which these actors appear. Among the factors on the supply side which determine these numbers are: economies of scale, absolute costs, control over technical knowledge, government policies and government control over the resource. Factors influencing numbers on the demand side would be similar.

Related to market structure are the implications which the structure has for the trading countries involved. These implications relate principally to the nature of the bargaining situation and the subsequent division of gains. A bargaining situation can be defined as the conditions which affect a mineral-producing country's effort to increase export earnings. These conditions are normally viewed in the context of the struggle between private firms or multinational mining companies (MMC) and host governments in mineral-exporting developing countries. Recently, these governments have successfully elevated their share of profits in mineral extraction, a trend which has notable implications for market control and price formation.[5]

Considered essential for analysing market implications are export dependence, size of investment projects, technology, control, processing opportunities, material share, obsolescing bargain, nature of competition, and government learning process.

Price information is particularly affected by the number of buyers and sellers in the market. For some combinations of competitive and monopolistic conditions, market prices can be determined; but for bilateral oligopoly, often found in mineral markets, price cannot easily be determined. The prices determined are contingent upon the capabilities of a few strong buyers, as they attempt to check the pricing actions of oligopolistic sellers.

State trading typically affects the components of the framework in several ways. Market conditions can be affected by restrictions in supply or export expansion by STOs. Market structure and bargaining power can be affected by changes in numbers and sizes of STOs, relative to other firms in the industry. Possibilities for producer or consumer cartels can be increased when STOs are present, since they are better suited to enter into restrictive types of international commodity agreements. In addition, STOs can promote particular price and distribution policies to aid certain countries or regions, possibly effecting the latter through integration. Regarding price formation itself, mineral markets typically embody several MMCs facing a number of smaller producers (in some cases the MMCs also are producers and thus deal with governments which control resources). As the STOs enter the market as sellers, the bargaining power of the MMCs changes. In the following discussions, the impact of such phenomena on mineral price formation can be seen.

STATE TRADING IN COPPER

Market Conditions. In the world market, copper is most often traded in its refined state, rather than as ore. For example, developing copper exporters, like Chile and Zambia, refine almost all of their output before selling it abroad. In 1975, world production of concentrate and refined metal amounted to 7.3 and 8.4 million short tons, respectively. The United States is by far the greatest producer, with 23 per cent of total production at the refined metal stage. Among the developing countries, Zambia accounted for 9 per cent of refined production, Chile for 6 per cent and Zaire for 3 per cent.

Marketing Structure and its Implications. The supply side of the copper market is a homogeneous oligopoly with a large competitive fringe. Copper-producing firms are highly concentrated; the eight largest firms account for 50 per cent of total mining capacity and for 44 per cent of the refining capacity.[6] On the demand side, primary copper is absorbed mainly by the fabricating industry, which transforms the refined copper bars or cathodes into various shapes and, in some cases, processes them even further.

This uneven concentration in the refined copper market is not a new phenomenon. Although the decision units were different, concentration among exporters was also very high, prior to the many nationalizations of the copper sector in Africa and Latin America over the past decade. Insofar as unrefined copper is concerned, concentration would probably be higher on the buying side, in view of the scale economies in smelting and refining. Although the prices applied in such sales are LME-based, deductions are made to cover the cost of processing the concentrate. The determination of these deductions gives the buyers the opportunity to use their negotiating strength and superior technical knowledge to their own advantage. Copper producers in the developing world have exhibited a strong tendency toward integrating forward to the refining stage, a movement probably resulting from a desire to eradicate the existing imbalance in negotiating power.

The desire to increase this power has been largely responsible for the nationalization of the copper industries, and for the formation of state trading in the copper-exporting developing countries.[7] In the late 1960s, when these efforts began to accelerate, the four largest privately-owned copper firms controlled about 50 per cent of the mine production of the market economies. In 1974, the corresponding figure was less than 20 per cent.[8] During the same period, the share of mine capacity held by majority- or wholly-state-owned mining establishments rose from practically zero to about 35 per cent of the total capacity of the market economies.

A listing of the more important of these establishments has been provided in Table 4.1, which also includes eastern Europe. The eastern European countries are primarily involved in trading and/or processing and semi-fabricating operations, but, because of a lack of data, their production capabilities could not be added to the market shares provided in Table 4.2. As of 1976, the total market shares, in production, of the state trading organizations was 39 per cent. The state owned copper corporation in Chile (CODELCO) is the largest

TABLE 4.1

Copper: State-trading organizations

Country	Name of the organization*	Basic functions
Chile	Corporacion Nacional De Cobre de Chile (CODELCO) Also: Compania Minera Andina – A Sub-division of CODELCO) (100%)	Mining and smelting
	Empresa Nacional De Minera (ENAMI) (Agency of the Chilean Government) (100%)	Mining
Zambia	Roan Consolidated Mines Ltd. (51%)	Mining
	Nchanga Consolidated Copper Mines (51%)	Mining and smelting
Bulgaria	Rudmetal (State Commercial Enterprise)	Trade in copper
	Tsvetna Metalurgia (State Economic Corp)	Trade and processing of copper
Zaire	La Generale Des Carrieres Et Des Mines Du Zaire (Gecamines)	Mining
Peru	Empresa Minera Del Peru (Minero-Peru) (100%) (State agent – State owned entity)	All phases of mining (production, refining marketing)
German Democratic Republic	Bergbau-Handel Intrachandels GMBN	Both trade in ores and refined copper
Hungary	Metalimpex	Trade in primary copper
Bolivia	Corporacion Minera de Bolivia (COMIBOL) (Bolivian State Mining Enterprise) (100%)	Mining
Taiwan	Taiwan Metal Mining Corporation	Mining Company
Iran	Sar Cheshmen Copper Mining Company	Copper mining
Italy	Entre Di Gestione Per Le Aziende Minerarie Metallurgiche (EGAM)	Copper mining
Uganda	Kilembe Mines Ltd. (100%)	Copper Mining
Poland	Impexmetal Minex	Both trade in copper and its products
Czechoslavakia	Metalimpex	Trade in copper and its products

* Figures in parenthesis represent interest held by state, where available.

TABLE 4.2

Ownership of Copper Companies (1976)

Organization*	Production (000 short tons)	Individual Market share (%)
Private:		
Anaconda (US)	164.1	2.8
Anamax (US)	95.7	1.6
Asarco (US)	106.7	1.8
Duval Sierrita (US)	101.5	1.7
Kennecott (US)	346.4	5.9
Magma Copper (US)	149.0	2.6
Phelps Dodge (US)	330.9	5.7
Compania Minera de Cananea (Mexico)	54.0	0.1
Inco (Canada)	165.0	2.8
Mount Isa (Australia)	156.3	2.7
Palabora (South Africa)	105.4	1.8
Rio Tinto Patino (Spain)	95.7	1.6
Bougainville Copper	194.6	3.3
Others	1491.7	26.7
Total	3558.0	61.1
State Owned:		
Chile (CODELCO and ENAMI)	1020.3	17.5
Zaire (GECAMINES)	449.4	7.7
Zambia (Nchanga and Roan)	776.3	13.3
Uganda (Kitembe)	10.0	0.2
Others	10.1	0.2
Total	2266.1	38.9
Combined Total	5824.1	100.0

* Classification of companies is preliminary subject to revision.
Source: *Non-Ferrous Metal Data, 1976*, American Bureau of Metal Statistics, New York, 1977.

firm in the world, with sales exceeding twice those of its close competitor (Kennecott Corporation), even though it does not have a high
monopoly power. Jointly, the four largest firms in the world have a
share of slightly over 30 per cent of the market for primary copper,
which represents about 22 per cent of all refined copper supply.
Among the four largest copper producing firms, two other corporations, in Zaire and Zambia, are also state owned. Market concentration in copper production has been falling, due to the nationalization
of the MMCs.

The tool with which the copper STOs influence the course of
copper trading and development is the Intergovernmental Council of
Copper Exporting Countries (CIPEC).[9] The Council was established
in 1967 by the countries which presently constitute the largest of the
copper STOs: Chile, Peru, Zaire, and Zambia. The membership of
CIPEC undertook its first action to influence copper prices in late
1974. This action took the form of a 10 per cent joint reduction of
copper exports followed by a further 5 per cent reduction. In as far as
such action had no subsequent influence on price, one could argue that
the sellers have failed to take advantage of their market power by
relegating price determination to an outside institution like the LME.
As indicated by Eckbo, however, there are many factors which have
prevented the full realization of price control by international
cartels.[10] For copper-exporting developing countries, the dependence
on copper is so strong that they would probably be forced to yield to
and accept inferior terms, rather than face the threat of a halt or
reduction in trade flows.

Price Formation. Copper price formation takes place primarily at the
refined metal stage. Transactions are based on an annual contract,
specifying delivery times, payment periods and other conditions. The
price of copper is largely determined by the transactions on the
London Metal Exchange. Acceptance of LME prices, by the trade,
results in a uniform price level for all sellers and buyers. With a neutral
and uniform price, determined separately from bilateral contract
negotiations, it becomes virtually impossible for copper exporters or
importers to take any pricing initiatives. Nonetheless, the increasing
market shares of state-trading organizations make it possible, in
practice, for them to influence the LME prices to their short-term
advantage. Physical turnover on the LME is limited, and a few well-
timed sales or purchase orders could significantly affect price
developments.

The sensitivity of the LME, as a customary pricing facility, provides the STOs with a situation that could produce a favourable turn of events. STOs could, for instance, increase the LME prices systematically on the days they choose to price their copper sales. Traders on the LME claim that concerted action of this kind is uncommon, since an attempt by the STOs to influence LME prices could easily lead to comparable retaliatory measures by other sellers or by buyers. Awareness of the advantages of the LME as a neutral pricing medium may discourage such attempts.

STATE TRADING IN TIN

Market Conditions. The world tin market involves trade in concentrates as well as in the refined metal, including ingots, blocks, bars and slabs.[11] The world production of tin concentrate reached some 207 million tons in 1975. Most tin production has taken place in developing countries, with Malaysia accounting for 31 per cent, Bolivia for 13 per cent and Indonesia for 10 per cent. This reflects a high concentration in Southeast Asia, which (including Thailand) accounts for 63 per cent of world production. The other major producer is the USSR, with 12 per cent of the total.

Firms involved in tin production are plentiful. In Malaysia, about 1000 mines are active, although the majority of these produce only about 40 tons per year. In Thailand, there are about 600 mines, with most producing less than 30 tons per year. The two largest international mining companies are state-owned: P. N. Timah in Indonesia, with about 10 per cent of world output, and Corporation Minera de Bolivia (COMIBOL) in Bolivia, with about 9 per cent. The largest international privately-founded tin mining group, until 1976, was the London Tin Group, Ltd. It now operates under the wing of Malaysia's Pernas Securities and Charter Consolidated, as Malaysia Tin Berhad. It is now the largest tin-mining group in the world, with interests in 18 tin mining companies, located mostly in Malaysia, but also in Thailand and Nigeria. The group produced 27,332 tons of 70–75 per cent tin concentrate in 1976, representing approximately 11.5 per cent of world production.

Most of the tin produced is traded either in concentrates or metal, trade in the latter being the larger. Malaysia, Thailand and Indonesia have exported the most, amounting to some 48.5 per cent, 13.1 per cent and 8.6 per cent of total exports, respectively (1973). Although the United Kingdom is not a producer, its ore imports are sufficient to maintain its position as a major smelting country, accounting for some 11.2 per cent. Among importers of refined tin metals, the United States is the largest, with a share of 26.3 per cent. Japan is next with 22.1 per cent, followed by West Germany with 9.9 per cent and France with 8.2 per cent.

Market Structure and Its Implications. The structure of the tin market is generally considered to be a bilateral oligopoly. On the supply side, it is partially dominated by the major multinationals, while there is some joint action on the part of the developing producing countries. Concentration of smelting capacity is one of the highest, with the largest four firms accounting for 52 per cent of capacity, and the largest eight firms for 76 per cent. Although firms on the demand (or fabricating) side are equivalent in number, information regarding the extent of their concentration has not been readily available. The market power of buyers and sellers is believed to be roughly equivalent.

Two other characteristics of market structure distinguish tin from the other three minerals. First of all, multinational or foreign participation has been more prevalent at the level of horizontal integration than at the vertical integration level. This appears to have occurred because smelters have retained their traditional roles. Smelters, such as the Straits Trading Co., have shares in Malaysian mines which do influence long-run contractural arrangements, but this linkage is minimal. Similarly, they have not integrated forward into tin consuming plants. The second characteristic is that of international intervention in pricing The International Tin Council operates a buffer stock facility, which attempts to mitigate wide price fluctuations.

Nationalization, the forming of STOs, and joint producer country action are becoming more prevalent in the industry. A list of state trading organizations is provided in Table 4.3. Indonesia was one of the first to nationalize, taking over Dutch capital invested in the industry. It is also the only producer developing country in which vertical integration extends to international marketing. Although it provides sales information for its agents from its world offices, its principal function is to set rules for long-term contracts. Government control in Bolivia is more limited. There, as in parts of Africa, the multinationals still play a strong role, such as in investments relating to exploration or joint ventures. The most dramatic change in ownership has been Malaysia's recent move to form Malaysia Tin Berhad, demanding a shift of firm domicile to Kuala Lumpur.

TABLE 4.3

Tin: State-trading organizations

Country	Name of the organization*	Basic functions
Bolivia	Corporacion Minera De Bolivia (COMIBOL) (The Bolivian State Mining Enterprise) (100%)	Mining company
Indonesia	Perusaman Negara Tambang Timah (P. N. Timah) (Indonesian State Tin Enterprise) (Government Executive Agency (100%)	Exploration, mining, processing and smelting
Nigeria	Nigerian Mining Corporation (100%) (Statutory agency of the Federal Military Government)	Mining, processing and marketing
Malaysia	Perbadanan Nacional BMD (Pernas) (National Corporation of Malaysia)	Tin prospecting and mining operations
	Pernas Mining SDN. BMD. (wholly-owned subsidiary of Pernas)	Tin prospecting and mining operations
	London Tin (Malaysia) SDN. BMD (LIMB)	Mining company
	New Tradewinds SDN. BMD. (Associated with Pernas Securities, SDN. BMD.)	Mining company (trade)
Zaire	Compagnie Geomines (Till 1967 named 'Zairetain') (50%)	Cassitevite and tautalite concentrates
Rwanda	Societe De Mines de Rwanda (49%)	Cassitevite, ferberite and columbite production
Hungary	Metalimpex	Trade in primary tin
Bulgaria	Rudmetal (State Commercial Enterprise)	Trade in primary tin
	Tsvetna Metalurgia (State Economic Corp.)	Trade and fabrication in tin
Poland	Impexmetal Minex	Both trade in primary tin and its products
Czechoslovakia	Metalimpex	Trade in primary tin and its products
German Democratic Republic	Bergbau-Handel Intrachandels Gmbh	Both trade in primary tin and its products

* Figures in parenthesis represent interest held by state, where available.

These recent attempts by governments to control production have not been so prevalent in smelting. As shown in Table 4.4, STOs account for only 27 per cent of all ownership, with private companies accounting for 73 per cent. This would suggest that governments are rarely in a position to exert bargaining power in the market. Some leverage can still be attained, however, in individual bargaining between host governments and foreign investing firms.

Price Formation. Tin possesses no single marketing structure.[12] Tin can be purchased directly by the consuming firms from smelters in the producing countries, or from tin merchants who buy tin in the producing areas and sell it via brokers to the consumers. Merchants usually have their own brokerage firms, so that they can deal directly on the LME; other brokers represent the consumer. Although different producer-consumer arrangements can be found, most often the consumer will deal directly with a smelter, or will have a contract with the merchant. Usually, the role of the merchant is to buy the tin-ore or metal, to ship it, and to finance the 'entire transaction until it is delivered to the consumer.

The foundation of world tin prices stems from the physical market at Penang (Malaysia). Prices on this market are also closely coordinated with those of the LME and other world markets. Although most trade on the Penang market is between producers and the two smelters representing Malaysian mines, a smaller amount of ore does come from Africa, Burma, Indonesia and Thailand. Penang, while not a true spot market in the sense of the LME, still does guide the world tin price. The LME price for large volume transaction is, basically, the Penang price plus costs of shipping, insurance and finance, together with a mark-up.

Among minerals, the pricing of tin is an unique process, where an attempt is made to control extreme price fluctuations through an international agreement between producing and consuming nations. This is accomplished through the International Tin Council (ITC), which strives to balance production and consumption, so as to stabilize both long- and short-term price fluctuations.[13] The process is consummated through a buffer stock operation in which a stock manager buys for and sells from the buffer stock, according to floor and ceiling price guidelines.

Control of the tin price in this manner, however, has not been very effective, particularly in the regulation of ceiling prices. Some attempt to control price fluctuations has also been made by the United States

TABLE 4.4

Ownership of tin smelting capacity (1976)

Organization*	Smelting capacity (000 metric tons)	Individual Market share (%)
Private:		
Belgium – Soc. Gen. Metallurgique de Hoboken	18.0	4.7
Federal Republic of Germany – Berzelius Metallhutten GmbH	3.5	0.9
Portugal – Neostano-Nova Empresa Estanifera-de Mangualde, SARL	0.8	0.2
Spain – Metalurgica de Noroeste	3.0	0.8
Minero-Metalurgica del Estano	2.0	0.5
Electrometalurgica del Agueda	1.0	0.3
Japan – Mitsubishi Metal Mining Co. Ltd.	2.5	0.6
Rasa Kogyo K.K.	1.0	0.3
Malaysia – Sharikat Eastern Smelting Bhd.	70.0	18.2
Straits Trading Co. Ltd.	60.0	15.6
Thailand – Thailand Smelting & Refining Co. Ltd.	25.0	6.5
Argentina – Soc. Min. Pirquitas, Picchetti y Cia. SA	1.5	0.4
Brazil – Cia. Estanifera do Brasil	6.8	1.8
Mamore-Mineracao e Metalurgia Ltda.	2.4	0.6
Comp. Industrial Fluminense	0.6	0.1
Mexico – Cia. Estano Electro, SA de CV	1.2	0.3
Cia. Estanera Mexicana	0.5	0.1
United States – Gulf Chemical & Metalurgical Corporation	20.0	5.2
Nigeria – Makeri Smelting Co. Ltd.	12.0	3.1
United Kingdom – Capper Pass & Son Ltd.	18.0	4.7
Australia – Associated Tin Smelters Pty. Ltd.	10.5	2.7
Others	19.8	5.3
Total	280.1	72.9
State Owned:		
Peoples Republic of China – Yunnan Tin Corp.	25.0	6.5
Ping Kwei Mining Association	10.0	2.7
Indonesia – Indonesian State Tin Enterprise (P.N. Timah)	13.5	3.5
Bolivia – Empresa Nacional de Fundiciones (ENAFBOL)	11.0	2.9
German Democratic Republic–State owned	1.5	0.4
USSR – State owned	39.0	10.1
Zaire – Zairetain (Geomines Cie)	4.0	1.0
Total	104.0	27.1
Combined Total	384.1	100.0

Source: G. S. Barry. *Tin*, Report No. 51, Canadian Department of Energy, Mines and Resources, Ottawa, 1976.

with adjustments of its strategic stockpile. Recently, the US stockpile has proved to be the most effective stabilizing agent in the world tin market.[14] In such a market structure, STOs are presently unable to exert substantial control over tin price formation.

STATE TRADING IN BAUXITE

Market Conditions. The world bauxite and aluminium industry is dominated by six major multinationals, vertically integrated from bauxite mining to smelting and even to the fabrication of aluminium end-products.[15] There are also a number of independent companies. The transformation of bauxite into aluminium requires an initial conversion to alumina, which is then smelted into refined aluminium. In bauxite trading, some 7.5 million tons in metal content were shipped in 1975, half of which came from countries around the Caribbean, and another quarter from Australia. The big deficit areas were the United States, Canada and Japan, who together absorbed 75 per cent of the total. Europe appears to be almost self-sufficient in bauxite, with the import requirements of Germany, Italy, United Kingdom and other countries being equal to the exports of Yugoslavia, Greece and Hungary. Of the significant aluminium producing countries, only France and the USSR satisfy a major proportion of their bauxite requirements from internal sources.

Market Structure and Its Implications. As indicated, the world bauxite industry is dominated by the six major multinationals, which are vertically integrated from the production of bauxite to the manufacturing of aluminium. These include: Alcoa, Kaiser, Reynolds, Alcan, Pechiney-Ugine-Kuhlman and Alusuisse. The market share accounted for by the largest eight firms amounts to 56 per cent of mine capacity, 67 per cent of alumina capacity, and 53 per cent of aluminium capacity.[16] These shares, however, have been declining as a result of the acquisition of capacity by various governments, including STOs, and because of the growth of independent firms. The latter comprise the remainder of the market share.

Because most of the world trade in bauxite consists of shipments within the six major firms, no adequate price information exists. Transaction prices are arranged to meet goals of individual firms. Thus, an imputed import price must be used as an indicator of market value. To understand price formation at the ore-producing level, the relative bargaining power between firms and governments must be examined. Obviously, taxing and leasing arrangements are the typical bargaining levels. But relating this to any bauxite price has been difficult, since past agreements have been based on a fixed income tax per long dry ton (LDT) of bauxite exported, rather than on sales or costs.

To assess bargaining power, we must look at recent change in taxation, notably the increases in taxation imposed by the Jamaican government in May 1974.[17] The extent to which such taxes can be increased depends on several factors, and implies the ability of either party to inflict losses on the other.

On one hand, the extent of the direct investment made by bauxite users ties them to the exporting countries. On the other hand, there is a limit to the effectiveness of taxation and threats of nationalization. Taxation on bauxite production can lead to shifts in supply sources and processing locations, shifts in cost structure, and shifts in investment patterns. For example, the World Bank suggests that the 1975 pattern of bauxite production in the high tax-rate nations reflects a production reduction and a shifting of demand from these producers to the low tax-rate producers.[18] Other countries seeking entry to the market could also give better terms of taxation to attract firms. Translating this into variable cost changes among different producers, one finds that producers may have the option to reduce the break-even levels of production in the higher cost sources by shifting their supplies.

To show state ownership, Table 4.5 lists the major STOs in bauxite. The share of the STOs, in total ownership, is further shown in Table 4.6, and amounts to only 27.0 per cent. This is less than one-half of the 59.0 per cent in private hands. While many STOs have enabled host governments to increase their individual bargaining power, their collective strength has not been equivalent. The principal mechanism for collective bargaining power is the International Bauxite Association, composed of the major exporting developing countries. Members include the Dominican Republic, Jamaica, Haiti, Surinam, Ghana, Guinea, Sierre Leone, Yugoslavia and Australia. Already, its formation has led Jamaica to initiate a tax increase. Since other members imitated this action, the organization of the IBA suggests that co-operation among the countries can lead to a greater extraction of resources rents and a concomitant increase in value-added.

Price Formation. Bauxite and aluminium transactions are normally carried out by (1) transfers within the six major multinationals,

TABLE 4.5

Bauxite: State-trading organizations

Country	Name of the organization*	Basic functions
Ghana	Ghana Bauxite Company (55%)	Mining company
Guinea	Kindia Project (100%)	Mining company
	Compagnie Des Bauxites De Guinee (49%)	Develop bauxite deposits, calcined bauxite
Guyana	Guyana Bauxite Company Ltd.	Mine and refinery (1975 = 7,000,000 tons)
	Berbice Mines (100%)	Mining company
German Democratic Republic	Bergbau-Handel Intrachandels GMBH	Both trade in ores and ingots
Indonesia	P.N. Aneka Tambang (100%)	Mining company
Jamaica	Kaiser Bauxite Company (51%)	Mining company
	Reynolds Jamica Mines Ltd. (51%)	Mining company
Taiwan	Taiwan Aluminium Company (TALCO) (100%)	Primary aluminium (mining)
Venezuela	Corporacion Venezolana de Guyana (CVG) (100%)	Mining and smelting
Hungary	Mineralimpex	Trade bauxite and aluminium
	Metalimpex	Trade aluminium ingots, semi-finished products
Bulgaria	Rudmetal (State Commercial Enterprise)	Trade aluminium
	Tsvetna Metalurgia (State Economic (Corporation)	Trade and processing of bauxite and aluminium
Poland	Impexmetal Minex	Both trade in aluminium and its products
Czechoslovakia	Metalimpex	Trade in aluminium and its products
	Kerametal	Trade in bauxite as well

* Figures in parenthesis represent interest held by state, where available.

TABLE 4.6

Ownership of bauxite mining capacity (1973)

Organization*	Production (000 long tons)	Individual Market share (%)‡
Private:		
Alcoa*	11530	14.7
Kaiser*	8516	10.9
Reynolds*	5267	6.7
Rio Tinto (Conzinc)	4725	6.7
Alcan	4034	5.1
Pechiney†	4300	5.5
Alusuisse	2952	3.8
Royal Dutch/Shell (Billiton)	2800	3.6
Anaconda*	792	1.0
Revere*	500	0.6
Olin*	495	0.6
Martin Marietta*	479	0.6
Subtotal	46390	59.0
State-Owned:		
Guyana	4500	5.7
USSR	4400	5.6
Guinea	3283	4.2
Yugoslavia	2500	3.2
Jamaica	2091	2.7
Hungary	2057	2.6
Indonesia	1218	1.6
Peoples Republic of China	845	1.1
Subtotal	21434	27.0
Other (Private and State)	10520	14.0
Combined Total	78343	100.0

* Domestic US bauxite production capacity allocated among US based firms according to their US alumina conversion capacity in 1973.
† All bauxite capacity in France is assumed to be controlled by Pechiney.
‡ Subtotals may not be exact because of rounding error.
Source: United Nations Report E/C.7/51. Prepared by the Centre for Development Planning, Projections and Policies of the Department of Economic and Social Affairs of the United Nations, New York, 1975.

(2) long-term contracts, or (3) joint venture. Only very small marginal quantities are traded through commodity dealers. As a consequence, there is no spot market with public prices, nor is there a representative 'posted' or 'listed' price. For bauxite in particular, pricing is further complicated by the need to account for alumina content, access to shipping terminals, proximity to consuming markets, the composition of the impurities, and the quantity and payment terms specified in the purchase arrangements.

Radetzki suggests that the ownership structure of the industry implies that the real trading partners are the governments of exporting countries on the one hand, and the companies on the other.[19] Taxes and other government levies assume the role ordinarily played by prices in striking a buyer-seller agreement. Any quoted export prices, therefore, do nothing but reflect the transfer prices of the multi-nationals, adjusted upwards or downwards to reflect their objectives.

Recent experience demonstrates that governments can use STOs to affect bauxite price formation. In addition to the price increase forced by Jamaica through increased taxation, similar agreements have been reached by Surinam, Haiti, the Dominican Republic, Guinea, Guyana, Indonesia and Sierre Leone.

STATE TRADING IN IRON ORE

Market Conditions. In the world iron ore market, most of the ore traded has undergone extensive processing. This 'usable' ore comes in several forms: calibrated lumps, concentrates, sinter feed, pellet feed and pellets.[20] In 1975, world iron-ore production reached some 501 million tons in iron content. Among the shares held by the major producing countries are the USSR with 25 per cent, Australia with 11 per cent, Brazil and the United States with 10 per cent each, China with 6 per cent, and India with 5 per cent. Canadian production is believed to have risen sharply in 1976, and so Canada would again be among the six leading producers.

Some 47 per cent of the world production of iron ore was traded internationally in 1975, about twice that traded a decade earlier. The pattern of iron ore trade has undergone very important changes in the post-war period. In the 1950s and early 1960s, a greater degree of self-sufficiency was prevalent in the major steel-producing countries. The trading which took place was primarily regional; Venezuela and Canada covered the lack of natural supply in the United States,

Sweden became the major exporter to West Europe users, and Japan's somewhat limited needs were satisfied by diverse sources in South and East Asia.

Market Structure and Its Implications. The eight largest firms accounted for 57 per cent of total iron ore shipments in 1974. The market could be typified as a weak oligopoly, including a large number of small producers, many of whom were organized as state-trading enterprises in exporting developing countries. Concurrently, the industry appeared as one dominated by the major multinationals, with the organization of the major ore suppliers becoming more centralized and increasingly more oligopolistic.

As with other minerals, it is difficult to measure the concentration of iron one on the demand side. It is believed to be roughly equal to that of the supply side. A large proportion of the traded iron ore is sold to countries where the steel industry has organized itself into purchase cartels or is represented by STOs. Even where this is not the case, such as in the United States, the iron ore purchase contract agreed upon by the major mills will strongly influence the negotiations of other steel producers. Concentration in steel production itself is not a good surrogate for the demand side.

Since the 1960s, the international market structure has appeared to change in three ways.[21] First, the development of the new large mines was dependent on substantial investment contributions from international sources. To safeguard their capital, the international investors required that the new mining firms sign delivery contracts with steel producers in the industrialized world for periods of 10–15 years or longer. This supposedly assured the mines of the cash-flow required for their debt service. These contracts commonly specified not only volumes but also prices, in US dollars, for a substantial part of the duration of the contract period. The contracts invariably failed to anticipate accelerating world inflation in the late 1960s and early 1970s, and the repeated dollar devaluations. From 1970 onwards, therefore, a sharply widening gap emerged between the prices tied for long periods of time on the one hand, and the annually negotiated price levels on the other.

A second change in the market structure has been a gradual weakening of the price-leading role of the annual German-Swedish negotiations. This is the result of Sweden's decreasing importance in the world iron-ore market. Its place has been taken by Brazil, which is poised for major expansion of its market share. On the whole, one might say that, during the last decade, 'anything goes' in the annual negotiations where sales volumes and prices for the following year are determined.

The third important change is the increasing involvement of governments in the iron ore sectors of most major exporting countries. Consequently, outright nationalizations of iron ore mines in countries like Mauretania, Peru and Venezuela have reduced the output share of captive mines. In 1974, large-scale export-oriented captive mines existed only in Canada and Liberia. The output of such mines has decreased to less than 25 per cent of world exports.

If some division of the proportion of trade now transacted can be made, the following is probably the most representative one: (1) 20 per cent or less of international ore trade is captive; (2) 40 per cent or more of the trade is transacted under contractual arrangements of 10–15 years' duration (as a result of the traumatic inflationary experiences during the recent past, prices are commonly negotiated every two years in these contracts); and (3) the remaining 40 per cent of world iron-ore exports are sold under short-term contracts, with both quantities and prices renegotiated annually.[22]

In addition to the market's changing structure regarding the three major contractual arrangements, there has also been a movement towards control by the exporting developing countries. Although substantial foreign ownership still remains, governments have acquired a strong equity interest in the iron ore mines of these countries. In some cases, such as Venezuela, the takeover has been complete. Although a substantial number of STOs are reported on in Table 4.7, many of the related projects are still in the development stage. Their share, together with new expansions of private companies, are thus not part of the compilation given in Table 4.8. The latter tabulation reports that STOs presently are partner to only 21 per cent of total estimated shipments. This data implies that STOs are less influential in the iron ore market than in the copper, tin and bauxite markets.

Brazil is likely to demonstrate the influence of STOs in the coming years, since its market share is expected to increase from 16 to 30 per cent by the late 1980s. Brazil has emerged as the second largest world exporter of iron ore since the early 1970s and, through an aggressive marketing strategy, has been able to increase its market share even during 1975–7 when world exports declined because of the steel crisis. Brazil has the comparative advantage of possessing the largest known deposits in the world of high grade ore (sinter feed), which is becoming increasingly scarce. Since economies of scale are extremely impor-

TABLE 4.7

Iron ore: State trading organizations

Country	Name of the organization	Basic functions
Brazil	Companhia Vale Do Rio Doce (CVRD)	Mines, railroads, pelletizing plants
	Companhia Siderurgica Nacional (CSN) (Brazilian National Steel Company)	Steel products
Chile	Compania De Acero Del Pacifico (CAP)	Iron mining
Hungary	Metalimpex	Pig iron and raw steel
Peru	Empresa Minera Del Peru	Iron mining
Bulgaria	Rudmetal (state Commercial Enterprise)	Trade in raw steel products
	Cherna Metalurgia (State Economic Corp.)	Imports iron ore and iron concentrate
Venezuela	Orinco Mining Co. and Iron Mines Co. (Nationalized in 1975)	Iron mining
USSR	Promsyrioimport	Trade in iron and steel products
Sweden	Luosavaara-Kiirunavaara. AB (LKAB)	Iron mining, concentrating, and pelletizing plants
India	Minerals and Metals Trading Corporation	Iron mining
	Mindusian Steel Ltd.	Pig iron and smelting
Liberia	Liberian American-Swedish Minerals Company (LAMCO)	Iron mining
South Africa	South Africa Iron & Steel Industrial Corporaion Ltd (ISCOR)	Pig iron and steel
German Democratic Republic	Metallurgiehandel GMBH	Trade in pig iron and raw steel
	Bergbau-Handel Intrachandels GMBH	Both trade in ores and concentrates
Poland	Stalexport	Export of iron and steel products
	Minex	Trade in iron and steel products
Argentina	Mierro Patagonico De Sierra Grande SA MIPASAM) (Government controlled steel company)	Steel company
Iran	National Iranian Steel Industries Corp. (NISIC)	Smelting company
Angola	Companhia Mineria Do Lobito	High grade calibrated iron ore
Czechoslovakia	Ferromet	Trade in iron and steel products

TABLE 4.8

Ownership of iron ore companies (1974)

Organization*	Shipments (000 long tons)	Individual Market share (%)
Private:		
United States Steel Corp. (US)	54,112	10.9
Bethlehem Steel Corp. (US)	52,795	10.6
National Steel Corp. (US)	26,498	5.3
Inland Steel Co. (US)	6,498	5.3
Youngstown Sheet and Tool Co. (US)	36,928	7.4
Republic Steel Corp. (US)	34,464	7.0
Armco Steel Corp. (US)	30,867	6.2
Cleveland Cliffs Iron Co. (US)	25,956	5.2
Hanna Mining Co. (US)	31,830	6.4
Hamersley Iron Pty. Ltd. (Australia)	31,811	6.4
Mt. Newman Mining Co. Pty. Ltd. (Australia)	30,252	6.1
Iron Ore Company of Canada (Canada)†	21,510	4.3
Quebec Cartier Mining Co. (Canada)†	14,138	2.8
Total	398,034	80.0
State-Owned:		
Brazil (Companhia Vale do Rio Doce-CVRD)	51,601	10.4
Brazil (Companhia Siderurgico Nacional)	3,240	0.6
Liberia (Liberian American-Swedish Minerals Co. – LAMCO)	12,900	2.6
Sweden (Luossavaara-Kiirunovaara – LKAB)	30,000	5.4
Total	97,741	20.0
Combined Total	495,775	100.0

* This list is incomplete. It is based on the best information available to the author.
† 1976.
Source: W. Skinner, *Mining International Yearbook, 1976*, Financial Times Ltd., London, 1977; and US Federal Trade Commission, *The US Steel Industry and Its International Rivals*, Washington, DC: US Government Printing Office, 1977.

tant in iron ore mining, Brazil's expansion strategy is based on the exploitation of these large deposits which would allow Brazil to reduce its already low average production costs. Such plans, however, have been slowed down by world market conditions. Thus, Brazil is still in the process of completing financing arrangements for its project at Carajos, the single largest iron ore project presently planned in the world.

Governments have made some attempt to act collectively. In 1975, an Iron Ore Exporters Association was agreed upon; but its rather wide geographic distribution, the existence of substantial reserves, and the availability of scrap have not given it much bargaining power.

Price Formation. Since iron ore is not traded on any of the world's commodity exchanges, there is no market, as such, where price quotations provide an indicator of market equilibrium. There are, however, several standard quotations which serve as suitable guides. For example, domestic iron ore suppliers in the United States indicate a basic price, in terms of a fixed iron (Fe) content, for a number of major types of ore. The Lake Superior Mesabi price and the Lake Superior pellet price are often referred to in this context. These domestic prices also provide the basis for the pricing of Canadian exports to the United States, as well as for the prices paid for West African and South American ores and for former captive ore supplies from Chile and Venezuela. The Kiruna D price, CIF Rotterdam and the Brazil price, CIF North Sea Ports are also worth noting.

Price formation, in the long run, depends on the long-term contracts now being negotiated by new mines to assure them of an income from which investment loans can be repaid. There are, however, linkages between these long-run prices and short-run prices. Previously, contract prices were tied throughout the contract period, which could range from 10 to 30 years. Now, economic instability has led the contracts to stipulate a price renegotiation every two years. It has been suggested that such long-term contracts have become merely long-term quantitative arrangements, but even the quantitative element has been subject to renegotiation when supply has been unstable.

It is difficult to analyse the bargaining power found in the long-term contracts negotiated between Japan and such countries as Australia, Brazil and India. Here, because of the ability of the Japanese to adopt joint buying techniques and the advantages previously mentioned, their bargaining power could be assessed roughly as that of a monopsonist.

In assessing the ore shipped from captive mines to parent companies, price formation is similar to that found in any vertically-integrated industry involving transfer pricing, etc. The large investment needed to secure long-term contracts for collateral in mine financing, however, has elicited the emergence of a consortium approach to mining among consumers. This consortium approach is nearly as significant as the trend toward longer-term contracting. European and American steel companies have formed co-operative joint-ventures for the mining of ore. Although mining control still rests with steel companies, pricing policy may be different in a joint-venture than in a truly captive situation.

Any influence which STOs may have on price formation, in any of these trading modalities, is probably stronger in long-term than in short-term contract negotiations. It seems that governments have not used STOs to precipitate any major price increases; this probably has been the result of guarantees for increased domestic processing.

CONCLUSIONS

Although the market share of state trading organizations has increased in all of the mineral cases studied; the impact of this phenomenon has varied in each market. Only in the bauxite market has one country, Jamaica, taken the lead in influencing price formation. Since then, other bauxite exporting, developing countries have followed suit. In the copper and tin markets, prices are determined on competitive markets of a public nature, and these prices serve as guidelines for the industry. Sufficient retaliatory reaction still exists in these markets to prevent any STOs from bargaining for substantial price increases. Prices in the iron ore market are not set publicly; the ability of STOs to influence prices depends on particular contract negotiations.

It is difficult to determine whether the STOs will be able to expand their influence in these markets. The above information suggests that they have helped to increase competition, but that some attempt at price control could occur. An opposing influence is that the multinational mining companies still dominate new mineral investment.[23] While the STOs have been successful in taking over and running facilities already in production, few have demonstrated an ability to develop new mines. For example, the only copper mining venture in Peru, at present, is the Caujoue project, which is being carried out by a private firm, Southern Peru Copper. Similarly, the STOs of Zaire, Zambia and Chile have not been able to bring major, new deposits on-stream. The most likely way for STOs to overcome these obstacles is by pursuing joint ventures with private firms. Brazil, for example, has developed a major iron ore deposit with multinational mining companies as partners.

As STOs become more important as investors, the factors affecting mineral investment decisions will change. For example, the STOs will be less concerned about risks and mineral taxation; nor will they be overly anxious about expected profits. Their goals will centre more around foreign exchange earnings, new skills and jobs, and stimulation of other sectors of the economy. The subsidization involved is likely to depress mineral prices and, thus, to reduce export earnings. Through the building of excess capacity, the mineral STOs could give their countries an advantage over countries whose mineral sector relies on private and multinational investment.

A general implication of STO presence has been the fortification of the international producer associations to which they belong. Whether or not STO presence can impel these associations to demand a greater transfer of resources to host governments will depend on the continued presence of mineral firms in the industrialized countries who are major mineral producers. It also appears that the STOs have recognized the importance of joint ventures and cooperation; this is likely to dissuade them from taking any cartel-like actions.

NOTES AND REFERENCES

1. The basic analytical framework presented derives from two previous works by the author: 'Market Structure and Market Power in Resource Price Formation', presented at the Wisconsin Seminar on Natural Resource Policy, Madison (1978); and *Market Structure, Bargaining Power and Resource Price Formation* (Lexington, Mass.: Heath Lexington Books, 1980).
2. See M. M. Kostecki, 'State Trading in the Industrialized Countries and the Developing Countries: The Background', *Cahiers on C.E.T.A.I.* no. 77–03 (Montreal, 1977); and D. P. Ghai, *Current Problems of Economic Integration*, TD/B/436, UNCTAD (New York, 1973).
3. The possibilities for utilizing an approach, such as the present one based on industrial organization theory, was first suggested by J. Behrman, 'International Commodity Market Models', in F. G. Adams and J. Behrman (eds.) *Econometric Modeling of World Commodity Policy* (Lexington: Heath Lexington Books, 1978), pp. 9–46. The problem has also been addressed by A. McCalla and A. Schmitz, 'State Trading in Grain', in Adams and Behrman (eds.) op. cit.

4. Only a brief summary of 'Market Conditions' is provided in the commodity analyses which follow, since basic market descriptions are readily available in a number of sources. For example, see *Mineral Facts and Problems*, Bureau of Mines Bulletin no. 667, US Department of the Interior, Washington, DC, 1975.

5. R. Vernon, 'Foreign Enterprises and Developing Nations in the Raw Materials Industries', *American Economic Review, Proceedings* (1970), pp. 122–6.

6. This discussion derives from Walter C. Labys, *Market Structure, Bargaining Power and Resource Price Formation* (Lexington, Mass.: Heath Lexington Books, 1980), Copyright, Heath Lexington Books, pp. 2–17.

7. See T. H. Moran, *Multinational Corporations and the Politics of Dependence: Copper in Chile*, (Princeton University Press, 1974).

8. See UNESCO, 'Future Demand and the Development of the Raw Materials Base for the Copper Industry', E/C. 7/65, (New York: United Nations, 1977).

9. Labys, op. cit., pp. 2–22.

10. P. L. Eckbo, 'OPEC and the Experience of Previous International Commodity Cartels', Energy Lab. Working Paper no. 75–008WP, (Cambridge, Mass.: Ins. of Tech., 1975).

11. Production and smelting figures reported below appear from K. L. Harris 'Tin', in US Bureau of Mines, *Mineral Facts and Figures, 1975*. (Washington, DC: Department of the Interior, 1976).

12. Labys, op. cit., pp. 4–31.

13. A complete description of the ITC, the history of tin agreements, and buffer stock price control appears in W. Fox, *Tin: The Working of a Commodity Agreement*. (London: Mining Journal Books, Ltd., 1974).

14. See G. W. Smith and G. R. Schink, 'The International Tin Agreement: A Reassessment', *Economic Journal* no. 86 (1976), pp. 715–28.

15. A more complete, but dated, description of the aluminium market can be found in M. Brown and J. Butler, *The Production, Marketing and Consumption of Copper and Aluminium* (New York: Praeger, 1968); and S. Brubaker, *Trends in the World Aluminium Industry* (Baltimore: Johns Hopkins University Press, 1967).

16. Labys, op. cit., pp. 5–15.

17. A detailed description of bauxite taxation and its likely effects can be found in World Bank, 'Market Structure of Bauxite/Aluminium', Commodity Paper no. 24, (Development Policy Staff, IBRD Washington, DC, 1977).

18. Ibid.

19. M. Radetzki, *Market Structure and Bargaining Power – A Study of Three International Mineral Markets*, (Stockholm: Institute of International Economic Studies, 1976).

20. See G. Mannors *The Changing World Market for Iron Ore 1950–1980* (Baltimore: Johns Hopkins University Press, 1967), p. 167.

21. Labys, op. cit. pp. 6–20.

22. Ibid., pp. 6–23.

23. See J. Tilton, 'Changing Patterns of Mineral Exports in World Trade'; Working Paper, (Pennsylvania State University, 1977).

5 State Trading and the Politics of Oil

Øystein Noreng

State trading in oil prevails when oil trade flows are conducted on government-determined terms of transaction (see Chapter 1). State trading in crude oil and oil products has become a frequent occurrence in the contemporary international markets and, as such, has greatly affected the political relationships of the trading partners involved.

This chapter will focus on the political implications of state trading in oil, beginning with a short history of that subject. Secondly, the current significance of that state trading will be evaluated, and the objectives motivating its maintenance considered. Finally, the issue of trade through politics and politics through trade will be discussed, demonstrating its influence on the larger system of relations among the trading countries.

HISTORICAL BACKGROUND

For many decades the non-competitive pattern of trading prevailed in international oil markets. That market has been characterized by low-price elasticities of supply and demand, at least in a short-term and medium-term perspective.[1] Historically, there is little evidence that changes in the price of oil have a significant short-term impact upon patterns of supply and demand, nor is there any systematic relationship between the price of oil and costs of production,[2] making the price mechanism a fairly inefficient regulator of international supply and demand for oil.[3] Instead, changes in the price of oil are crucial to the distribution of oil-related income, or the oil rent, defined as the sum of profits and income to be made from oil.[4] This makes vertical integration particularly attractive to the oil industry, because when all aspects of the trade, from production to marketing, are controlled by the same corporate entity, the impact of price changes upon total corporate income is limited.

In this century, only a small portion of the international trade in crude oil and its products has brought about open 'arms-length' transactions between mutually independent sellers and buyers.[5] Instead, the bulk of internationally traded oil has been subject to transfers between different parts of the same corporate entity, with the transfer price being of limited significance. Furthermore, joint ventures and non-competitive behaviour have figured prominently in the oil industry, suggesting a desire to avoid risk and a hope to stabilize prices and markets.

With a trading pattern characterized by close cooperation between a limited number of vertically integrated corporate entities,[6] the international oil market has behaved differently from most other commodity markets. Short-term fluctuations in supply and demand have had little impact upon prices. In a historical perspective, the evolution of the price of oil is characterized by discontinuities, primarily caused by institutional changes.

The strategic importance of oil as an energy supply to industrial economies has made the industry a politically powerful one, as is demonstrated for example by the long-standing position of Standard Oil in the United States. Because the oil industry is essentially an international one, with production and consumption taking place in different countries, vertical integration has increasingly proceeded across borders, rendering any single government powerless to control it.[7]

For importing countries, increasing use of imported oil caused an increasing dependence upon the international oil industry, subjecting them to discriminatory pricing and consequent transfers of income judged as excessive.[8] For the exporting countries, dependence upon oil as the major source of foreign exchange implied a dependence upon foreign oil companies, giving them limited means to defend national economic interests. The boycott of Iran by the international oil industry during the years 1951–3 and the overthrow of the Mossadeq government demonstrate that international oil trade has often been involved in political power relations and, in extreme cases, has been the reason for the rise and decline of governments.

At the same time, there has been a contrary trend. Given the limited ability of the price mechanism to regulate oil supply and demand, as well as the importance of stable oil supplies for economic activity, regulation was a typical occurrence in the oil markets.[9] Internationally, the regulation, until the 1960s, was essentially carried out by a cartel of international oil companies. In the 1970s the control and the regulation of the international oil market was taken over by the Organization of Petroleum Exporting Countries, OPEC. Long before the 1970s, however, several governments felt that oil was too important to be left to market forces alone, which, in this case, meant the international oil industry. State trading in oil originated with governments who wished to secure oil supplies without the assistance of private oil multinationals.

Oil trading began in Western Europe. In 1914, upon the recommendation of Winston Churchill, the British government took part ownership of the Anglo-Persian Oil Company (new British Petroleum), with the explicit purpose of securing supplies of foreign oil, primarily for military needs.[10] The alternative, to rely upon foreign suppliers such as Standard and Shell, was considered unacceptable for reasons of national security. After the First World War, several other European countries established national oil companies in order to secure foreign oil supplies. France took over the ex-German part of the old Turkish Petroleum Company, now the Iraq Petroleum Company, receiving oil concessions in the Middle East for the first time. Government intervention was required to create a viable, French, oil company, and in 1929 the French government became the major shareholder of the Compagnie Française des Petroles, CFP. In Italy, the government created a wholly state-owned oil company, Agip, in 1926. Likewise, Spain in the 1920s created a state oil company, Campsa. After the Second World War, France established two new state entities, BRP and RAP, to explore for oil in French overseas territories. In 1966 they merged into Elf-ERAP. In Italy, the state oil industry was reorganized after the Second World War, and ENI was established as a new company to serve the purpose of exploring in Italy and of handling oil imports. A semi-public oil company, VEBA, was also established in West Germany after the Second World War. Furthermore, a considerable number of oil-importing developing countries have established their own national oil companies, to import foreign oil and to explore and eventually produce oil at home, as is the case for example with Petrobras of Brazil.

State trading by oil-exporting countries is a more recent phenomenon, and its development has been of a more dramatic character. The

Soviet Union nationalized its oil industry after the revolution and a Soviet oil-exporting firm, Nafta, was operating in some European countries in the 1930s. Mexico nationalized its oil industry in 1938, but exports were discontinued as a result of foreign boycott. The first oil nationalization in a significant oil exporting country took place in Iran in 1951. This led first to an international boycott and, subsequently, to the overthrow of the regime, as mentioned earlier. After 1953, under changed political circumstances, the new national oil company, NIOC was reorganized in a way that left marketing and international trading to the international oil companies. Indonesia created two national oil companies in 1957, and in 1960 nationalized its oil industry. In 1968 the two companies were merged into Pertamina. In the 1960s a number of oil-exporting countries established national oil companies: Venezuela in 1960 (CVP), Saudi-Arabia and Kuwait in 1962 (Pertamina and KNPC), Algeria in 1963 (Sonatrach), Iraq in 1964 (INOC), and Libya in 1968 (Lipetco, later NOC). In the early 1970s other exporting countries followed: Abu Dhabi and Nigeria in 1971 (ADNPC and NNOC) and Qatar in 1972 (QPNC). In 1971, the OPEC countries represented about 85 per cent of the oil entering international trade, but this oil was essentially traded by foreign companies. The question of take-over was becoming more urgent; and in 1972 an agreement was concluded between the OPEC countries and the major international oil companies, stating that the former would gradually take an increasing participation in their oil industry, with 51 per cent ownership being reached by 1981.[11]

In the meantime, Libya had partly nationalized its oil industry in 1970, and Algeria followed in 1971. In 1972, Iraq fully nationalized its oil industry. The events of 1973–4 showed that the power relations in the world oil market had changed decidedly, and so most OPEC countries moved to nationalize their oil industries. This also meant that the state, or the state oil companies, got control of the international oil trading. There are a few exceptions to this rule today, such as Gabon and Ecuador, but they are of little importance. Libya retains some foreign concessions; Saudi-Arabia, Nigeria and the United Arab Emirates only have a majority participation. However, in all but a few cases, there is a fairly strict control of export marketing, which gives the OPEC governments a significant role in international oil trade. It is significant of the new realities of the world oil market that marginal oil exporters outside OPEC also opt for a high degree of state participation in their oil industry, and consequently for a high degree of state trading. Great Britain, Malaysia and Norway have state oil companies that produce oil for domestic use and for export. Canada has a national oil company whose fate at the moment is unclear; but it seems that state trading of oil will be maintained.

The oil crisis of 1973–4 has also been described as the 'oil revolution'.[12] Property relations in the international market have changed significantly with the oil exporting countries taking over their own industry, and engaging directly in oil exportation. In this way, the old pattern of trading in oil, based upon vertical integration and private trading, has been broken down. A new pattern of oil trading is emerging; it is largely based upon state trading.

CURRENT IMPORTANCE OF STATE OIL TRADING

Establishing statistics on state trading in oil is impeded by problems of definition and the scarcity of relevant and reliable data. In Table 5.1, two types of state exports of oil are distinguished: exports by the state oil companies of the producing countries, and exports by state oil companies of other countries. The data are calculated on the assumption that domestic needs are covered by the local state oil company.

In Table 5.1, all oil exports going through the Iranian NIOC are counted as state-traded exports. In the case of Saudi-Arabia, the 60 per cent nationalized share of Aramco is likewise counted as state oil exports. This can be disputed, as Aramco's oil essentially is shared by its four US minority shareholders, Exxon, Texaco, Socal and Mobil, on a fairly settled pattern of transactions. The Saudi-Arabian share of Aramco oil was about 5147 mbd in 1978, accounting for 18 per cent of total OPEC oil exports. Even discounting this as state trading, one concludes that the majority of OPEC's oil exports are handled by national oil companies. This trend has been reinforced in 1979, by the nationalization of BP in Nigeria and by the reorganization of the NIOC after the Shah's fall. In 1979 the Saudi-Arabian state oil company Petromin has been taking directly about a fourth of Aramco's allowable production, 2.3 out of 9.5 mbd, leaving Aramco's four minority shareholders with 7.2 mbd.[13] The state trading in oil exports is mostly generated by the French companies (CFP and Elf) in Algeria, Gabon, Indonesia, Iran, Libya, Nigeria, Qatar and the UAE. It is also due to the presence of British BP in Nigeria, Qatar and the UAE, as well as the operation of the Japanese Japex in Indonesia. The presence of the Brazilian Braspetro in Algeria, although less significant, should also be mentioned.

TABLE 5.1

Oil exports of OPEC countries by types of companies (1978)

Country	Total	National oil companies	Foreign state oil companies	Private oil companies
Algeria	1080.7	954.1	126	0.6
Ecuador	140.8	65.8	—	75.0
Gabon	36.4	36.4	131	26.0
Indonesia	1386.8	480.6	42	864.0
Iran	4530.3	4004.5	525.8	—
Iraq	2411.2	2411.2	—	—
Kuwait	2088.3	1963.3	—	125.0
Libya	1954.0	1177.0	96	681.0
Nigeria	1830.9	975.9	322.1	532.9
Qatar	480	477	2	1
Saudi-Arabia	8063.5	4632.5	—	3431
UAE	1819.6	1167.6	339	313
Venezuela	1934.0	1934.0	—	—
OPEC Total	27913.5	20279	1583.9	6049.5
Percentage	100	72.6	5.7	21.7

Source: OPEC, *Annual Statistical Bulletin*, 1978.

Among the new marginal exporters, which were of minor importance in the 1978 world oil market, are oil exports from Mexico, 0.7 mbd, handled by the state oil company Pemex. Those from Great Britain, about 0.5 mbd, were handled by the national oil company BNOC at a rate of about 50 per cent. In 1978 Norway's Statoil and Malaysia's Petronas had small shares only.

Among the importers, the tendency to state trading in oil is less pronounced. In 1978, about one-half of France's oil imports, 1 mbd out of 2 mbd, were handled by state oil companies, and about two-thirds of Italy's, 1.3 mbd out of 2 mbd. In other West European countries, state trading in oil was of minor importance, with the exception of Finland and Spain, where a state monopoly imports oil; and Portugal and Greece, where state oil companies had a large share of oil imports. Outside Europe, the trend toward state trading in oil is remarkable. In Japan, the state oil company Japex currently has an import share of about 45 per cent, about 2.5 mbd. out of 5.5 mbd. In the Third World outside OPEC, there is a more pronounced trend toward handling oil imports by state companies, for reasons of supply security; however, these countries still represent only a minor fraction of the world's oil imports. In North America, Canada handles a minor part of its oil imports through a state oil company.

Data are not readily available on flows of oil between producers and consumers, but certain preliminary conclusions can be drawn. Japan is increasingly supplied with oil from state oil companies, or under the auspices of state-to-state deals, from Indonesia, Iran, Iraq, Kuwait and Qatar. France, too, is presumably supplied with oil handled by state oil companies in Algeria, Gabon and Iraq. In the same way, Italy is supplied with oil from Libya, Algeria, Iran and Kuwait. For Germany, the importance of oil handled by state oil companies, or transacted under the auspices of state-to-state deals, is increasing, within limitations.

OBJECTIVES OF STATE OIL TRADING

For the oil importing countries, the basic objective behind state trading in oil has been supply security. There have also been economic considerations. When national oil companies produce oil abroad to be sold in foreign markets, the proceeds offset the cost of oil imports from other sources, having a beneficial effect upon the current balance. As an example, for a long time, BP has produced more than enough oil than was needed for British domestic consumption. An important objective of French oil policy has been to let French companies produce abroad quantities of oil at least corresponding to the domestic French oil consumption. In the case of Italy, an important objective has been to secure oil supplies on terms better than those offered by the private international oil companies.[14]

For the oil-exporting countries, the objectives behind state trading in oil have been both economic and political. At first, when the world oil market was not very politicized, the basic objective of oil exporters was to earn money; and in some cases, state trading was seen as a useful instrument in this respect. More recently, as the world oil market has been increasingly politicized, with scarcity threatening, the bargaining power of the oil exporting countries has increased and, consequently, political objectives have become more pronounced. In this perspective, state oil trading and state-to-state deals are seen as indispensable instruments.

The rapid change in oil-property relations in the 1970s gave the exporting countries free rein in deciding their own depletion policies and marketing patterns. For the consumers, the significance of the change was not fully felt, as established trading patterns were largely maintained. The new oil-trading policy of the OPEC countries announced some important changes, to be implemented gradually from 1979 to 1980. The basic principles of the new policy seem to be the following:[15]

— crude oil will be sold by the national oil companies of the OPEC countries to foreign refiners on long-term contracts;
— contracts will have a destination clause, forbidding the resale of oil by the refiner without the specific permission of the supplier;
— the lifting of crude oil is to take place regularly throughout the year, with little tolerance for seasonal variations or liftings above or below the volume contracted;
— there will be some kind of preferential treatment for the national oil companies of the oil importing developing countries, usually by indirect methods rather than by price discounts;
— The role of intermediaries, such as traders and brokers, will be considerably reduced; this will also reduce the role of the spot market;
— there will be a close supervision of profits made on oil by refiners and marketers;
— there will be an increasing effort not to sell crude oil alone, but

only in the form of oil products, i.e. introducing progressively 'package contracts';

— there is likely to be some preferential treatment of national oil companies of the industrialized countries, although this is less certain and more subject to local variations than other principles of the new policy.

The economic goal of the new policy is to secure financial stability, as well as a greater part of the oil rent in the long run. The political aim of the policy is to strengthen the OPEC countries' control of the international oil market, and to improve their bargaining position with the industrialized oil importers. From an OPEC point of view, the spot market, based upon intermediaries such as brokers and traders, is in many ways a nuisance. It is an important element of instability. Furthermore, spot sales are usually associated with large windfall profits, increasing the total oil rent, with a corresponding part of it going to intermediary, at the expense of both producers and consumers. With the breakdown of the old oil regime, the spot market has increased in volume and significance. A large spot market is risky for OPEC since it can limit its freedom of action. For example, in the spring of 1979, the cutback of Iranian oil exports made spot market prices soar to levels two or three times above the OPEC price; this was seen as undesirable, as the producers' part of the oil rent was diminishing because of higher profits made by traders. As a result a surcharge was introduced, in order somehow to close the gap between the OPEC price and prices quoted in the open market. Later, in June 1979, there was a general increase in OPEC oil prices. However, both the surcharges and the price rise were moderate compared to the spot market price, which demonstrated that, for OPEC, the objective of short-term income maximization is not the dominant one.

POLITICS THROUGH TRADE AND TRADE THROUGH POLITICS

The direct trading of oil between the state oil companies of the OPEC countries and foreign clients, on long-term contracts which limit the right to resale and impose a certain regularity of liftings, can be seen as a mean to reduce the significance of the spot market and to increase stability in the world oil market. The economic objective for the OPEC governments is a greater regularity of income, facilitating budgeting and planning. The new trading pattern also has important consequences for the long-term relationship between producers and consumers of oil, and in this way it also has a political character. It transfers from the producer to the refiner and marketer the burden of adjusting to seasonal demand variations. Thus, the refiner and marketer will increasingly face the burden of either keeping large inventories at a high cost, or of not being able to cope with demand. The limitation of the right to resale works in the same direction. This might lead either to price increases for consumers or to a profit squeeze for refiners and marketers, or both. For the OPEC governments, the political benefit is that their bargaining position with oil importers, governments and companies, will be strengthened. With reduced flexibility of the intermediary market, consumers will have to deal more directly with OPEC state traders. When scarcity persists, the consumer countries may have to address themselves directly to OPEC governments, and perhaps consent to price increases or propose political favours in return for marginal increases of oil exports above contracted volumes. The weakened bargaining position of the oil importing countries will also make it easier for the OPEC state traders to seal combinations of crude oil and products. Finally, the new pattern of state oil trading by the OPEC countries prepares the ground for more overt political competition for oil supplies among consumer governments.

Recently, several OPEC countries have made direct political interventions in their state trading in oil. In the autumn of 1979, Iraq notified several customers that contracts would be terminated at the end of the year. This especially affected the international majors, whereas customers covered under state-to-state deals appears not to be affected.[16] For the renewal of contracts, Iraq demanded a boycott clause concerning Israel and some other countries. Iraq's relationship with France also deserves special mention. France took a fairly understanding attitude when Iraq nationalized the oil industry in 1972, for which the French CRP was granted a long-term contract with a slight price discount.[17] In 1979 Nigeria nationalized BP's shares of concessions, allegedly for breaking commitments not to trade with South Africa. The available volumes were used by Nigeria's state oil company to give preference to other state oil companies.

Historically, several West European countries, such as France, Italy, Spain and Finland, have a record of state-to-state deals for oil supplies. It is significant of the present tend that the West Germany and Japanese governments are becoming more directly involved in the oil industry, and in direct dealings with the oil exporting countries.

France, however, remains as the outstanding example of a state trader in oil among the consumers; it has quite successfully managed its relations with the oil-exporting countries and has enjoyed a high degree of supply security. Two French national oil companies that serve as instruments for government policy confirm the advantages of state trading in assuring national oil-policy goals.

The increasingly direct state trading in oil between the OPEC countries and the developing oil importing countries has important political aspects. In the past, the latter group of countries has been supplied by the private oil companies, often at high cost. In the 1970s there have been many third-party arrangements, with the state oil companies of the oil-importing developing countries receiving oil supplies from the international majors which they, in turn, have purchased from the OPEC countries. These deals are being phased out rapidly, partly because several of the international oil companies have supply problems and give a priority to the industrialized consumers, and partly because the oil-importing developing countries have learned that they can get oil at better terms, and with a high security of supply, directly from the national oil companies of the OPEC countries. So far, there is no coherent OPEC policy on deals with other developing countries, but there is a systematic trend of giving some kind of preferential treatment. Kuwait has introduced price controls on oil exports to countries with a GNP per capita of less than $1000. Saudi-Arabia recently diverted some volumes of exports from Aramco to Petromin, to some extent in connection with direct state-to-state deals with developing countries. This shift could mean less low-priced oil for the United States. For some time, Saudi-Arabia has given a preference to the United States, probably in order to induce the United States to exert pressure on Israel to reach a Middle East settlement acceptable to Saudi-Arabia. For the OPEC countries, the relationship with the rest of the Third World is of great political importance, as they see themselves as champions of a wider cause, that of a new world economic order. The OPEC countries, without the alliance with other developing countries, would be left alone to face the pressure from the industrialized consumers, possibly finding themselves in a situation of double pressure, from both industrialized and developing consumers. The new direct state trading with oil between OPEC countries and developing consumers, with preferential treatment, is likely to increase the political cohesion of the Third World, which again could have an important effect upon the global system of international relations.

In conclusion, the rapid expansion of state trading in oil in the 1970s has created a new situation in the world oil market, one of profound dualism. On one hand, there is 'politics through trade', where governments pursue political goals using oil commerce as a means to secure them. This is the case of many OPEC countries, which reputedly give some preferential treatment, particularly on supply security, to oil importing countries that are willing to do them political favours. At a more discrete level, this is also typical of the state oil trading policies of newcomers such as Mexico and Norway. On the other hand, there is what can be described as 'trade through politics', where oil importing governments are willing to give political favours in return for secure oil supplies, or some kind of preferential treatment. This is the case of many OECD countries, with France as the prime example; but also of countries such as Italy, West Germany, Japan, etc. In addition, this is also becoming very common with the oil-importing developing countries. In both cases, governments pursue political goals usually of a long-term character, surpassing the time horizon of simple oil transactions. This implies a politicization of international oil trading with individual oil importing or exporting countries, coupling oil trade with other issues. In this sense, there has been a fragmentation of the world oil trading, which also gives a higher degree of selectivity. Governments engaged in oil trade are able to formulate their interests and goals more specifically now than before. In this way, the 'new' oil market is characterized by a multitude of transactions involving states, revealing a variety of political interests.

It should be stressed that oil trading's 'political' implications are not recent, but, under the past regime, the international oil companies tended to serve the collective interests of the oil consumers, not those of individual consuming countries. In the history of international oil trading, the changes that have taken place in the 1970s are remarkable. The organization of the marketplace and its institutions has changed drastically, with governments and state oil companies playing an increasingly dominant role. The major uncertainty now concerns the future role of the international oil companies. On the one hand, their loss of equity in the trade of crude oil with the exporting countries and the new OPEC trading pattern tend to have a negative impact upon their profits and long-term stability. On the other hand, the international oil companies still have a comparative advantage over state oil companies in technological capability. This makes them attractive partners for oil exporting governments that need assistance; this has been demonstrated recently by both Brazil and the Soviet Union.

In any case, the increasing politicization of the international oil trading, with more state intervention and participation, reflects a historical situation in which the market is characterized by looming scarcity, or at least by substantial price rises. In such a situation, the consumers are anxious about future supplies, and producers are concerned about getting the full benefit for their oil. To some extent, the absence of a futures market in oil means that secure oil supplies, over a longer period of time, are considered more valuable than current supplies, so that the current price of oil does not indicate its full value. Consequently, there is a political rent attached to secure supplies of oil, and this is the basis for both 'politics through trade' and 'trade through politics'.

NOTES AND REFERENCES

1. Douglas R. Bohl and Milton Russell, 'Some Economic Effects of the United States Import Quota', in Ragaei El Mallakh and Carl McGuire (eds.) *U.S. and World Energy Resources: Prospects and Priorities*, (Boulder, Col.: ICEED, 1977), pp. 1–19.
2. Ibid, p. 4.
3. Øystein Noreng, *Oil Politics in the 1980s* (New york: McGraw-Hill, 1978), p. 2.
4. Jean-Marie Chevalier, *Le Nouvel enjeu petrolier* (Paris: Calmann-Levy, 1973), p. 14.
5. Jens Evensen, *Innstilling om oljepolitiske spørsmol*, (Oslo: Ministry of Industry, 1971), p. 7 ff.
6. Robert Engler, *The Brotherhood of Oil* (The University of Chicago Press, 1977), p. 146 ff.
7. Raymond Vernon, 'The Influence of the U.S. Government Upon Multinational Enterprises: The Case of Oil', in Antoine Ayoub (ed.), *Le Nouvel Ordre Petrolier*, (Quebec: Les Presses de l'Universite Laval, 1976), pp. 44–79.
8. For example, there is evidence that during the late 1950s and the 1960s, oil imported to Norway was priced substantially higher than oil imported to Sweden by the same companies. Reasons are, essentially, the companies' leverage with Norway because of the tanker fleet operating largely for the international oil companies, and the fact that low-priced Soviet oil was not imported into Norway because of the NATO membership.
9. Robert Mabro, *The Role of Government in Regulating Energy Markets*, internvention at OPEC seminar, 'OPEC and Future Energy Markets', Vienna, 3–5 October 1979, p. 3.
10. Christopher Tugendhat and Adrian Hamilton, *Oil – The Biggest Business* (London: Eyre Methuen, 1965); p. 68.
11. Chevalier, op. cit., p. 110.
12. Mabro, op. cit., p. 6.
13. *Petroleum Intelligence Weekly*, 29 October 1979; p. 1.

14. Chevalier, op. cit., p. 42.
15. Francisco R. Parra, *OPEC Oil: Recent Developments and Problems of Supplies*, Supplement to *Middle East Economic Survey*, (24 September 1979), pp. 1–7.
16. *Middle East Economic Survey*, (10 September 1979), p. 1.
17. J. E. Hartshorn, *Objectives of the Petroleum Exporting Countries*, (Nicosia: Middle East Petroleum and Economic Publications, 1978), p. 121.

6 State Trading and the Theory of International Trade

P. J. Lloyd

Direct participation by the state in international trading activities is only one of very many forms of state intervention in the flow of commodities across national borders. All forms of intervention distort the pattern of trade from what it would have been in the absence of intervention. There is a well-developed theory of intervention which quantifies the magnitude of government interventions and predicts their effects on the quantities traded, consumed and produced of commodities. Somewhat surprisingly, in view of its significant share of total global commodity trade,[1] state trading has not been widely analysed in the terms of international trade theory. The only extensive analyses of state trading, as far as I am aware, are those of Meade (1955) and Humphrey (1959).[2] Most of the literature on state trading has been concerned with trade in which either the Soviet Union and other centrally-planned economies or the developing countries provide at least one of the trading partners. This seems to have promoted a tendency to regard state trading as a problem in comparative systems, even though state trading is widespread (see Kostecki, 1978, 1979).[3]

Recent advances in the theory of trade policy can be applied, with some adaptation, to state trading. In particular, the standard notions of the ranking of instruments and the relations of equivalence/non-equivalence between pairs of instruments of government policy can elucidate some of the effects and problems of state trading. The notion of equivalence was put forward formally by Bhagwati (1965) in

117

his comparison of the effects of a tariff and a quota and has been developed subsequently by Bhagwati (1969) and others.[4] This paper seeks to interpret the effects of the instrument of state trading in terms of equivalence and non-equivalence, with the instrument of *ad valorem* trade taxes. This comparison in turn gives us some indications as to why state trading is the preferred instrument for some governments in the regulation of trade in particular commodities.

WHAT IS STATE TRADING

There is no agreed definition of state trading. As a sample, state trading has been defined variously as 'state conduct of foreign trade' (Hazard, 1959);[5] 'the practice of some governments . . . of monopolizing foreign trade in certain commodities' (Baldwin, 1970);[6] 'a state trading enterprise is defined simply as one which is either wholly or partly owned by the State' (Ghai, 1973).[7] Clearly, there are significant differences between these conceptions. While the assumption of a monopoly or an element of monopoly is frequent in the literature of state trading, direct participation or ownership in trading activities implies nothing about the absence or restriction of competition. State traders may be in competition with private traders in all or some of the commodities they trade. Even if the rights to import particular commodities are assigned exclusively to state enterprises there may be some competition among state enterprises within an economy. Panglaykim and Palmer (1969), discuss varying forms of 'specialization' of functions and commodities among Indonesia Bhaktis and Niagas.[8] In regional economic integration schemes (Ghai, 1973) or centrally-planned economies state trading companies may be restricted to importing or exporting with particular countries or groups of trading partners.[9] On the other hand, in Tanzania some exclusive import rights have been assigned to the nationalized concerns which produce these goods locally, thus eliminating all competition from local and imported commodities (Hazelwood, 1973).[10] Similarly, the ownership basis does not imply that control is exercised by the state over the state-trading organization or agency in the determination of the commodities which are purchased or sold and the terms of the purchase or sale.

The range of state-trading organizations which has been examined in empirical studies of state trading is wide. It encompasses the centralized buying agencies set up in the UK after the Second World War to make bulk purchases; primary product marketing boards in developed countries such as Australia and New Zealand which regulate export prices and/or quantities (sometimes by direct negotiation and sometimes by licensing private traders) but leave the actual exporting to the principals; state-trading organizations which handle all aspects of the international movement of the commodities, and enterprises which are integrated backwards to the production of the commodities traded or forwards to the wholesale and retail distribution of the traded commodities.[11]

The dominant theme is that there exist in virtually all countries, state or parastatal organizations or agencies which trade in commodities under government direction; that is, the quantities they may import from or export to other countries and/or the price and other terms of sale or purchase are determined or controlled by the government. They may or may not be owned by the government, they may or may not have a monopoly in the trade of the commodities, and they may or may not conduct the actual shipment of the commodities. This direct government control of the prices and quantity of commodities traded via some state or parastatal agency may be used to pursue objectives of government policy other than the maximization of profits from trade which is taken to be the predominant concern of private traders. Most writers on state trading provide a list of the objectives for which state trading may be used as an instrument.[12] These lists include the following objectives – protection of domestic producers, improvement of the terms of trade, raising revenue for the state, promotion of domestic price stability, health and national security, export expansion, the implementation of exchange controls or bilateral trading or foreign aid agreements with other countries, and the indigenization of foreign trade or wholesale and retail trade activities. This is what Kostecki called the 'functionalist' approach to the definition of state trading.[13] Allen proposed the same basis for the definition: 'state trading exists when national, in contradistinction to private, interests are primarily being pursued'.[14] Viner had made the same point eloquently: 'Private enterprise, as such, is normally non-patriotic, while government is automatically patriotic'.[15] This view leads to the following definition.

Definition. State trading occurs when there exists a trading organization for which the prices and/or quantities of international transactions in commodities are determined as an instrument in the pursuit of the objectives of government policies.

This definition focusses on the government *control* of foreign trade flows, rather than the ownership or management of the companies or agencies actually engaged in the trade.[16] The objectives of government policy should be left open-ended in order to allow for variation among countries in objectives and the evolution of new objectives. It encompasses organizations such as state-owned production enterprises which trade internationally part of their outputs or inputs but are not primarily trading enterprises when the prices and/or quantities of these commodities are determined by the state. I shall refer to all such trading organizations as state traders. Conversely, it excludes state-trading enterprises which are autonomous in terms of deciding themselves the quantities and prices of commodities traded, even though they may be owned wholly by governments and subject to government regulation in other respects.[17]

Some writers on state trading specifically exclude commodities imported for government use, that is government procurement expenditures.[18] This exclusion is arbitrary. Government procurement policies have often been used to give supplementary protection to domestic private producers of defence and non-defence commodities and for other objectives of government policy, such as the maintenance of local employment or the conservation of energy inputs in the government sector.[19] Moreover, with this exclusion, the scope of state trading depends arbitrarily on the size of the public sector. Nevertheless, the inclusion of these commodities would simultaneously introduce the issue of the optimal supply of 'public' goods. Therefore, in the discussion below the 'commodities' will be understood as private marketable commodities or inputs into the production of *marketable* commodities (including nationalized industries), recognizing that government procurement policies pose the same questions of the choice of instrument as do state-trading activities as defined here.

COMPARISON OF STATE AND PRIVATE TRADING

With this definition, state trading is viewed as one of several instruments which might be used to pursue one or more objectives of government policy. The key economic question is what instrument(s) should be used for each objective. This approach brings the instrument of state trading into the discussion of non-economic objectives in which hitherto the choices contemplated have been confined to quotas or taxes, and the discussion of the ranking of instruments with economic objectives. More generally, the analysis of the economic effects of state trading is an example of the assignment problem.[20]

A basic implication of this approach is that it dispenses with a need for a special theory of state trading. Rather it treats the theory of a state-trading activity as an application of existing theory of (private) trading. Since the number of objectives to which state trading may be applied is large, I confine my account to a few examples.

As an example, consider a state organization which is a monopolist trader in the domestic market of a single homogeneous commodity. (Although it has been observed that monopoly is not a necessary attribute of a state trader, it is a typical one.) For the moment it is assumed that the state trader does not discriminate among his suppliers or his buyers. His monopoly powers will permit the buying and selling price to diverge and both prices may be different than the free trade (zero-intervention) single buying-selling price. While one would normally expect a monopoly trader to lower the buying price of imports or raise the selling price of exports compared to the free-trade market solution, the freedom of a state-directed monopolist does permit it to buy imports at a price exceeding the free-trade price or sell exports below the free-trade price, for example as part of a foreign-aid programme.

Such a monopolist may adopt, at the direction of the government, a *pricing rule* for a commodity traded. There are several alternatives, including:

(*a*) maximize aggregate profits;
(*b*) fix a profit margin per unit of sales;
(*c*) zero profits;
(*d*) a fixed price;
(*e*) maximize gains from trade.

All of these have been practised by the state traders. A state trader may, of course, use some combination of rules. If it trades multiple commodities it may apply one rule to one set of commodities with one or more other rules applying to other set(s).

Associated with a pricing rule for a commodity there will be a *market solution*, $S = (p^*, q^*, e^*)$. This is a vector whose elements are the domestic price (p) and foreign price (q) for the commodity and the quantity traded internationally (e). The simplest solutions are those in which the state trader allows the market to clear, but one may also contemplate situations in which the domestic price is fixed and the supply is rationed.

A market-clearing solution is given as the solution to the system of equations:

$$q = q(e) \tag{1}$$
$$p = p(e) \tag{2}$$
$$p = \text{price set by pricing rule} \tag{3}$$

In this rudimentary partial equilibrium model the foreign and domestic price functions given by Equations (1) and (2) are the inverses of the foreign and domestic excess demand functions, respectively, $e(q)$ and $e(p)$. The assumption that excess demand is a function of own price alone clearly implies that the prices of other substitutes and complements are unaffected by the pricing policy of the domestic trader. Equation (1) implies the foreign supply is competitive. Equation (2) rules out the situation for an imported commodity in which there is a local monopolist supplier of the same homogenous commodity. In this case there would be a duopoly whose solution might be obtained in one of many ways, but there would be no excess demand function. However, the assumption of equation (2) is fairly general. For example, it encompasses the polar cases in which there is no local production and that in which there is a perfectly competitive local industry. The first is appropriate for many of the state import monopolies established for revenue purposes. Transport costs and all other costs of importing/exporting other than the foreign supply buying price are ignored. For the moment the state trader is assumed to pay no tariff or export tax, or income tax.[21]

This model applies equally to state exports and imports, given parallel assumptions concerning the structure of markets. For expository purposes only I shall for the moment take the trade flows to be imports, that is, $e = m > 0$.

Suppose the rule is to maximize profits. The profit function is obtained from equations (1) and (2):

$$\begin{aligned}
\pi &= p(m) \cdot m - q(m) \cdot m \\
&= [p(m) - q(m)] \cdot m \\
&= \pi(m)
\end{aligned} \tag{4}$$

Price functions are assumed to be continuous, differentiable and strictly monotonic in each country, and for an importable commodity $p(0) > q(0)$. If a solution value of m exists, it is given by setting $d\pi/dm = 0$. The equilibrium values of p and q are given by equations (1) and (2). Differentiating (4), yields:

$$d\pi/dm = p(1 + 1/\epsilon) - q(1 + 1/\eta) = 0$$

where

$$\epsilon = (dm/dp \cdot p/m)$$

and

$$\eta = (dm/dp \cdot q/m)$$

are the elasticities of domestic and foreign inverse excess demand respectively.

Hence,

$$p/q = (1 + 1/\eta)/(1 + 1/\epsilon) > 1. \tag{5}$$

since $\epsilon < -1$. This is the Lerner form of the usual $MC = MR$ rule which expresses the divergence between the domestic and foreign price as a function of the elasticities.

Suppose instead that rule (b) is adopted; that is,

$$p(m) - q(m) = \bar{n} \tag{6}$$

The solution exists within limits for the unit profit margin (n). The upper bound for the profit margin is $n_{max} = p(0) - q(0)$. This margin would just prohibit all trade in the commodity. The lower bound is given by the margin which would lower the domestic price to zero, or if the price function does not intersect the axis to p_{min}. As a special intermediate case one gets the rule (c). The equilibrium import quantity here is given by the rule: average cost = average revenue. Given the downward slope of the domestic demand function and the upward slope of the foreign supply function, the zero-profit quantity imported is necessarily greater and the domestic price associated with it necesssarily less than those of the maximum-profit situation. If the pre-determined profit margin exceeds that implied by the aggregate profit maximization rule, the quantity imported will be necessarily less and the domestic price necessarily greater than that of the maximum-profit situation.

Under rule (d) the quantity imported is given simply from $p(m^*) = \bar{p}$ where $\bar{p}$ is the fixed price and the foreign price is given from $q = q(m^*)$. (If the profit/loss margin or the total loss is constrained, it may be necessary to introduce rationing.) Hence, this rule is equivalent to fixing, at the corresponding levels, the foreign price or the quantity of imports, or the foreign exchange expanded on imports of the commodity.

Under rule (e) the state-trading monopoly is instructed to use its monopoly power so as to restrict imports below the free-trade situation and thereby lower the unit cost to the nation of the imports of the commodity. Since this policy will bring a gain through the fall in the foreign price and a loss through the fall in the volume of trade there will be an optimum restriction. Trade should be restricted to the quantity such that the marginal social cost equals the marginal social benefit of imports. The marginal cost to the nation of buying additional imports exceeds the average cost when the foreign-supply function is not perfectly elastic. Under the assumptions that the domestic industry is perfectly competitive, there are no distortions in production or the allocation of the household's budgets, and aggregate consumers' and producers' surplus is a valid measure of welfare, the total benefit from imports is given by the gain from consumers' surplus minus the loss of producers' surplus and the cost of imports (which is equal to the area under the import demand function):

$$\Phi = \int_0^{\bar{m}} p(m')dm' - q(m) \cdot m \qquad (7)$$

The solution to the maximization of Φ is given by

$$d\Phi/dm = p - q(1 + 1/\eta) = 0 \qquad (8)$$

Hence the pricing rule is

$$p/q = (1 + 1/\eta) > 1 \qquad (9)$$

Contrary to what is sometimes supposed, this optimal pricing rule is not satisfied by the monopolist's behaviour of equating marginal (private) costs to marginal (private) revenue,[22] since marginal private revenue and marginal social benefit (= average private revenue) diverge. In fact, provided that the private demand is not perfectly inelastic, the socially-optimal price is lower and the socially-optimal quantity imported is greater than the corresponding private-optimal (profit-maximizing) values.[23] It also follows from equations (10) and (5) that the profit margin is less in the social optimum than in the monopolist's optimum.

(The cases (b) and (d) in which the price or price margins are arbitrarily pre-selected are left to the reader).

To compare the solutions under state trading with those under private trading the relation of equivalence is used.

Definition 1. One instrument is said to be *equivalent* to another instrument of government intervention in the market of a commodity if any market solution for the commodity which exists when the first instrument is set at some level can be replicated by the setting of the second instrument at some unique level, and *vice versa.*

Non-equivalence is the complementary relation.

This is a notion of equivalence which is similar to that of Bhagwati but there are several differences. First, following the later work of Fishelson and Flatters (1975) and Ohta (1978), equivalence is stated in terms of the multi-variable concept of a market solution rather than the single-variable concept of the level of imports (exports) as in Bhagwati (1965) or the level of domestic production as in Shibata (1968).[24] Equivalence in terms of several endogenous variables is obviously a more stringent requirement than equivalence in terms of only one variable. A less stringent version of the notion is defined by the relation of quasi-equivalence.[25]

Definition 2. One instrument is said to be *quasi-equivalent*, that is, equivalent in terms of one variable or a proper subset of endogenous variables, to another instrument of government intervention in the market of a commodity if any solution value(s) of this variable or subset of variables which exists when the first instrument is set at some level can be replicated by the setting of the second instrument at some unique level, and *vice versa.* In addition, existence and uniqueness have been added to the two definitions. Existence takes the strict form that there exists a level of the other instrument. This is important because it is possible that there may be a subset of values of one instrument for which a replicating value of the other instrument does not exist. (Note that neither existence nor uniqueness of a market solution has itself been assumed.) An example of this possibility is given later. Uniqueness is important because it removes the ambiguities involved in ranking two or more instruments which occur when there are multiple solutions.

Equivalence in terms of all variables determined by an equilibrium implies that there is no difference between the economic effects of the two instruments when they are set at the levels which ensure the equivalence. Equivalence in terms of one or any proper subset of selected variables allows the possibility that they may be non-equivalent in terms of the market solution but equivalent in terms of a subset of variables determined in the solution. In particular, if they are equivalent in terms of one variable and this variable is, or is related by a one-to-one correspondence to, an objective of government policy it is the difference in the other variables which permit the ranking of their effects on the social maximand (social utility or whatever).

As with earlier comparisons made between the pair of instruments consisting of the quota and tariff (Bhagwati, 1965, 1969 and others) and the subsidy and the tariff (for example, Corden, 1974, chapters 2 and 3), the instrument of state trading will be compared with that of the *ad valorem* tariff, or *ad valorem* export tax in the case of export trading.[26] A simple tax is the most obvious alternative instrument.

Each of the solutions to the cases (a) − (e) can be achieved by an appropriate level of tariff. In each case one simply obtained the required tariff rate (t) from the expression

$$t = p(m^*)/q(m^*) - 1 \tag{10}$$

which utilizes the definition of *ad valorem* tariff and the behavioural functions of equation (1) and (2). Competitive profit-maximizing behaviour by private traders will yield the solution value of m under state trading and the pricing rule which applies. Because of the restrictions imposed on the excess demand and price functions, t is unique. By derivation, this calculation yields the same solution values of p and q also. That is, it yields the same market solution as the state trading under the chosen pricing rule. The converse also applies for all cases (a) − (e). This has established the following proposition.

Proposition 1. Under the pricing rules (a) − (e) for a state trader, the instruments of state monopoly trading and an *ad valorem* tariff levied on competitive private trading are equivalent.

The substance of this proposition, though not the whole content or the terms of equivalence relations, was stated by Meade.[27]

The solution to (c) is identical to that of completely unrestricted or 'free' competitive private trading. The solution to (b) includes the case of a government directive to the state-trading monopoly to import zero quantity of a commodity, a situation which could be achieved by private trading plus a prohibitive tariff.

While the three equations are sufficient to determine the solution values for the three variables (p, q, m), it is of interest to consider whether the equivalence extends to other endogenous variables. In particular, one might consider the output of the domestic industry and the total revenue accruing to the state, since concern for these two variables prompts some government interventions. Both of these variables are determined simultaneously with the set (p, q, m) but the reduced form of the model in Equations (1) − (3) gives the solution in terms of the three variables only. That the equivalence does extend to domestic output and domestic demand is apparent from the derivation of $p(m)$ from its inverse function $m(p) = d(p) - s(p)$. *Domestic* demand and supply, are d and s respectively. If p is identical in the solutions under state trading and the tariff, so must be s and d. The response of the total revenue accruing to the state from an importable commodity sold by a state trader is slightly different. This total revenue (R) is the sum of the tax revenues and the profits paid to the state by the state trader. While this variable does not enter the determination of the other variables it is determined by the solution and the *tax rule*. If 100 per cent of the profits earned from the importation of this commodity are paid into the Consolidated Revenue of the state, it is immediately apparent from the definition of the profit margin in equation (4) and that of the tax rate in equation (10), that the equivalence extends to the revenue variable. Thus, the equivalence proposition above can be extended to the augmented market solution, $S (p^*, q^*, m^*, d^*, s^*, R^*)$. One consequence of this extension is that it is irrelevant to the state, under the set of behavioural relations postulated, whether a given total revenue is collected from a tax on private traders or a state-trading monopoly operating under the corresponding pricing rule. If a state monopolist must pay a positive tariff rate on imports of the commodity, the profit-maximizing market solution has the property that

$$p/q(1 + t) = (1 + 1/\eta) (1 + 1/\epsilon) \tag{11}$$

This implies a margin of profit-plus-tax which is greater than the profit- (or revenue-) maximising margin and a lesser quantity of imports. However, there exists a pricing rule and a tax rule such that the tariff-paying monopolist augmented market solution is identical to the revenue-maximizing or pure profit-maximizing solution.

The set of equivalent state trading and private trading situations can be extended considerably. Many complications might be introduced into the rudimentary model.

Consider, first, price discrimination by state traders. This appears to be common. Suppose the state-import monopolist is able to charge different prices in the domestic market to different groups of buyers. Such price discrimination is feasible only if these different markets can be segmented so that buyers are unable to trade between them. With an internationally-tradable commodity market segmentation also requires that there be no domestic source of supply which is competitive with the state monopolist. Let there be u segmentable sources of domestic demand. Now, the aggregate domestic demand (d) and the total revenue from the domestic sales of the monopolist (r) may be disaggregated:

$$d = \sum_{i=1}^{u} d_i(p_i) \tag{12}$$

and

$$r = \sum_{i=1}^{u} d_i p_i(d_i) = \sum_{i=1}^{u} r_i(d_i) \tag{13}$$

$p^i(d^i)$ are assumed to be continuous, differentiable and strictly decreasing functions. Aggregate profits are given by

$$\pi = \sum_{i=1}^{u} r_i(d_i) - c\left(\sum_{i=1}^{u} d_i \right) \tag{14}$$

$c = d \cdot q(d) = c(d)$ is the cost function which is also continuous and differentiable. The first-order conditions for the profit solution, if it exists, are

$$dr_i/dd_i - \partial c/\partial m = 0 \qquad i = 1, \ldots, u \tag{15}$$

The second-order conditions are satisfied if the marginal revenue from each market decreases less rapidly than marginal cost with output. The equality marginal revenues is the necessary and sufficient condition to maximize the total revenue from a given quantity sold. Equation (13) implies that the monopolist charges the maximum price which the market will bear. Substituting the relationship between price and marginal reveune in equation (15) gives the usual discriminating monopolist pricing rules.

$$p_h/p_i = (1 + 1/\epsilon_i)/(1 + 1/\epsilon_h) \qquad i \neq h \tag{16}$$

where ϵ_i is the price elasticity of demand in segment i. A discriminating-monopolist's profits are maximized if it charges higher prices in those segments of the market in which demand is more inelastic. His profits are greater (or if elasticities in all segments are identical no less) than those of the simple monopoly situation because the discriminating monopolist always retains the option of not discriminating. However, it is not true that the equilibrium quantity imported must be less than that of the simple monopoly situation.[28]

It may be that a state trader is not able to discriminate among his sellers, but as a sole importer has some monopsony power over his foreign suppliers. If the foreign market is segmentable into v segments, we have a case of discriminating monopsony which parallels that of discriminating monopoly above. The aggregate supply and the total cost of imports may be disaggregated and the monopsonist will maximize his aggregate profits

$$\pi = r\left(\sum_{j=1}^{v} m_j\right) = \sum_{j=1}^{v} c_j(m_j)$$

by following the rule of equating marginal cost of buying from each market:

$$dr/dm - \partial c_j / \partial m_j = 0 \qquad j = 1, \ldots, v \qquad (17)$$

Substituting the relationship between price and marginal cost gives the pricing rule

$$q_k/q_j = (1 + 1/\eta_j)/(1 + 1/\eta_k) \qquad j \neq k \qquad (18)$$

where $\eta_j > 0$ is the price elasticity of supply in segment j. Higher prices are paid in the more elastic segments of the market. Again the profits of the discriminating state monopsonist are greater than those of the non-discriminating state monopsonist and the quantity imported may be less or greater than, or equal to, that of the non-discriminating monopsonist.

As with simple monopoly there are other pricing rules which a discriminating monopolist may follow. In particular, what is the discriminatory pricing rule for the *social* optimum? With possible discrimination among both buyers and suppliers the social maximand becomes

$$\Phi = \sum_{i=1}^{u} \int_{o}^{d_i} p_i(d'_i)dd'_i - \sum_{j=1}^{y} c_j(m_j) \qquad (19)$$

Differentiating first with respect to the d_i

$$\partial \Phi / \partial d_i = p_i - q(1 + 1/\eta) = 0 \qquad i = 1, \ldots, u \qquad (20)$$

The social optimum, unlike the private optimum, calls for no discrimination among domestic buyers. Setting $p_i = p$, the first term of the social maximand in equation (20) is again the area under the aggregated import demand curve. Differentiating with respect to the m_j

$$\partial \Phi / \partial d_j = p - \partial c_j / \partial m_j = 0 \qquad j = 1, \ldots, v \qquad (21)$$

The social optimum, like the private optimum, calls for discrimination among the foreign suppliers. The relationships among the differentiated foreign prices are again given by equation (19). Price discrimination among suppliers is the necessary and sufficient condition for minimizing the cost of purchasing a given supply of imports. However, the absolute level of these prices is less than those of the profit-maximizer who discriminates among his suppliers since the left-hand sides of equations (17) and (21) are not identical. Again, as in the case of simple monopoly, profit-maximizing behaviour does not lead to the social optimal level of imports and gains from trade.

Another alternative is that the state issue instructions to the state trader that sales to some group(s) be made at a price lower than sales to other buyers. The margin might be set in absolute or relative terms. To enforce such discrimination the state would have to impose restrictions on the resale of the commodity by the subsidized group. The solution for this case is given by adding the price constraint to the system of equations in (16) for the appropriate market segmentation.

Each discriminating monopoly-monopsony situation has a solution or solutions $S(p^*, q^*, m^*)$. p^* and q^* are now vectors of prices in the discriminating monopoly or monopsony situation, respectively. Any discriminating monopoly or monopsony solutions may be attained equivalently by private competitive trading plus an appropriate set of taxes-subsidies levied on buyers and sellers. In the case of discriminating monopoly one sees from equation (16) that the appropriate set of taxes is a set of *ad valorem* sales taxes-subsidies which differentiate among buyers and create precisely the same divergences between the supply price and the sale prices as does the discriminating monopolist, viz $t_i = p_i/q - 1 = (\epsilon_i - \eta)/(\epsilon_i \eta + \eta)$. Similarly, in the case of the discriminating monopsonist, one sees from equation (18) that the appropriate set of taxes is a set of discriminatory tariffs which differentiates among suppliers in precisely the same way as does the discriminating monopsonist. Clearly these sets are unique for each market situation in both cases. These two sets of marginal conditions determine the market solution under discriminating state trading or under private trading. Hence, we have:

Proposition 2. For a given market segmentation, the instrument of a discriminating state trader and a set of *ad valorem* taxes-subsidies levied on competitive private trading are equivalent.

Until now the market situation has been unchanging. In reality, the demand and/or supply functions of the domestic and/or foreign markets change substantially over time, even over short periods. There are situations in which demand fluctuates over a cycle period or grows because of economic growth or declines because or the emergence of a new source of supply. These situations typically elicit some response from policy-makers in order to maintain output and employment in domestic industries or to prevent the price of an importable which is a significant item in the domestic household budget from rising, or to pursue other objectives of government policy. Therefore, it is important to consider whether equivalence between state trading and the tariff instruments extends to a changing environment.

Market shifts can be incorporated by modifying equations (1) − (3):

$$q = q(m, x) \tag{22}$$
$$p = p(m, y) \tag{23}$$
$$p = \text{price set by pricing rule} \tag{24}$$

The restrictions on the price functions in equations (1) and (2) are maintained. (x, y) are the respective shift factors which are here presented as shifting the inverse price functions and regarded as non-stochastic. Given a particular state of the world $(\bar{x}, \bar{y})$, and the pricing rule, one can obtain the market solution. Given the sequence of values of $(\bar{x}, \bar{y})$ one can obtain the sequence of market solutions. It follows from one-period analysis that, for any of the pricing rules which is chosen, there exists a sequence of sets of tariffs which replicates the sequence of market solutions under state trading, and *vice versa*. Thus the equivalence of private trading under a tariff regime, and state trading in the presence of market shifts, is maintained. This equivalence over time requires a time differentiation of the equivalent tariffs which parallels the spatial differentiation of taxes required to replicate the solution of the spatially-discriminating state trader.

Equivalence of a price-discriminating monopolist and a set of taxes over a number of periods follows by the same argument. We may prove, analogously, equivalence between a state-export monopolist who follows a certain price policy and a regime of private competitive export trade with appropriate export taxes. For example, a state-export monopsonist may improve the country's terms of trade by restricting trade. It may improve it further by discriminating among export markets. Export price discrimination is widespread because tariffs and other barriers to inter-country trade enhance the segmentation of national markets. In particular, dumping, which is discrimination in favour of overseas buyers, is common in agricultural trade. Marketing boards have a monopoly over sales in both domestic and foreign markets typically (see Chapter 2 in this volume) and since the domestic market is normally relatively inelastic, they dump in foreign markets. This suggests that such boards have operated in the interests of the producers alone. The pricing of exports lower than the competitive solution increases the volume and, if the foreign segment is elastic, the value of exports; but it worsens the terms of trade and, as the theory of dumping has recognized, it reduces the welfare of the exporting country.

All of the results obtained so far are subsumed in the following proposition.

Proposition 3. For any sequence of market solutions obtained by an exclusive state importer or exporter operating under some specified pricing rule, there exists a unique sequence of sets of *ad valorem* trade taxes-subsidies which yields an identical sequence of competitive private market solutions. Conversely, for any sequence of market solutions obtained by competitive trading under some specified sequence of sets of *ad valorem* trade taxes-subsidies, there exists a unique sequence of pricing rules which yields an identical sequence of state trading solutions.[29] That is, the instruments of state trading and the trade taxes are equivalent. Single-period monopoly is included as a sequence of one.

Although equivalence has been proven in the market situations considered so far, it does not always hold. In the comparison of the quota and tariff instruments which others have examined quite thoroughly it has been shown that the equivalence which can be established for a simple model breaks down if one introduces the complications of either monopoly in domestic production or foreign supply (Bhagwati, 1969), or if the foreign supply is uncertain (Fishelson and Flatters, 1978; Pelcovits, 1976), or if there is foreign retaliation to the changes in instrument levels (Rodriguez, 1974).[30] These complications introduce the possibility of non-equivalence in the comparison of the state-trading-tariff pair of instruments too. Some developing countries have introduced state-export monopolies in part to countervail the bargaining power of large multinational corporations' buyers, especially in the field of mineral exports. For example, the introduction of pure monopoly in foreign buying (or selling) in the model above would create a bilateral monopoly situation whose solution would be non-equivalent to private trading, which will remain competitive as long as there are alternative sources of supply. Uncertainty could be introduced into the model immediately by regarding the shift parameters in equation (22) and (23) as random variables. The outcomes of the state and private trading situations will then depend on many factors, including the method of adjustments to change in the supply and demand and attitudes to risk.

Cases of non-equivalence, which are perhaps more realistic, can arise in other ways too. Consider, for example, the introduction into the model of the simple monopolist of a fixed price and assume, unlike the case (d) above, that the monopolist seeks to maximize his aggregate profits subject to this additional constraint. If the maximum price is set at a level below that at which $AR = MC$, the profit-maximizing monopolist will import only up to the quantity such that the rising marginal cost equals the fixed price. This will result in excess demand for imports at this price and necessitate rationing of some form. Under this pricing rule, the instruments of state trading and the tariff are not equivalent with respect to non-price variables.

The proofs of equivalence above also assumed that the state-trading organization was identical to the private traders in having access to foreign buyers/sellers on equal terms and being equally efficient as private traders. It is often argued that state enterprises are not equal in efficiency to private enterprises, usually that they are less efficient and, occasionally, that they are more efficient. Any differences in efficiency would cause the supply functions to differ between private and state trading situations and produce non-equivalence.

Another breakdown of equivalence occurs with shifts in the market situation over time if there are constraints on the variability of the instrument levels. For example, a government may be able to adjust a tariff downwards but not upwards because of tariff binding, or it may be able to make only one or a small number of changes to the instrument levels. When the feasible set of instrument levels is restricted in this way they will not generally be equivalent.[31]

It is quite probable that non-equivalence may arise when the directions from the government to the state trader take the form of *quantity rules* rather then the pricing rules analysed above. These may introduce elements of non-competition in domestic or foreign supply. This non-equivalence is even more probable in situations in which state trading is combined with a web of controls on the domestic prices and quantities produced and/or traded, as in commodity price or income stabilization schemes.

Hence the proofs above which began with the standard simple model of international trade theory exaggerate the extent of equivalence. Yet, in these cases of non-equivalence, except that in which the feasible set of instrument levels is restricted, the instruments of state trading and the tariff may remain quasi-equivalent. Thus the state still has a choice between these two instruments in order to achieve a single objective. However, quasi-equivalence is not certain for any two instruments. As an example, consider the pair of instruments, state trading and a production subsidy, as alternative instruments to attain a specified level of output of the domestic industry. The maximum output that may be induced by a non-discriminating state monopoly is that at which the pricing policy becomes equivalent to a prohibitive tariff. For any level of output subsidy which induces an output greater than this, there does not exist a pricing policy which has the identical effect on domestic output. Thus state trading and a production subsidy are not quasi-equivalent with respect to output. The tariff which is equivalent to state trading is also not quasi-equivalent to the production subsidy.[32]

REASONS FOR PREFERRING STATE TRADING

Given the possibility, in all trading situations, of equivalence and the likelihood in many situations of quasi-equivalence between state trading and a regime of private trading with *ad valorem* trade taxes, it is important to consider why state trading has been used so extensively.

If the instruments are equivalent, there is no reason to prefer one to the other on the basis of their economic effects. By the same token, the state-trading instrument is redundant in these situations. More-over, the equivalence of state trading and trading taxes is realizable only if the appropriate pricing rule is followed, that is, if the state-trading enterprise does not operate autonomously. If the instruments of state trading and trade taxes are not quasi-equivalent in terms of some objective of government policy, state trading may be preferred to a trade tax-subsidy simply because a target level of this objective is unattainable by means of a trade tax-subsidy. However, there may be other instruments which could be set to attain the target. This choice may be greater than appears. In instructing the state trader to follow a particular rule the ultimate concern of the government is likely to be the welfare of some group of income earners or consumers. It is preferable to state the ultimate objective explicitly because there may be other non-state trading instruments which also attain the objective; for example, direct income supplements.

The theory of policy interventions stresses that it is possible to rank instruments which have been described in this paper as quasi-equivalent but not equivalent. It also clearly demonstrates that the first-best interventions should be related as closely as possible to the ultimate objective;[33] for example, income distribution or consumption distortions should be remedied by the use of direct income payments or consumption taxes-subsidies. Interventions based on trade flows, by means of either state trading or trade taxes-subsidies are first-best only for distortions which originate in international trade flows. The sole cases which could justify state trading or (quasi-)equivalent trade taxes as the first-best instrument are the presence of national bargain-ing power in international trade, and the taxation of imported luxury goods which are not produced domestically. While the desire to improve the terms of trade and to tax luxury importables have been motives for some state trading, in many other instances state trading appears to have been used to pursue domestic income distributional objectives.

There are several reasons why non-first-best state trading may be the chosen instrument of government policies. Some preference for state trading may derive from muddle-headedness over the ultimate objectives of government policy and the range of instruments availa-ble. A second possible set of reasons for preferring one of two quasi-equivalent instruments arises from the monopoly profits earned by the state trader. Unlike the receipts from quasi-equivalent (or equivalent) tax(es), these profits may not be paid 100 per cent or immediately into the Consolidated Revenue of the state. This creates an opportunity for empire-building or other expenditures on the part of the managers of the state enterprise. Once created, there are groups of income-earners whose vested interests may make it difficult to restrict the activities of the enterprise. Corruption may be more difficult to detect and combat than the non-payment of taxes collected. Or, with an enterprise in which the managers cannot have an equity and the ultimate equity-holders, the people of the nation, have no knowledge of and no direct say in the management of the enterprise, it may encourage managerial inefficiencies.

There are aspects of instruments, in addition to those considered in the questions of equivalence and non-equivalence, which may be crucial in determining the choice of instrument. Another feature of the state-trading instrument, by comparison with taxes or subsidies, is that price effects which are equivalent or quasi-equivalent are not visible when the intervention takes the form of state trading. For example, the increase in the producer price under state trading, the implicit tariff, may be very high by comparison with tariffs normally levied on imports. Such differentially high tariff rates may not be acceptable to the public – if they are aware of them. This difficulty applies *a fortiori* to state schemes which discriminate in favour of foreign consumers. The transparency of tariffs and taxes which are specified in schedules and in most countries require validating legislation may be one reason why state trading and other non-tariff forms of intervention are frequently preferred to taxes. Empirical estimates of some forms of non-tariff restrictions, such as those applied on agricultural imports in the US (Wipf, 1971), Japan (Bale and Greenshields, 1978) and the EEC (Sampson and Yeats, 1977)[34] indicate that the implicit tariffs of these non-tariff barriers, many of which involve state trading, are commonly many times higher than tariffs on other agricultural and manufactured imports in these countries. It would be interesting to know the implicit rates of protection granted to domestic producers who have been protected by the operations of state traders.

A second 'advantage' of state trading over taxes which is often quoted is its flexibility.[35] It is much easier to issue instructions to a state trader which, for example, increase the restrictiveness of import barriers implicit in the operations of a state trader, than to debate and legislate a tariff change. This feature is also linked to that of invisibility because the changes made may be invisible. Hence, where adverse foreign reaction is feared or retaliation is possible, state trading may be preferred. It might also provide a method of circumventing the binding of tariffs and subsidies either multilaterally or preferentially within a regional trade agreement of the non-discriminatory obligations of a Contracting Party to GATT. The GATT Articles dealing with state trading are based on the principle that state traders should have the same obligations as private traders, and in particular state trading should not discriminate among trade partners and it should not be used to nullify tariff concessions. It has proven more difficult to enforce these obligations on traders who are usually owned by the state and subject to trade restrictions by means of invisible administrative decree.[36]

Indeed, there is an interesting historical incident which illustrates how basic the perceived advantage of flexibility has been in the development of state trading. After the Russian Revolution, Lenin advocated the use of state-trading monopolies to develop the infant industries of the Soviet Union, whereas Bukharin argued that the same goal could be achieved by using high tariffs.[37] Lenin's concern appears to have been that the cartels of rich imperialist countries would deliberately undercut Soviet producers and prevent their continuation, a tactic which today we call predatory dumping. In his view, the tariff was not likely to be 'effective' in such situations. A quota is more 'effective' in that it sets a maximum limit to imports.[38] In situations of changing demand or foreign supply a quota ensures that the imports do not increase beyond this maximum,[39] whereas the maintenance of a constant level of imports or production would require a continually changing tariff. State trading is an even more flexible instrument than the quota.

Invisibility and flexibility are not advantages from an economic point of view. They increase the possibilities of harmful interventions as well as those of beneficial interventions. The outcome of the choices of an invisible flexible state administrator will depend on the wisdom of these choices. The concepts of equivalence and non-equivalence have given precision to the economic analysis of these choices, but only empirical studies can decide whether this freedom of choice has been exercised soundly.

NOTES AND REFERENCES

1. 'In quantitative terms, its importance is probably equal to that part of world trade internal to multinational producing enterprises', M. M. Kostecki, 'State Trading in Industrialized and Developing Countries', *Journal of World Trade Law*, no. 12 (May–June 1978), pp. 187. The sparsity of the

literature on state trading is in stark contrast to the volumes on the 'equally important' subject of the MNCs.

2. J. E. Meade, *Trade and Welfare* (London: Oxford University Press, 1955), chapter 1. D. D. Humphrey, 'The Economic Consequences of State Trading', *Law and Contemporary Problems*, no. 24 (Spring 1959), pp. 276–90.

3. Kostecki, op. cit., pp. 187–207 and Chapter 1 in this volume.

4. J. Bhagwati, 'On the Equivalence of Tariffs and Quotas' in R. E. Baldwin *et al.* (eds.), *Trade, Growth and the Balance Payments: Essays in Honor of Gottfried Haberler* (Amsterdam: North Holland, 1965). J. Bhagwati, 'On the Equivalence of Tariffs and Quotas' in J. Bhagwati (eds.), *Trade, Tariffs and Growth* (London: Wiedefeld and Nicholson, 1969).

5. J. N. Hazard, 'State Trading in History and Theory', *Law and Contemporary Problems*, no. 24 (Spring 1959), p. 242.

6. R. E. Baldwin, *Non-tariff Distortions of International Trade* (Washington: Brookings Institution, 1970), p. 11.

7. D. P. Ghai, *State Trading and Regional Economic Integration Among Developing Countries* (New York: United Nations 1973), p. 9.

8. J. Panglaykim, and I. Palmer, *State Trading Corporations in Developing Countries with Special Reference to Indonesia and Selected Asian Countries* (Rotterdam: Rotterdam University Press, 1969).

9. Ghai, op. cit.

10. A. Hazlewood, 'State Trading and the East African Customs Union', *Oxford Bulletin of Economics and Statistics*, no. 35 (May 1973), pp. 75–89.

11. For example see, Panglaykim, and Palmer, op. cit., and Ghai, op. cit.

12. For example, R. L. Allen, 'State Trading and Economic Welfare', *Law & Contemporary Problems*, no. 24 (Spring 1959), p. 258. Baldwin, op. cit. ECAFE, *State Trading in Countries of the Asia and the Far East Region* (New York: United Nations, 1964), pp. 1–2. Ghai, op. cit., pp. 9–11 and Kostecki (1978), op. cit., p. 188.

13. Kostecki (1978), op. cit., p. 188.

14. Allen, op. cit., pp. 257–8.

15. J. Viner, 'International Relations between State-Controlled National Economies', *American Economic Review*, no. 34, supplement (March 1944), p. 439.

16. Matejka also distinguished between ownership and control, but chose the opposite course of defining state trading as the activities of the set of enterprises which are owned, but not controlled, by the state. See H. Matejka, 'State Trading: Instrument of Object of Trade Control', *Journal of World Trade Law*, vol. 8, no. 2 (March/April 1974), pp. 209–14.

17. There are some grey areas. For some enterprises the prices and/or quantities of goods traded may be determined by the state in only some instances. Or the prices and/or quantities may be regulated within margins or subject to surveillance by the state rather than precisely determined.

Quantitative restrictions, such as quotas and import licensing, are not state trading, since these constrain the actions of private traders rather than determine the actual quantities and prices of the traded commodities.

18. For example, see Gai, op. cit., p. 9.

19. See Baldwin, op. cit., Ch. 3; or I. J. Tether, *Government Procurement and Operations* (Cambridge, Mass.: Ballinger, 1975).

20. There are, of course, substantial differences between state trading and the instruments which intervene in private trading, other than the economic effects considered here. In particular, there are major differences in commercial and international law. I shall ignore these in the main, although they do, themselves, have subsidiary economic consequences. It was the uncertain and disruptive effect of direct state participation in trading activities, together with the creation of monopolies, which led Viner, op. cit., p. 44 to condemn the 'evil pattern of behaviour' associated with state trading.

21. Economic costs of administration, transport, etc., and taxes based on income derived from trade in the community can be incorporated into the model with no change, simply by redefining the supply price as the price including these costs as well as the purchase price paid to the overseas supplier. These would shift the $q(m)$ function upwards once-for-all and all the properties of the model would carry over. This assumes that these costs would be identical for state and private traders. To judge from passing comments in the literature, some state traders pay the normal duties which would be levied on private imports of the same commodities and some are exempt from import duties. For a discussion of income taxation of state-trading enterprises, see the chapter by Floyd.

22. However, as is well-known, this social optimum is achieved by the behaviour of a perfectly discriminating monopolist with the sole difference that under the latter the intra-marginal buyers pay a higher price.

23. This proposition is proven under non-restrictive general equilibrium conditions by R. E. Caves, and R. W. Jones, *World Trade and Payments: An Introduction* (Boston: Little, Brown and Company, 1973), p. 266. Some of the other propositions stated in the text have also been proven under general equilibrium conditions. The partial one-good equilibrium model of the text can be interpreted as a general equilibrium model of a purely competitive economy with a single-market intervention by interpreting the excess demand functions as the general equilibrium excess demand functions. Since the granting of privileges to state traders tends to be rather selective in non-socialist countries, and for reasons which are specific to the commodity markets concerned, little is gained by using general equilibrium models.

24. G. Fishelson, and F. Flatters, 'The (Non) Equivalence of Optimal Tariffs and Quotas under Uncertainty', *Journal of International Economics*, vol. 5, no. 4 (November 1975), pp. 385–94. H. Ohta, 'On the Ranking of Price and Quantity Controls under Uncertainty', *Journal of International Economics*, vol. 8, no. 4 (November 1978), pp. 543–50. H. Shibata, 'A Note on the Equivalence of Tariffs and Quotas', *American Economic Review*, vol. 58, no. 1 (March 1968), pp. 137–41.

25. This definition is not quite that of Bhagwati (1965, 1969), though it carries the same implications. In his definition equivalence is said not to hold if two instruments (tariff and quota), when set at appropriate levels, yield the same level of one endogenous variable (quantity or imports) but the implicit tariff of the non-tariff (quota) instrument is not equal to the tariff. Since it is the implicit tariff which determines p and therefore domestic consumption, and with competitive local supply the domestic output, the instruments are not equivalent in terms of their effect on local consumption and output.

Bhagwati equivalence is a case of quasi-equivalence in my terminology. For the purpose of comparing instruments, it seems more direct to state in the definition the variables which are equal for corresponding levels of the two instruments.

   G. Yadav, 'A Note on the Equivalence of Tariffs and Quotas', *Canadian Journal of Economics*, no. 1 (February 1968), pp. 105–10 and J. Bhagwati, 'On the Equivalence of Tariffs and Quotas', in *J. Bhagwati, Trade, Tariffs and Growth* (London: Weidenfeld and Nicolson, 1969) pp. 255–8. and Bhagwati (1969, pp. 255–58) have considered the Bhagwati equivalence of the tariff and quota when all imports are conducted by a state monopoly but that is not the comparison considered in the paper.

26. W. M. Corden, *Trade Policy and Economic Welfare* (Oxford: Clarendon Press, 1974) Chapter 2.

27. Meade, op. cit., p. 176.

28. There is no simple rule which indicates the conditions under which the quantity sold by a discriminating monopolist is greater or less than that sold by a non-discriminating monopolist. Even in the simplest case of only two market segments, this relationship depends on the relative concavity-convexity properties of the segmented demand functions. J. Robinson, *The Economics of Imperfect Competition* (London: Macmillan, 1933), Chapter 16.

29. Uniqueness of the market solution was not proven for the case of price discrimination. It occurs if there is only one intersection of the aggregated marginal revenue and the marginal cost functions.

30. M. D. Pelcovits, 'Quotas versus Tariffs', *Journal of International Economics*, no. 6 (November 1976), pp. 363–70. G. Fishelson and F. Flatters, 'The (Non) Equivalence of Optimal Tariffs and Quotas under Uncertainty', *Journal of International Economics*, vol. 5, no. 4 (November 1975) pp. 385–94. C. A. Rodriguez, 'The Non-equivalence of Tariffs and Quotas under Retaliation', *Journal of International Economics*, vol. 4, no. 3 (August 1974), pp. 295–316.

31. P. Dasgupta, and J. E. Stiglitz. 'Tariffs vs. Quotas as Revenue Raising Devices under Uncertainty', *American Economic Review*, vol. 67, no. 5 (December 1977), pp. 975–81. This paper demonstrates this in the case of tariffs or quotas which are used to raise revenue for the state.

32. P. J. Lloyd, *Non-Tariff Distortions of Australian Trade* (Canberra: Australian National University Press, 1973), pp. 161–3.

33. J. Bhagwati, 'The Generalized Theory of Distortions and Welfare', in J. Bhagwati *et al.* (eds.), *Trade, Balance of Payments and Growth*: Papers in International Economics in Honor of Charles P. Kindleberger (Amsterdam: North-Holland, 1971.)

34. L. J. Wipf, 'Tariffs, Nontariff Distortions and Effective Protection in US Agriculture', *American Journal of Agricultural Economics*, vol. 53, no. 3 (August 1971) pp. 423–30. M. D. Bale, and B. L. Greenshields, 'Japanese Agricultural Distortions and Their Welfare Value', *American Journal of Agricultural Economics*, no. 60 (August 1978), pp. 59–64. G. P. Sampson, and A. J. Yeats. 'An Evaluation of the Common Agricultural Policy as a Barrier Facing Agricultural Exports to the European Economic Community', *American Journal of Agricultural Economics*, no. 59 (1977), pp. 99–106.

35. See Allen, op. cit., p. 274. D. D. Humphrey, 'The Economic Consequences of State Trading', *Law and Contemporary Problems*, no. 24 (Spring 1959), pp. 276–290; and Ghai, op. cit., p. 11.

36. See Bernier Chapter 12 in this volume.

37. The literature is cited by Hazard, op. cit., p. 245.

38. In Australia there has been a similar argument about the 'effective tariff' which predates the contemporary meaning of the term. For more than fifty years the Australian Industries Protection League, the predecessor of the current Australian Industries Development Association, argued periodically that the quota was a more 'effective' instrument than the tariff because it ensured that the total quantity imported did not exceed that stipulated in the quota.

39. Unless the quota is subject to upward revision. The uncertainty of the quota itself may be quite great when it is one of many in a comprehensive set of quotas which are determined annually or bi-annually to manage the balance of payments, but as an instrument to protect a single commodity, the level of imports is likely to be more certain under a quota than a tariff.

7 Trade-Policy Instruments, State Trading and First-Best Trade Intervention

Harriet Matejka

In the literature of trade policy, state trading is often classified as a trade-policy instrument. Meade, for instance, refers to state-trading monopolies as 'another instrument through which a government can control the volume of trade'[1] and goes on to state that the effects of state trading in a competitive regime 'are essentially similar to the consequences of state intervention through taxes or subsidies and through quantitative restrictions'.[2] Comparable statements can be found elsewhere[3] and the assertion is also made implicitly by describing state trading as a substitute for other trade-policy instruments.[4]

The identification of state trading with an instrument implies that, like other commercial policy instruments, it can be used for trade intervention. This, in turn, means that it may be used for intervention which is optimal, that is first-best, or sub-optimal, that is second-best or worse. Both the contention that state trading is an instrument and the proposition that it can be used for first-best trade intervention are discussed below.

Section 1 demonstrates that it need not be an instrument, but can be an object of trade policy like private trading. Section 2 shows that, in the special case where a state-trading unit is government-operated and has price-making power, it can serve as a trade-policy instrument, and lists its characteristics. Section 3 compares state trading and other trade-policy instruments in the achievement of optimal intervention. Section 4 argues that, given present international conventions, state trading is the most readily available measure for optimal and sub-optimal intervention especially on the export side, but that it cannot be the universal trade policy instrument. Section 5, finally, considers the implications of the analysis for the international regulation of state trading and, in particular, suggests a revision of Article XVII of the General Agreement on Tariffs and Trade.

(1) AN OBJECT OF TRADE POLICY

State trading will be defined in what follows as the activity of enterprises or agencies that engage in foreign trade and that are fully owned, whose ownership is controlled, that are managed, or which are both owned or controlled and managed, by the state. The restrictive definition of many authors which stresses the element of central functional control in state trading, that is the government's power directly to determine the quantities, prices and other terms of sale or purchase of state-traded commodities,[5] will not be adopted here. For it excludes most of what is commonly understood under the term of state trading.[6] Moreover, by focusing on only one type of state trading, it has caused considerable confusion[7] and can lead to erroneous conclusions with respect to the international regulation of state-trading enterprises.

To identify the truth contained in the assertion that state trading is an instrument of commercial policy, it is necessary first to show that the mere substitution of state trading for private trading is not sufficient to change the level of trade achieved by private traders. Consider, to begin with, a number of privately owned, privately managed, profit-maximizing trading enterprises which are price-takers on both domestic and foreign markets and which import a given good into a given economy. They will equate marginal cost to marginal revenue, that is foreign to domestic price and, in the absence of tariffs or other trade-policy instruments, determine the free-trade level of imports. Suppose they are then replaced by state-owned, state-managed enterprises which, except for state ownership and the state personnel managing them, are identical with the private enterprises they replace, and trade under identical conditions of demand and supply: the level of imports determined under state ownership and management will be the same as under private ownership and management, that is, the competitive free-trade level.

Suppose next that a single, privately owned, privately managed, profit-maximizing importer, which is a price-maker on both domestic and foreign markets replaces the competitive importers. It will equate marginal cost to marginal revenue and determine the free-trade level of imports, which will lie below the competitive free-trade level because of the exploitation of the price-maker's monopsony and monopoly power. If the privately owned, privately managed importer is then replaced by a state-owned, state-managed enterprise which, except for these characteristics, is identical with the private trader, the state trader will determine exactly the same level of imports as its private predecessor, that is the free-trade level under monopsony-monopoly conditions. As in the case of the private trader, this will lie below the competitive level, but not because of state trading. It will be because the state trader exploits its price-making power, like the private trader.

In both the cases considered, therefore, the mere adoption of state ownership and management will not alter the level of trade achieved under private ownership and management. For imports to be restricted below, or expanded beyond, the free-trade level, given state trading, will require the central authority to intervene by means of tariffs, subsidies, quotas, or some other trade-policy instrument. In other words, it will be necessary for the trade authority to treat the state-trading enterprises as it would private-trading enterprises, that is, not as instruments but objects of trade policy.

Two subsidiary conclusions follow. The first is that state trading need not be an obstacle to trade, although this is often supposed and conventionally provided for.[8] The case of the competitive state traders makes this clear. The second is that where state trading does restrict trade, this may be due only to the state enterprise's price-making power which can be wielded as effectively by a private enterprise operating under the same conditions. The example of the monopsony-monopoly importer demonstrates this.

(2) THE CENTRALLY OPERATED STATE-TRADING ENTERPRISE

The preceding analysis omits a distinctive feature of state trading, however. This is that the state enterprise, unlike the private enterprise, can be operated by the government. It is this second form of state trading which, as indicated, has dominated much of the analysis of the subject. The reason, no doubt, is that economists were thinking of systems in which economic activity was essentially private and state transactions were central, or government transactions. The examples of state trading to which they could refer, notably in the industrialized countries during war-time or following the depression, supported this view. But, as the preceding section shows, centrally operated state trading is not necessary. Nor, nowadays, is it empirically the rule.

A centrally operated state-trading enterprise may, providing it has price-making power,[9] restrict the level of trade below, or expand it beyond, the free-trade level and, thus, introduce rates of divergence between domestic and foreign prices. In other words, it can create the same effects as would be achieved if the trade authority, instead of operating the enterprise, were explicitly to employ tariffs, subsidies, quotas or other trade-policy measures. Nevertheless, government-operated state trading differs essentially from such instruments in at least three ways.

First, the centrally operated state-trading enterprise can substitute for any other trade-policy instrument. It can serve to introduce an *ad valorem* rate of divergence between domestic and foreign prices and hence replace an *ad valorem* tariff or subsidy. It can be operated so as to levy or disburse an equalizing tax or subsidy, to impose a quantitative limitation on imports or exports, or to ensure the import or export of a given quantity or value of goods. Its Protean qualities mean, further, that a single enterprise can substitute successively for a number of instruments. Thus a government-managed enterprise, operating so as to maintain an *ad valorem* tax on imports, can convert the tax into a quota should the foreign price of the importable fall rapidly and threaten to disrupt the domestic market.

Secondly, the centrally operated enterprise, when it effectively introduces trade taxes or controls, directly affects only those trade flows which it transacts itself. By contrast, when tariffs, trade subsidies or controls are resorted to by the central authority, they directly affect the transactions of the population of enterprises subordinate to the authority and subject to the measure.

Thirdly, as a consequence of their directly regulating only their own transactions, government-managed enterprises may operate in secrecy. Thus, if quantitative restrictions are necessary, there will be no need for the central authority to publish lists of commodity quantities or of types of licence, and if import taxes are to be introduced, parliamentary approval will not be necessary as it might be in the case of tariffs.

Although the two are often confused, the government-managed state-trading enterprise also differs from the trading enterprise which is subject to government directives or instructions. This is not always apparent, both because the literature stressing central functional control in state trading does not distinguish between the two cases and because, in practice, the two may have equivalent effects. Thus a trading enterprise which has a monopoly of the import of a certain commodity will be government operated whether it is state owned and government managed, or privately owned, privately managed and subject to directives during some national emergency for instance. Nevertheless, it is necessary to distinguish between the two situations.

To start with, it can be shown that a directive is equivalent to a competitively allocated quota.[10] Thus to classify enterprises subject to government directives as state-trading units would require the identical classification of enterprises subject to competitively allocated quotas. Yet, this is contrary to present usage.[11]

Further, a population of enterprises may be subjected first to directives and later to tariffs. To identify enterprises subject to directives as state-trading units would require the change to be described as an abandonment of state trading. Yet it may be more accurate[12] to consider it simply as the substitution of one form of trade-policy instrument for another, given the same ownership and management of the trading enterprises concerned.

Thus, while recognizing the practical difficulty of separating government managed units from those subject to central directives, it seems analytically desirable to maintain a clear distinction between the centrally-operated enterprise, on the one hand, and all other enterprises on the other which, whether state trading or not, are subject to centrally applied trade-policy instruments ranging from directives, through quotas, to tariffs and subsidies.

(3) CENTRALLY OPERATED STATE TRADING AND FIRST-BEST TRADE INTERVENTION

Whenever a state-trading enterprise is centrally operated as well as a price-maker and, hence, is available as a trade-policy instrument, it can be used for optimal trade intervention like other instruments. Optimal, or first-best, intervention, is action on the part of the policy authority which eliminates a divergence between marginal social cost and marginal social value without creating an associated distortion. Trade intervention, in turn, may be defined as action on the part of the policy authority which directly affects trade and so both the production and consumption of tradeables. Optimal trade intervention is thus action by the policy authority which removes a divergence attached to trade and, in so doing, affects both the production and consumption of the tradeable good.

A trade divergence will arise either because positive or negative external effects are attached to trade or because the trading country, though not its traders, is a price-maker on the international markets on which it transacts. If the divergence is attached to imports, marginal social-domestic cost and marginal social value will be equal, but will exceed or fall short of the marginal social cost of imports. If it is attached to exports, marginal social cost and marginal social domestic value will be equal, but will exceed or fall short of the marginal social value of exports.

Figure 7.1 illustrates the use of a tariff and of a centrally operated state-trading enterprise for optimal intervention in the case of a negative external effect, such as pollution, attached to trade. D_m is the demand for imports, that is, the difference between the demand for and the domestic supply of importables at all prices below P_e, the price at which the two are equal. It is assumed that there is no divergence between the marginal private and social value, or between the

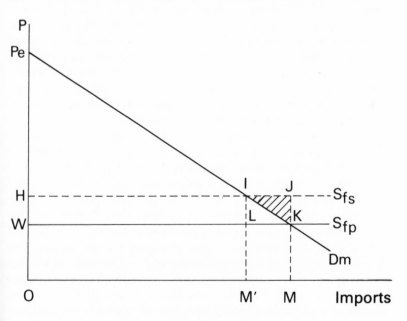

FIGURE 7.1
Optimal tariff or state-trading intervention

marginal private and social domestic cost, of importables, so that D_m indicates the marginal social value of imports. It is further assumed that traders are perfectly competitive, that is, price-takers. S_{fp} is the foreign supply of imports as it appears to the traders and is assumed to be infinitely price-elastic at price OW. The importing country, in other words, is small. There is a divergence between the marginal private cost of imports, indicated by S_{fp}, and the marginal social cost of imports, indicated by S_{fs}, because of the negative external effect attached to foreign trade activity. S_{fp} thus lies below S_{fs}.

In the absence of central intervention, importers consider the marginal private cost of imports and equilibrium is at world price OW and the level of imports OM. As marginal private cost is inferior to marginal social cost, imports exceed the level required for optimal allocation. The country thus suffers a loss which is represented by IJK, that is the excess of the marginal social cost of imports over the marginal social value and domestic cost of importables.

To eliminate the loss and restore the optimal situation, the central trade-policy authority can introduce a tariff at the rate $OH-OW/OW$. This reduces the level of imports to OM', and equates the marginal social cost of imports to the marginal social value and domestic cost of importables. All are now equal to OH. The gain which results may be ascertained by considering the redistribution of income which the transition from the second- to the first-best situation occasions. The consumers lose real income to an amount equal to $WHIK$,[13] the government reaps $WHIL$ in tariff revenue, those who suffered from the external diseconomy gain $LIJK$ from the reduction in pollution. The net gain to the economy is thus IJK.

Alternatively, the central-policy authority can create a single state-trading enterprise to replace the competitive traders and operate it so as to reduce the level of imports to OM' and to create a rate of divergence between domestic and foreign prices equal to $OH - OW/OW$. Again, consumers lose $WHIK$, the government-operated trading enterprise reaps a profit of $WHIL$, those suffering from pollution gain $LIJK$, and the country reaps a net benefit of IJK.

Figure 7.2 illustrates the use of an export tax and of centrally operated state trading for optimal intervention in the case of a price-making country. S_x is the trading country's supply of exports, that is the difference between the domestic supply of, and demand for, the exportable at all prices above P_e, the price at which the two are equal. It is assumed that there is no divergence between the marginal private and social cost, nor any between the marginal private and social

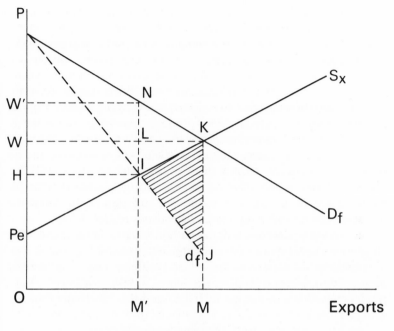

FIGURE 7.2
Optimal export tax or state-trading intervention

domestic value, of the exportable, so that S_x indicates the marginal social cost of exports. It is further assumed that trade is undertaken by competitive, that is price-taking, traders. D_f is the foreign demand curve but it does not indicate the social value of the country's exports. For the country that has price-making power: by varying the amount that it sells abroad, it varies the price of its exports. The marginal social value of its exports is thus indicated by d_f, the marginal curve corresponding to the average curve D_f.

In the absence of central intervention, the competitive traders in the exporting country will act as though D_f were the country's export demand curve and will equate marginal cost to marginal revenue, that is, domestic to foreign price. Equilibrium will thus be at price OW and the level of exports OM. As the marginal private value exceeds the marginal social value of exports, these will exceed the level required for optimal allocation. The country will thus suffer a loss equal to IJK, that is the excess of the marginal social cost and domestic value of exportables over the marginal social value of exports.

To eliminate this loss, the central trade-policy authority can intervene by means of a tax at a rate of $OW' - OH/OW'$. This reduces exports to OM' and restores the equality between the marginal social cost and marginal social domestic value of exportables, on the one hand, and the marginal social value of exports on the other. All are now equal to OH. The gain associated with the transition from the second- to the first-best situation is determined by the redistribution of income which it occasions. The producers suffer a loss equal to $HWKI$.[14] The government reaps revenue equal to $HW'NI$ which can be divided into two parts. The first is $HWLI$ which would be the tax revenue assuming constant foreign prices. The second is $WW'NL$ which is equal to the increase in real income resulting from the improvement in the terms of trade. The net gain to the country is therefore equal to $WW'NL$ minus LKI, *that is to* IKJ.[15]

Alternatively, the central policy authority can create a state-trading enterprise which replaces the competitive traders, and operate it so as to reduce the level of exports to OM' and to create a rate of divergence between domestic and foreign prices equal to $OW' - OH/OW'$. Again producers suffer a loss equal to $HWKI$ and the government reaps a gain equal to $HW'NI$ which can be divided into two parts. The first is the profit of the enterprise assuming constant foreign prices. The second is $WW'NL$, the terms of trade gain. The net benefit to the country is therefore equal to $WW'NL$ minus LKI.

The preceding case may be modified to consider the optimal explicit export subsidy or the implicit subsidy afforded by the operations of a centrally-operated state-trading enterprise. In Figure 7.3, S_x as before is the trading country's export supply curve and indicates the marginal social cost of exports. Traders are assumed to be price-takers. D_f is infinitely price-elastic at price OW and indicates the marginal private value of exports. Because there is a positive external effect, such as foreign goodwill associated with exports, D_{fs}, indicating the marginal social value of exports, lies above D_f intersecting the vertical axis at W'.

In the absence of central intervention, exporters respond to the marginal private value of exports and determine the level of exports OM, which falls short of the level required for optimal allocation. The country thus suffers a loss equal to the excess of the marginal social value of the exports foregone over the marginal social cost and domestic value of exportables, that is geometrically to the triangle IJK.

In order to eliminate this loss the central authority can intervene by

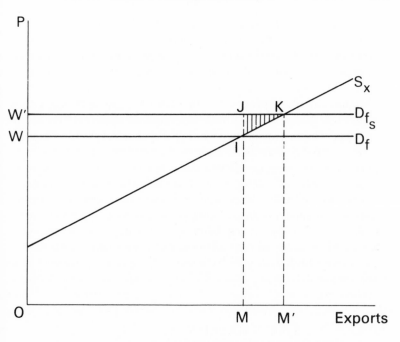

FIGURE 7.3
Optimal export subsidy or state-trading intervention

means of an export subsidy at a rate equal to $OW' - OW/OW$, or can create a state-trading enterprise to replace the competitive exporters and operate it so as to determine the same rate of divergence between domestic and foreign prices. In both cases, exports increase to the level OM', the equality between the marginal social value of exports, on the one hand, and the marginal social cost and domestic value of exportables, on the other, is restored, and the country reaps a net gain equal to triangle *IJK*.

In all the cases considered, therefore, a centrally operated, price-making state-trading enterprise has been used as a perfect substitute for trade taxes or subsidies for the purpose of first-best intervention. In the first two cases, the same demonstration could have been under-taken had the substitution been between quotas, or restrictive direc-tives, and state trading and, in the third, had it been between an expansionary directive and state trading. Moreover, the exercise could have been pursued for still other trade policy instruments and for second-best, instead of first-best, trade intervention.

A feature of the three cases presented has also been that the centrally operated state-trading enterprise has not only had price-making power, thus being able to vary the amount of exports it has put on, or of imports it has taken off, the international market, but that it has wielded that power so as to achieve the social optimum instead of maximum enterprise profits. In other words, it has operated so as to equate marginal social cost and value and not marginal private cost and value. This has meant that where the demand curve for, or supply curve of, imports or the demand curve for, or supply curve of, exports has represented marginal social value or cost, the state-trading enterprise has operated along it instead of along the corresponding marginal private value or cost curve which would have been appropriate for the maximization of enterprise profits. This may be seen in all diagrams. The enterprise behaviour they depict is the necessary condition for the use of centrally operated state trading as an alternative to other trade-policy instruments in first- and second-best trade intervention.

(4) CENTRALLY OPERATED STATE TRADING AND OTHER INSTRUMENTS IN PRACTICE

In theory, all the trade-policy instruments just considered, as well as others, can be used for first-best intervention and, moreover, be varied to maintain the optimal situation. In practice, however, the extent to which they can be applied at all, or adjusted in response to varying conditions, is severely limited by international convention. This, however, is more true of the chief trade-policy instruments than of government-operated state trading.

About 95 per cent of the tariffs of the developed countries, to start with, are bound following the successive rounds of negotiation held under the auspices of the General Agreement on Tariffs and Trade (GATT). In addition, the General Agreement requires tariffs to be effectively abandoned within the boundaries of a customs union or a free-trade area.[16] Quantitative restrictions, in turn, are prohibited except for specific purposes.[17] And export subsidies on industrial goods have ceased to be granted by seventeen countries in accordance with the provisions of Article XVI, paragraph (4) of the Agreement. Exchange controls on current payments and differentiated exchange rates, finally, are proscribed by the Charter of the International Monetary Fund for countries applying Article VIII.

State trading is also subject to international regulation under the provisions of the General Agreement. Article XVII requires state-trading enterprises to behave solely in accordance with commercial considerations,[18] and countries with state-trading enterprises to inform contracting parties of import mark-ups or, failing that, of the prices charged on the resale of products.[19] And it is true that the strict application of the first provision would effectively eliminate centrally operated state trading as a trade-policy instrument. For, if the centrally operated enterprise were obliged to behave in accordance with commercial considerations, it would be unable to introduce either an *ad valorem* rate of divergence between domestic and foreign prices or a restrictive quota.[20] But no agreement seems to have been reached on the meaning of the phrase,[21] and it has played little or no part in the international control of state trading. Moreover, while the Agreement attempts to control state trading in imports, it is far more discrete on the subject of exports. Significantly, the provisions of the Agreement do not expressly ban the implicit subsidization of exports discussed in the previous section. Nor does the associated Code on Export Subsidies and Countervailing Duties negotiated during the Tokyo Round.

Thus, state trading emerges as less subject to limitations by international convention than other trade-policy instruments. Bearing in mind that the centrally operated enterprise can take the place of any other instrument for optimal or sub-optimal intervention, and do so in secrecy, it consequently appears to be the supreme instrument and in a position to replace all others. But this would be to overlook the limitations impeding its own universal use.

The first, as already noted, is that the centrally operated state-trading enterprise must have price-making power if it is to serve as a trade-policy instrument. In other words, it must be a monopoly, and a monopoly not only in the sense that it is responsible for all or most imports, exports, or both of a particular commodity, but that its trade constitutes a sufficiently important share of domestic or foreign supply for it to influence prices.

The second limitation arises because, if centrally operated state trading were to replace all other instruments, the central trade-policy authority would transact, perhaps not all, but at least most, trade. Foreign trade decisions would be virtually concentrated in one body, and foreign trade be centrally planned. But the experience of fifty years of central planning has led to two conclusions. One is that it is not possible for the central authority to determine the optimum level and pattern of trade both because the necessary information cannot be collected and *a fortiori* kept up to date, and because it cannot be processed.[22] The other is that, for the same reasons, the central authority cannot make consistent decisions so that it can transact all or a significant share of trade only with considerable waste.

The third limitation stems from the secrecy with which the state-trading enterprise can be operated and which appears as an advantage to the national trade authority. For secrecy both breeds suspicion and prudence on the part of trading partners and makes it difficult to regulate centrally managed state trading internationally. As a result, it hinders trade.

Thus, despite its attractions, centrally operated state trading cannot be the universal trade-policy instrument. It must be restricted to markets on which the state-trading enterprise has monopoly or monopsony power. It should be limited to the trade in which the central authority is better able to assess social costs and benefits than the private enterprise. It should also be confined to cases in which divergences or distortions cannot be satisfactorily corrected by price-mechanism devices or direct controls, but require the continuous intervention of the central authority. All three conditions may be fulfilled in a developing country for the import or export of a new product. They may be fulfilled in any country for the import of necessities where, in times of shortage, private traders may be tempted to exploit their private monopsony power. They will often be fulfilled in all countries for strategic goods where divergences between marginal private and social costs and benefits are particularly pronounced if only for political reasons, and trade requires continuous central supervision. In most other instances, however, there would seem to be less justification for the central authority to trade itself. Actual transactions would seem best left to private- or state-trading enterprises and central intervention reserved for a regulation of their operations by means of tariffs, quantitative restrictions and other trade-policy instruments.

(5) CONCLUSIONS AND SOME INFERENCES FOR THE INTERNATIONAL REGULATION OF STATE TRADING

The argument of the preceding pages has been that there are two types of state trading. The one, which has been overlooked by the literature, is an object of trade policy like private trading. The other, which has been focussed on by writers on the subject, is an instrument of trade policy, like tariffs or quantitative restrictions. For the state-trading enterprise to be of this second variety requires it to be government-operated and a price-maker. It will then be available for first- and second-best intervention and constitute an attractive, though by no means universal, trade-policy instrument.

The distinction drawn has implications for the international regulation of state trading. To begin with, the state-trading enterprise which is an object of trade policy will not require specific provisions. Its operations will be subject to tariffs, quantitative restrictions and other measures, and it will be these expressions of national policy which will require international control, but not the enterprise itself. For it will be operated like its private counterpart.

It may be objected, however, that the state-trading enterprise, though an object of trade policy, will restrict and therefore be an obstacle to trade because of its price-making power. This can and does occur. But if monopsony or monopoly power is to be the justification for international control, then it should be extended to private traders with price-making potential. For they have the same ability to restrict international trade as their state-trading counterparts. In other words, here again, there is no reason for discriminating between the private and the state trader.

On the other hand, it may be that the state enterprise perturbs trade because it is of the second variety, that is because it is centrally managed, has price-making power and is operated so as to achieve the same effects as would otherwise be achieved by price-mechanism devices and direct controls. In this case, it will require specific regulation in the same way as other trade-policy instruments, such as tariffs, export subsidies and quantitative restrictions, do. Given the secrecy which surrounds the transactions of government-operated enterprises and which makes them difficult to control, this could be implemented in the following ways.

First, a notification requirement could be established which would request member countries with centrally operated state-trading enterprises to provide information to the secretariat of an international agreement on, or including, state trading. Secondly, a complaints procedure could be introduced as part of the international convention, and penalties imposed upon countries with centrally operated state-trading enterprises which acted against the interests of other parties. Thirdly, the secretariat of the agreement, or an independent body at its request, could collect data about state-trading enterprises which were thought to be centrally operated. This could include data on, for instance, the evolution of trade flows and rates of divergence between domestic and foreign prices. As comprehensive results could not be expected from any one of the methods, a combination of the three would be advisable.

These considerations, in turn, suggest a revision of Article XVII of the GATT. In its present form, it neither distinguishes between state trading as an object and as an instrument of trade policy nor, within the first alternative, between price-taking and price-making enterprises. Paragraph 1, to start with, requires all state-trading enterprises without exception to behave commercially and competitively, which is confusing. For either the state enterprises referred to are objects of trade policy, in which case the same obligation should be imposed upon private enterprises and there is no justification for a separate article dealing with state-trading units. Or the state enterprises in question are trade-policy instruments, and there is a justification for a separate article, but it should at the same time be recognized that the enterprises can neither act commercially nor competitively.

Paragraph 4(b) goes on to require countries with import monopolies to inform other contracting parties on request of import mark-ups or of prices charged on the resale of products. But, again, either the trading enterprises referred to are objects of trade policy, in which case the same obligation should be imposed upon private import monopolies and there is no justification for a separate state-trading article. Or the state enterprises concerned are instruments of trade policy, and there is a justification for specific regulation, but account should be taken of the fact that import margins are only one way in which the government-operated enterprise can intervene in foreign trade, quantitative limitation and export subsidization being others. For if the centrally operated enterprise is to be internationally controlled, its ability to substitute for any trade-policy instrument should be recognized expressly.

The revised formulation of Article XVII should thus so define state trading as to exclude those state enterprises which are the object of trade policy intervention by means of tariffs, quantitative restrictions and other measures. For the regulation of these instruments is already provided for elsewhere in the Agreement. It should instead refer to the centrally operated state-trading enterprises, whose operations could be controlled in the three ways described above. In other words, it should concentrate, like much of the literature, on those state-trading enterprises which may be used to achieve national policy objectives and may in doing so perturb trade, and which, like other trade-policy instruments, consequently require international regulation.

NOTES AND REFERENCES

1. James E. Meade, *The Theory of International Economic Policy, Volume Two: Trade and Welfare* (London: Oxford University Press, 1955), p. 176.
2. Ibid., p. 176.
3. See, for example, Charles P. Kindleberger, *International Economics*, fourth edition (Homewood, Ill.: Richard D. Irwin Inc., 1968 (The Irwin Series in Economics)), p. 130.
4. A Panel of the GATT has regretted that an enquiry into state trading did not 'permit the CONTRACTING PARTIES to judge the extent to which such enterprises serve as a substitute for other measures covered by the General Agreement, such as quantitative restrictions, tariffs and subsidies'. *Basic Instruments and Selected Documents*, ninth supplement (Geneva: GATT, February 1961), p. 183.
5. See in this volume for instance, Robert W. Floyd, 'Income Taxation of State Trading Enterprises'; and Peter J. Lloyd, 'State Trading and the Theory of International Trade'.

The conception presented is not always as clear, however. Thus Carter Murphy states that state-trading agencies 'must be governed by decisions actually or potentially dominated by government officials', but, when considering the organization of state trading, acknowledges that outside the British Commonwealth 'The semi-autonomous, limited liability, public corporation, which may or may not have the same legal status as private corporations, predominates'. J. Carter Murphy, 'State Trading', *International Encyclopedia of the Social Sciences*, vol. 8 (Macmillan and Free Press, 1968), pp. 136 and 138.
6. For instance, state-owned enterprises which compete with private firms and are managed like other businesses; also, many of the state-trading enterprises in what are referred to as state-trading countries, that is the socialist countries. In Yugoslavia, the trading enterprises are state owned and state managed, though by executives subordinate to the central authority and thus not by the government itself, and their transactions are regulated by tariffs and quotas. In other, small Eastern European countries, the trend is in the Yugoslav direction with trading enterprises being increasingly required to maximize profits subject to quotas, tariffs and export subsidies.
7. Thus Meade, who considers only government trading monopolies, is led to assert that an essential difference between state trading and the control of trade by taxation, subsidization and quantitative limitation is the creation of a state import monopoly in one country in response to the existence of a state export monopoly in another country, that is the creation of a bilateral monopoly. But this can occur only if the government monopolies have price-making power not only on domestic markets, but also on foreign markets, which is not necessarily the case. Moreover, assuming that they do have such

power, the creation of bilateral monopolies is not a problem essential to state trading, but one essential to monopolist trading regardless of whether trade is conducted privately or by the state.

See Harriet Matejka, 'State Trading: Instrument or Object of Trade Control?', *Journal of World Trade Law*, vol. 8, no. 2 (March/April 1974), pp. 209–14.

8. See *The General Agreement on Tariffs and Trade*, Article XVII, paragraph 3, which states that 'The contracting parties recognize that enterprises of the kind described in paragraph 1(a) of this Article might be operated so as to create serious obstacles to trade; thus negotiations on a reciprocal and mutually advantageous basis designed to limit or reduce such obstacles are of importance to the expansion of international trade'.

9. That this is a necessary condition for the centrally managed state-trading enterprise to operate as a trade-policy instrument does not seem to be generally recognized, although it is implicit throughout Meade's analysis.

10. Harriet Matejka, *Trade Control in East Europe*, Thèse no. 265, Univesité de Genève, 1973 (Genève: Médecine et Hygiène, 1978), pp. 244–6.

11. The GATT provisions relating to quantitative restrictions and to state trading differ. Moreover, trade-policy treatises always consider quantitative restrictions, but do not always discuss state trading and, when they do, consider it as distinct from quantitative restriction.

12. Not to say more acceptable: the smaller socialist countries of Eastern Europe, which are gradually shifting from directives to tariffs, while retaining the state ownership of their trade enterprises and state management at executive level, reject the notion that they are abandoning state trading. For this would suggest the abandonment of the collective ownership of the means of production in an important sector of the economy.

13. This is equal to the reduction in the segment of consumers' surplus contained within the area bounded by the demand and domestic supply curves.

14. This is equal to the reduction in the segment of producers' surplus contained within the area bounded by the supply and domestic demand curves.

15. This may be shown by making use of the fact that total social value may be measured either by the area under D_f or under d_f, and by considering the change in total value as imports are reduced from OM to OM'.

16. *General Agreement*, Article XXIV.

17. *General Agreement*, Articles XI, XII, XVIII, XX, XXI.

18. *General Agreement*, Article XVII, paragraph 1(b).

19. *General Agreement*, Article XVII, paragraph 4(b).

20. This may be shown formally for both the perfectly competitive, that is price-taking, and the monopolistic or monopsonistic, that is price-making, state-trading enterprise.

Let

S_D	= domestic supply;	P_D	= domestic price;
S_F	= foreign supply;	P_F	= foreign price;
D	= demand;	r	= price-maker's rent;

and assume that the state-trading enterprise imports and, behaving commercially, maximizes profits. The two assumptions are convenient but not essential. The state-trading enterprise could be exporting and maximizing not profits, but another variable such as sales.

The system given state traders who are price takers is then the following:

$$S_D = S_D(P_D) \tag{1}$$
$$S_F = S_F(P_F) \tag{2}$$
$$D = D(P_D) \tag{3}$$
$$D = S_D + S_F \tag{4}$$

where the first equation states that domestic supply is a function of domestic price, the second, that foreign supply is a function of foreign price, the third, that demand is a function of domestic price, and the fourth, that demand equals the sum of domestic and foreign supply. The price-taking state-trading enterprise will import to the point at which its marginal cost, that is foreign price, is equal to marginal revenue, that is domestic price. It will therefore be unable to introduce the wedge between domestic and foreign price which would, for instance, be necessary to maintain an *ad valorem* tax or be consistent with a restrictive quota.

In the case of state traders who are price makers, the system is as follows:

$$S_D = S_D(P_D) \tag{1}$$
$$S_F = S_F(P_F) \tag{2}$$
$$D = D(P_D) \tag{3}$$
$$S_F = D - S_D \tag{4}$$
$$\frac{d(P_D - P_F)S_F}{dS_F} = 0 \tag{5}$$
$$P_D = P_F(1 + r) \tag{6}$$

where the first three equations are the same as in the perfectly competitive case, the fourth states that foreign supply is equal to the demand for imports, the fifth expresses the profit-maximizing condition for the price-making importer, and the sixth asserts that domestic price is equal to foreign price plus the importer's monopsony and monopoly rent.

The price-making enterprise will import to the point at which marginal cost equals marginal revenue and will determine r. But this cannot substitute for a tariff. For if equation (1), (2) or (3) change because of changing supply or demand conditions, so will the value of r. For r to be converted into a tariff would require the central authority to operate the state-trading enterprise not so as to maximize profits (or some other variable), but so as to maintain r equal to a given *ad valorem*, specific or equalizing tariff.

The satisfaction of equations (1) to (6) is not compatible, either, with the introduction of a restrictive quota. For this would mean that

$$\frac{d(P_D - P_F)S_F}{dS_F} > 0$$

in other words, that equation (5) was not satisfied. For a given quantitative limitation to be established would again require the central authority to operate the state-trading enterprise not so as to maximize profits, but to achieve a particular limitation.

21. See Ivan Bernier, 'State Trading and the GATT', Chapter 12 in this volume.

22. Thus, in Poland, the fact that linear programming has been used to determine the optimal trade pattern in only three instances is attributed to the impossibility of collecting the necessary data. In addition, and independently, the statement has been made that 'As a realistically formulated overall optimization problem would involve approximately 100,000 commodities to be allocated to approximately 3–100 currency areas, it may give rise to a linear programme with several millions of possible variables subject to hundreds of thousands of constraints. Such a problem is outside the possibilities of solution of any existing linear programming computing code, the solution time for which increases approximately by the cube of the number of linear constraints'. Witold Trzeciakowski, *Systems of Indirect management in a Planned Economy; Effectiveness Models and their Application in Poland* (Lodz: Universytet Lodzki, 1973), p. 43.

8 State Trading and Domestic Distortions in a Mixed World Economy

Klaus Stegemann

(1) THE PROBLEM

The Economist reported in early 1979 (20 January, p. 50) that the EC Commission was getting ready 'for an attack on the devious ways in which member governments distort competition by pumping money into state-owned industries'. The Commission's draft directive was reported to be focussed on 'public enterprises operating in competition with other countries' state companies (e.g., ship-building) or with private companies (e.g., the motor industry)'. The problem requiring attention is that governments increasingly direct publicly controlled companies to sell below 'full' cost (or to purchase domestic products at a premium), and that the resulting losses are absorbed, more or less directly, by the public purse. It should be noted that in this paper the concept of public control will be interpreted widely. The crucial aspect is the state's influence on the terms of sale or purchase rather than the government's ownership of the means of production. Trading at state-directed terms has become a major irritation that seriously affects commercial relations among mixed economies not only within the European Common Market but elsewhere as well.[1]

The contention that state trading at unprofitable prices 'distorts' competition is accepted without much questioning by the general public and by most economists. The public generally appears to agree with the businessmen's code which holds that selling at less than full (long-run) cost is 'unfair' – and that it is twice unfair if the resulting

161

losses are absorbed by the public purse. The business community is primarily concerned about the 'unfair' advantages that open or concealed subsidies provide for publicly controlled competitors. Hence the cited article in the *Economist* suggested that any definition of 'distortion of competition' would have to be based on 'some rule of thumb about profitability'. Furthermore, the public generally equates losses of state-owned industries with social losses, i.e., a waste of national resources. Economists, while realizing that such losses may largely represent a transfer of income from taxpayers to people directly or indirectly employed by state enterprises, are concerned about the concomitant waste of resources resulting from price distortions defined in the usual welfare-economic sense.

It is the purpose of this paper to demonstrate that a rule requiring publicly-controlled enterprises to sell at prices covering their long-run cost would cause waste of a country's national resources under circumstances that are not at all uncommon. At times of under-utilization of capacity, full-cost prices tend to be distorted in the sense that they exceed the short-run marginal social opportunity cost of production. The social optimality of marginal-cost pricing acquires an additional dimension when we consider an open economy. A country that has control over the prices of domestic producers can avoid wasteful imports and encourage socially advantageous exports by directing firms to sell at short-run marginal social cost. State trading thus is regarded as a policy instrument to deal with domestic price distortions. This view complements the more common argument that state trading (especially for agricultural staples and resource-based products) can enhance national welfare by exploiting a country's strength as a buyer or seller in international markets.[2]

I do not intend to make an argument in favour of state ownership of manufacturing industries. It is simply assumed that such ownership or other forms of public control exist in certain countries, and it is shown that the socially optimal pricing policy of state enterprise in certain (not uncommon) circumstances differs from the pricing policy that private owners would adopt. This paper deals only with pricing policy, other aspects of state trading will be disregarded.[3] My principal point essentially is a short-run argument, though an argument of recurrent importance for all cyclical industries, and long-run implications will also become apparent. Furthermore, it should be noted that the argument will be developed from the point of view of an individual country's national welfare. It will be shown that pricing policies that other countries may find disturbing are in the interest of the state-trading country as a whole, rather than merely in the interest of certain pressure groups or the political party in power.

Conflicts of interest between countries arise mainly because trade occurs in a mixed international economy. Countries with different degrees of control over domestic producers depend on different policy tools to maintain domestic employment when capacity exceeds demand at current prices. The international rules of respectable trade conduct try to prevent 'beggar-my-neighbour' policies in order to avoid escalating trade restrictions and to force countries to overcome unemployment primarily by stimulation of demand. It should be recognized that most 'fair trading' rules, countervailing measures, or *ad hoc* negotiations that are aimed at preventing beggar-my-neighbour situations in effect are aimed at organizing international market sharing. 'Organized free trade', to use the French prime minister's much despised term, is the order of the day whenever international capacity exceeds demand at current prices, for important industries such as steel, shipbuilding, fibres or electronics. This paper will show that aggressive price cutting by state-controlled enterprise is not necessarily the villain of the piece.

(2) DOMESTIC PRICE DISTORTIONS CAUSE WASTEFUL IMPORTS

As Dam (1970, p. 318) has pointed out, state trading fits poorly into the GATT system because the system 'presupposes that importation and exportation are handled by private firms which, stimulated by profit motives, are guided by commercial considerations'. Given this underlying principle, it stands to reason that attempts to integrate state enterprise into the prevailing order of international trade are typically based on the postulation that state enterprise ought to behave like private enterprise. Article XVII (1) (b) of the GATT requires state enterprises to make any purchases or sales involving either imports or exports 'solely in accordance with commercial considerations'. Similarly, Articles 4 and 7 of the previously mentioned draft directive of the EC Commission (1978) refer to profits and losses and 'the principle of a market economy'.

In this section, I plan to demonstrate how, at times of under-utilized domestic capacity, a country encourages wasteful imports if it depends on private enterprise or on state enterprise guided by commercial considerations. Conversely, later sections will exemplify how state trading that is guided by social considerations can avoid wasteful imports. Imports are defined as 'wasteful' if equivalent goods could be acquired at a lower social opportunity cost if they were produced domestically.

In the absence of corrective government intervention, wasteful imports will occur if the prices of import-competing domestic goods are 'distorted', in the sense that the prices quoted in the domestic market exceed the marginal social opportunity cost of domestic production. It will be useful to distinguish two principal types or components of domestic price distortions: (i) the prices quoted by domestic producers exceed their marginal private short-run opportunity cost because the domestic market is not perfectly competitive, and (ii) the producers' marginal private opportunity cost exceeds the marginal social opportunity cost because input prices, in the short-run, exceed the marginal opportunity cost of using the inputs for the production of import-competing goods. I maintain that, for sectors where state trading could be relevant, the adherence to 'commercial considerations' almost invariably implies that both types of distortions will occur whenever a substantial proportion of domestic resources is unemployed.

Whatever might be the appropriate interpretation of adherence to 'commercial considerations' in pricing, it almost certainly is not one that requires producers to sell at short-run marginal cost when a substantial proportion of their capacity is idle. Pricing at short-run marginal cost would presuppose conditions of perfect competition. Industries for which state trading is relevant typically perceive domestic demand to be inelastic at current prices, at least in the short-run. Even if price cutting develops as a consequence of excess capacity, prices would rarely approach the level of short-run marginal cost. More typically, rival producers, at times of weak demand, tend to collaborate to avoid price cutting in the domestic market.[4] To establish peaceful pricing behaviour, rival producers might adhere to a code of ethics that requires 'full-cost' pricing. In that event, the first type of domestic price distortion would be equal to the difference between the short-run marginal cost and the long-run average cost, as viewed by private producers.

The second type (or component) of domestic distortion is often added to the first because, at times of weak demand, the marginal private cost of production tends to exceed the marginal social cost. Even if competition is sufficiently strong for producers to price close to short-run marginal private cost, the prices of import-competing goods would still exceed the short-run marginal social opportunity cost of domestic production, to the extent that input prices are distorted. Wages, for example, are a short-run private opportunity cost when labour can be laid off. The social opportunity cost of labour is, however, much less than the wages paid because alternative employment is not readily available at times of slack economic activity, and because workers who expect to return to their previous jobs are reasonably reluctant to accept alternative employment. Indeed, considering the investment in job-specific human capital, non-vested pension benefits, and the cost of relocating homes and families, it would generally be wasteful for workers to change jobs when they are laid off temporarily. With generous unemployment benefits, workers are hardly stimulated to accept temporary work, even if it is available. The short-run opportunity cost of labour would thus consist of the value of backyard projects and the enjoyment of free time, minus the cost of aggravation and public unrest that could be caused by major layoffs. The net social cost of maintaining production, in the short-term, might be only a fraction of the cost to employers, and it might even be negative. Prices of intermediate inputs would also tend to be distorted in the short run because producers of these inputs charge more than their marginal cost and because their own input prices, e.g., wages, exceed the short-run marginal social opportunity cost.

The adherence to commercial practices, which would not necessarily appear to be monopolistic under long-run considerations, could cause prices of import-competing goods to substantially exceed the marginal social cost of domestic production. Let us assume that the marginal social opportunity cost of imports is equal to the prices paid for imports (adjusted for non-price differences in case of differentiated goods). Domestic buyers respond to relative prices, rather than to relative marginal social opportunity costs, assuming that buyers are guided also by commercial considerations. If the prices of domestic goods are distorted, private buyers will thus import goods that could be acquired at a lower social opportunity cost if they were produced at home. In other words: The market mechanism may fail to achieve the best use of the importing country's resources. This point is best elaborated with the aid of a diagram.[5]

In Figure 8.1, the quantity of a product, say steel of a certain shape and quality, is shown on the horizontal axis, and the domestic producers' price for this product is drawn up on the vertical axis. Let us assume that the domestic producers are quoting a price OP and that they stick to this price at all times.[6] The domestic producers' rate of sales (and output) is determined as the difference between the total quantity demanded by domestic buyers and the quantity of imports

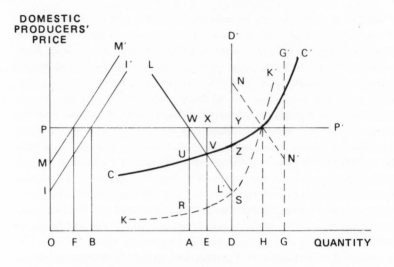

FIGURE 8.1
Domestic distortions causing wasteful imports

that domestic buyers purchase after having compared the prices of foreign suppliers to the domestic producers' price. In the interest of simplifying the diagram, I have assumed that domestic demand is completely inelastic in the short-run; thus, short-run demand curves are vertical for the relevant price range. In Figure 8.1 two such demand curves are shown: the broken line *GG'* represents total domestic demand during a boom period, whereas the line *DD'* represents demand during a slump period.

The positively sloped line *MM'* shows the quantity of imports that domestic buyers purchase, as a function of the domestic producers' price, during a boom period. The line *II'* represents the corresponding curve for a slump period, when the foreign suppliers' quotations are more attractive, relative to the domestic producers' price. As the concept of an 'import sales curve', to my knowledge, has not been used before, let me emphasize that *MM'* and *II'* are *not* supply curves for imports. Each of these curves represents the quantity of imports purchased by domestic buyers as a function of the domestic suppliers' price, *ceteris paribus*. The *ceteris paribus* assumption includes the prices of foreign suppliers, that means foreign prices are assumed to be given, in the sense that they are not a function of the quantity imported.

The foreign prices are not shown in Figure 8.1. Presumably they are lower than the domestic producers' price, at least in times of weak demand. As I have pointed out elsewhere, domestic buyers will not completely switch to imports, when import prices fall below the domestic prices.[7] The slope of the import sales curve reflects the experience that for a higher domestic price a larger percentage of domestic sales is replaced by imports *ceteris paribus*, because in the view of some buyers the increased price advantage of imports exceeds the value of the non-price advantages offered by domestic suppliers. The import sales curve shifts if import prices or relative non-price differences change. In Figure 8.1, the curve is assumed to shift from *MM'* to *II'* because at times of slack demand the prices of (at least some) foreign suppliers are lower than in the boom. Accordingly, the rate of imports will be *OF* during the boom and *OB* in the slump, if domestic producers hold their price at *OP*.

Figure 8.1 is to be used to demonstrate that domestic price distortions may result in the purchase of imported goods, even when equivalent goods, if domestically produced, could be acquired at a lower opportunity cost. Consequently, curves representing the marginal social cost of imports and of domestic production are necessary. The marginal social cost of domestic production is represented by either *CC'* or *KK'*, depending on which type of domestic distortion prevails. *CC'* is the short-run marginal cost curve of the industry and is defined as the horizontal sum of the short-run marginal cost curves of all domestic production facilities.[8] The *CC'* curve is the relevant domestic cost curve, if private cost equals social cost, i.e., the prices of variable inputs equal their marginal social short-run opportunity cost. If the input prices paid by domestic producers exceed the marginal short-run opportunity cost of the inputs, a lower curve, such as *KK'*, is used to indicate the marginal social cost of domestic production.

The *KK'* curve might join or intersect the *CC'* at a higher level of capacity utilization. For Figure 8.1, it has been assumed that *KK'* lies above *CC'* for output rates larger than *OH*. This could happen, for example, because of an increased incidence of accidents at higher utilization rates, or because pollution cannot be kept in check when utilizing older, standby capacity. Furthermore, it has been assumed, for the time being, that the domestic industry does not export; or alternatively, that the cost curves have been shifted to the left by a given rate of exports. The *CC'* and *KK'* curves thus represent the marginal cost of import-competing domestic production.

How can the marginal social cost of imports be represented? It is a convenient property of the import sales curve that, in the absence of trade intervention, it can be interpreted as the marginal social cost curve for imports. For any domestic price, the cost of buying the marginal unit of imports is just equal to the domestic producers' price, since, at the margin, buyers are just indifferent between foreign and domestic supplies. The cost of using the marginal unit of imported steel (rather than domestic steel) comprises the price quoted by the foreign supplier and the cost of non-price differences. The latter would include such items as differential transport costs and differential storage costs (if a greater dependence on imports requires holding larger inventories to ensure adequate supply). It is assumed that the marginal private cost of imports is equal to the marginal social cost of imports. This is true under the assumption that exports that are used to pay for imports, and that the resources used to overcome non-price differentials are priced at their marginal social opportunity cost. It is also assumed that the prices of imports are not distorted by tariffs or other types of government intervention in the importing country.

Now, the social cost of importing a given volume of steel can be compared to the social cost of producing it at home, except that it would be convenient to place the relevant curves one above the other in such a way that the difference in cost can immediately be read off. The curve LL' corresponds to II', and NN' corresponds to MM'. The economic interpretation of this construct is that, in each case, I have deducted the import sales from the relevant total demand curve. Thus $LL'D$ represents the residual demand for domestic steel in a slump, and $NN'G$, the residual demand curve for domestic steel during a boom period.

Let us first examine the slump situation. If the domestic producers quote price OP, the rate of imports during a slump period is OB. Domestic suppliers sell the residual BD, which equals OA, since AD equals OB by construction. For a domestic output rate of OA, the marginal social cost of domestic production equals AR or AU, depending on whether KK' or CC' is the relevant curve. In either case, the marginal social cost of imports is given by the LL' curve, which is the mirror image of the II' curve. Thus, for an import rate of OB (equal to AD), the marginal social cost of imports is AW (OP). The marginal waste of importing steel is measured by the distance RW or UW, depending on whether KK' or CC' applies. If KK' represents the marginal social cost of domestic production, all imports are wasteful, since the KK' curve lies below the LL' curve for the relevant incremental output AD. The area $RSL'W$ could be saved by producing the quantity *AD* domestically, instead of importing it. If *CC'* represents the marginal social cost of domestic production, not all imports are wasteful, because *CC'* intersects *LL'* at point *V*. In this case, the total waste of national resources is given by the area *UVW*. It could be avoided by an intervention that results in expanding domestic production from *OA* to *OE*, which implies that imports would have to be reduced by *AE*.[9]

Wasteful importation results from domestic price distortions. It can be shown that, in the absence of optimal corrective intervention, any positive rate of imports will result in some waste if the domestic price of an import-competing good exceeds the marginal social opportunity cost of domestic production. On the other hand, without domestic distortions, imports cannot be wasteful, no matter how low or high are the (given) import prices and the share of imports. The 'boom version' of Figure 8.1 illustrates these points. Given a boom demand *GG'*, and an import sales curve *MM'*, the price *OP* permits domestic producers to sell and produce at rate *OH*. For that rate of output, the domestic producers' price is not distorted; it equals the marginal social short-run opportunity cost of domestic production for both the *CC'* and *KK'* cases. Consequently, there are not wasteful imports when the domestic industry produces at rate *OH*. The marginal social cost of imports equals the domestic producer's price which in turn equals the marginal social cost of production. For any higher or lower rate of output, however, a domestic price *OP* would imply a price distortion and some waste of national resources.[10]

(3) HOW STATE TRADING CAN ELIMINATE WASTEFUL IMPORTS

(A) THE STATE AS A BUYER

Let us return to the slump situation in Figure 8.1, letting domestic demand shift to *DD'* and the import sales curve to *II'*. For sake of simplicity, it was earlier assumed that the domestic producers, during the slump, would maintain the same price *OP* that they charge in the boom. A slump price *OP*, it should be noted, is clearly not too high from a short-run profit-maximizing point of view, as the residual demand *LL'D* is inelastic at this price. The profit-maximizing rate of domestic production would be about one-half of the output *OA* that is actually produced. In this context, it is not necessary to question why domestic producers might charge less than the profit-maximizing price. All that matters is that, at times of weak demand, the domestic prices almost inevitably exceed the marginal social opportunity cost of domestic production. As demonstrated above, wasteful imports are the consequence of domestic price distortions if buyers, as well as sellers, follow commercial considerations.

It is now fairly obvious how state trading guided by social (national) considerations, can prevent wasteful imports. Let us first take the case of a state enterprise that could purchase either domestic or imported goods, for example, a national railroad company purchasing rails or rolling stock. For simplicity, let us assume, initially, that there are no private domestic buyers of the products in question. Socially wasteful imports can then be avoided by instructing public purchasers to buy imports only if their marginal cost, as measured along the LL' curve, is less than the marginal social opportunity cost of domestic production. If we assume that the latter is indicated by the CC' curve in Figure 8.1 (i.e., input prices are assumed to be undistorted), the public purchasers must buy imports only at rate ED. Domestic sales and production can thus be expanded from OA to OE. Output rate OE is socially optimal, and the remaining imports are socially advantageous, because to the right of point V the marginal social opportunity cost of imports is less than the marginal social opportunity cost of domestic production.

The substitution of imports AE by domestic production saves national resources measured by the triangle UVW. Domestic factors of production employed to produce AE receive their opportunity cost as indicated by the area $UAEV$. Because of government intervention, domestic producers (employers) gain net revenues equal to the area $UVXW$. They thus collect the social gain UVW (the value of national resources that would be spent unnecessarily if AE were imported), plus area VXW. The latter represents a transfer from domestic purchasers to domestic producers. If domestic purchasers were following commercial considerations, they could reduce their expenditures by the area VXW since imports AE are cheaper than equivalent domestic goods. The commercial implication of the transfer of area VXW to domestic producers is a reduction in the national railroad company's profits, or an increase in its losses. From a national point of view, area VXW is a premium that must be paid for domestic goods in order to avoid wasteful imports, given that the domestic price OP exceeds CC'.

Nearly the same considerations apply if we assume that the marginal social opportunity cost of domestic production in Figure 8.1 is represented by the *KK'* curve (i.e., the marginal private opportunity cost *CC'* is assumed to exceed the marginal social opportunity cost because input prices exceed the marginal social opportunity cost of the inputs that would be used to make import-competing goods). In this case, purchasers who support national interests should not buy any imports, because the *LL'* curve lies above the *KK'* curve for the relevant range *AD*. Substituting domestic production for imports *AD* saves a value of national resources that is represented by area *RSL'W*. Inputs employed to make the extra output *AD* receive area *ADZU*, which means that their income exceeds their opportunity cost by an amount equal to area *RSZU*. Producers (employers) gain area *UZYW*, and domestic purchasers lose area *L'YW*. As in the previous case, area *L'YW* is a transfer or premium that publicly controlled purchasers pay for domestic goods in order to avoid wasteful imports.

In both cases, the comparison between commercially-oriented and nationally-oriented purchasing has revealed substantial implications of an intervention for income distribution in the importing country. Indeed, income maintenance may often be the chief motive in protective government intervention during weak demand periods. It could even be argued that the anticipation of protective intervention contributes to the distortion of domestic prices. The preceding argument's decisive point, however, is that, in circumstances where domestic price distortions would prevail without intervention, protective government purchasing serves the national interest and accommodates domestic producers (including workers) as well, whose income is increased by the intervention. Protective purchasing is in the national interest in the sense that domestic producers gain more than domestic purchasers lose. Purchasing under commercial considerations would lead to a 'deadweight' loss that can be avoided if state purchasing is guided by national considerations.[11]

So far, it has been assumed that only state-controlled purchasers would consider importing the goods in question. The same goods could be imported by private firms which, presumably, would serve their own interests. State purchasing in this situation can still benefit the country even though all wasteful imports cannot be prevented. Assuming that *CC'* in Figure 8.1 represents the marginal social opportunity cost of domestic production, state purchasing can eliminate all wasteful imports only where state-controlled purchasers, in the absence of intervention, would buy all the socially wasteful imports that we find on the *WV* segment of the *LL'* line, and private purchasers would buy only socially advantageous imports along the *VL'* segment. It must also be assumed that private purchasers do not pick up socially wasteful imports when public purchasers refuse to buy them. Such circumstances are conceivable, e.g., as the consequence of locational differentiation, placing private buyers closer to the source of socially advantageous imports. In general, however, state purchasing will achieve only a partial improvement.[12]

(B) THE STATE AS A SELLER

Let us now reverse the situation and assume that all domestic production of the import-competing good is state-controlled and all domestic buyers are private firms that follow solely commercial considerations. Think, for example, of a national steel company selling autobody sheets to domestic automobile producers who may choose freely between domestic and imported products. In this case, wasteful imports can be avoided if the government instructs state-controlled producers to disregard commercial considerations and to sell at prices that just cover the marginal social opportunity cost of domestic production. In the slump situation assumed for Figure 8.1, this rule implies that domestic producers must reduce their price from OP to EV, if the CC' curve represents the marginal social opportunity cost. At the lower price, sales and output of domestic producers expand to OE, as buyers move along the LL' curve. We saw before that OE is the optimal rate of domestic production. The result is not surprising, because the state-controlled producers have been instructed to set perfectly competitive prices. Wasteful imports disappear because the domestic price distortion disappears.

Similarly, if KK' is assumed to represent the marginal social opportunity cost of domestic production, state-controlled producers must reduce their price to DS (or at least DL').[13] The lower domestic price eliminates all imports and domestic production expands to OD. This result is socially optimal because any imports are wasteful, if the marginal social opportunity cost is given by KK'.

Compared to a situation where domestic producers follow commercial considerations, a country whose state-controlled producers sell at marginal social cost gains area $RSL'W$, if KK' is the relevant domestic cost curve, or area UVW, if CC' is the relevant curve.[14] The conservation of national resources is equivalent to that in the cases of corrective state purchasing discussed in subsection (A). The effects of government intervention on income distribution, however, are vastly different when the state controls the prices of domestic producers.

If the domestic producers sell quantity *OE* at price *EV*, domestic buyers reap a windfall because, without intervention, the cost of quantity *OE* would have been equal to area *OEVWP*, whereas, at the lower price, buyers pay only *OE* times *EV*. The gain to domestic buyers is even greater if state-controlled producers reduce their price to *DS* or *DL'*. In the latter case, domestic factors of production are employed to make the additional output *AD* gain area *RSZU*, which represents the excess of factor income over factor opportunity cost (area *ADSR*). The domestic producers (employers) are the obvious losers in either case, because their gross revenue decreases when intervention occurs (inelastic residual demand), whereas their total cost increases. If, for example, they are forced to sell at a price equal to *DL'*, the state-controlled producers' gross revenue falls from *OAWP* to *OD* times *DL'*, while total cost increases by area *ADZU*.

As in the case of state purchasing, the shift in income distribution is a by-product of an intervention that improves the use of the country's resources. The winners gain more than the losers lose. Part of the redistribution may be desired on equity grounds. A transfer of income from state-controlled corporations to factors of production may, indeed, be the prime reason for an intervention. Policy-makers presumably regard the use of public funds for purchasing and selling at 'non-commercial' prices as an alternative to other forms of transfer payments, such as unemployment benefits. Furthermore, the state will normally recover part of the windfall gains in the form of higher tax revenues.

If state-controlled producers are directed to sell at prices that do not cover their 'full' (long-run) unit cost, they inevitably incur losses, at least during times of weak demand. Compared to pricing under commercial considerations, state-directed pricing will always lead to lower profits, but state-controlled producers will not necessarily require transfers of public funds. By applying the literature on peak-load pricing (especially Williamson, 1966),[15] it can be shown that short-run marginal-cost pricing, in a cyclical market, can result in losses over the business cycle only if the industry's capacity exceeds the socially optimal size of capacity, or if domestic production is inefficient in the sense that it does not use the best methods, the optimal plant sizes, or the optimal locations (Stegemann, op. cit., 1977, pp. 290–305).

On the other hand, it does not necessarily follow that state-directed producers ought to be able to cover their total cost over the business cycle, nor is failure to do so necessarily an indication of permanent excess capacity or inefficient production. First, Williamson's peak-load argument was developed for the case of undistorted input prices (the CC' curve in Figure 8.1) and does not necessarily apply when producers who must sell at marginal social cost are paying input prices that exceed the marginal social cost (the case of the KK' curve). Secondly, state-controlled companies may be unable to cover costs over the business cycle if they are directed to sell at less than short-run marginal cost during boom periods. While such constraints may lead to wasteful domestic production, the existence of price distortions in the boom is no reason to retain price distortions during the slump.

Finally, I would argue that the occurrence of losses and the need for transfers of public funds ought to be divorced from the problem of socially optimal pricing. Pricing below full cost is necessary to prevent wasteful imports at times when domestic capacity would remain idle. Transfers of public funds to state-controlled producers could be required to: cover short-run losses due to marginal cost pricing in the slump, cover for past mistakes, provide for future expansion or modernization. In covering past mistakes, the allocation of resources is a bygone decision. If a state-controlled industry has over-invested, a transfer of public funds may be necessary to cover the industry's obligations, whether they concern existing legal arrangements or problems of income distribution. It would be wasteful to try to minimize losses (transfers of public funds) by directing producers to hold their prices above marginal social opportunity cost.

Decisions concerning future expansion and modernization of state-controlled industries ought to be made on the basis of a comparison of long-run costs and social benefits. Again, short-run pricing decisions ought to be divorced from the long-run investment decisions. A need for investment funds does not justify setting prices under commercial considerations. Conceivably, an expansion project could be in the social interest even if decision makers expect that total revenues will never cover total cost, because input prices in a certain region or industry are expected to be distorted for the duration of the project.

I readily admit that public ownership may create more distortions in input prices, or that it may cause a wasteful allocation of resources in the long run, because state-owned companies show more restraint than private companies in making unpopular decisions concerning closure, restructuring, or relocation of wasteful production. Such reservations merely suggest, however, that there may be more effective means of regional development policy or adjustment assistance than public ownership of the industries concerned. They do not alter my principal contention that, in the presence of domestic price distortions, it would be wasteful for state-controlled producers to set prices in accordance with commercial considerations.

For state-controlled selling to prevent wasteful imports, it is not necessary that all domestic production of the goods in question be government owned. If the government can direct a major producer to cut his price, others may follow because their residual demand becomes too elastic or because it becomes impossible to hold prices at *OP* by 'spontaneous coordination' of conduct. Any domestic price-cutting is a move in the right direction, so long as prices exceed the marginal social opportunity cost. Private producers, however, would not cut their prices to levels below the *CC'* curve in Figure 8.1. If the marginal social cost of domestic production is lower (as indicated by the *KK'* curve), price competition among producers cannot attain the optimal rate of domestic output. The imposition of a price ceiling cannot solve the problem either, because private producers would reduce output if the price were fixed at a level less than *AU*. A price ceiling-cum-subsidy for the use of overpriced inputs might approximate state-controlled selling.[16]

(4) HOW STATE TRADING CAN STIMULATE SOCIALLY ADVANTAGEOUS EXPORTS

(A) ASSUMING A PASSIVE ATTITUDE OF FOREIGN COUNTRIES

In this section, it will be shown how the domestic distortions problem is alleviated if an import-competing industry increases its capacity utilization by expanding exports during a slump period. 'Intra-industry trade' is a common phenomenon (see Grubel and Lloyd).[17] At times of excess capacity, the same product might be imported and exported simultaneously, because domestic producers in each country hold the home-market price at a level well above marginal cost, but may find it profitable to make price concessions in order to increase the penetration of export markets. Much of what follows in this section is built on the assumption of mutual dumping. That assumption is not implausible, because the importing countries, in accordance with Article VI of the GATT and the Antidumping Code, may take antidumping actions only if serious injury to domestic production can be established. And even if the legal requirements for antidumping action are fulfilled, countries may be reluctant to implement protective measures because the cure is worse than the injury.[18] Further-more, an Interpretative Note to Article XVII of the GATT states clearly that 'the charging by a state enterprise of different prices for its sales of a product in different markets is not precluded . . . provided that such different prices are charged for commercial reasons, to meet conditions of supply and demand in export markets'. (See Dam, pp. 322–3).

If it were possible to export at a constant (mill-net) price equal to the domestic price *OP*, distortions would disappear, because, in this case, domestic producers would expand output to *OH* in Figure 8.1. For that rate of output, the marginal private and social cost of domes-tic production equal *OP*. Thus the marginal social cost of domestic production would equal the marginal social cost of imports, *AW*. If we moved the *CC'* and *KK'* curves to the left by the distance representing the additional output, *AH*, there would be no price distortion and no area of waste. Intervention would be unnecessary, since commercial and social considerations would be identical.[19] It is, however, ex-tremely unlikely that, during a slump period, an industry beleaguered by imports would be in a position to expand exports at its domestic price. If the domestic producers are able to expand exports at all, they presumably have to resort to dumping.

Figure 8.2 repeats all the curves that were relevant for the 'slump portion' of Figure 8.1.[20] In the absence of intervention, an import-competing industry produces at the rate *OA* for domestic consump-tion, if no export opportunities are available, because total domestic demand is *OD* and imports are *OB* (equal to *AD*), when the domestic price is *OP*. Now let us assume that exports generate a mill-net price equal to *OQ* and that foreign authorities are not expected to interfere, although there would be a margin of dumping equal to *PQ*. In these circumstances, domestic producers who follow commercial considera-tions find it profitable to expand production to *OE* and to export *AE*. Because of the larger output, the divergence between *OP* and the marginal social cost of domestic production is smaller than it was in Figure 8.1.

The introduction of export opportunities implies that we have to consider two different margins in order to determine the scope for improvements by policy intervention. The first is the optimal rate of domestic production that is established by the intersection of the relevant marginal cost curve with the *QQ'* line in Figure 8.2. If *CC'* represented the marginal social cost (input prices are undistorted), *OE* would be an optimal rate of output, because the social cost of the

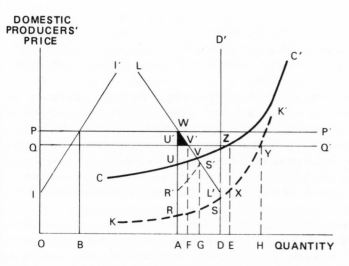

FIGURE 8.2
Intervention at two margins

last unit produced would equal the marginal social value obtained by
exporting it. If, however, we assume that *KK'* represents the marginal
social cost, *OE* is a suboptimal rate of output, because, for that rate,
the marginal social value exceeds the marginal social cost by *XZ*. The
country's welfare could be increased by area *XYZ* if exports were
increased by *EH* beyond the rate that is profitable under commercial
considerations. Secondly, the other margin that must be examined
concerns, of course, the optimal combination of imports and domestic
output for domestic consumption.

Under the second aspect, we previously compared the marginal
social cost of importing (represented by *LL'*) to the marginal social
cost of domestic production. Since domestic output now has an alternative use (it can be exported at price *OQ*), the marginal social
opportunity cost of consuming domestic output is represented by the
QQ' line. As seen in Figure 8.2, the marginal social cost of imports
(*LL'* line) exceeds the *QQ'* line for imports *AF*. These are the wasteful
imports, in the sense that consumption of an equivalent quantity of
domestic output would be cheaper. It is implied that imports *AF* ought
to be replaced by domestic goods which could have been exported at
price *OQ*. The shaded triangle *U'V'W* represents the waste that occurs

because domestic buyers, following commercial considerations, prefer imports AF to equivalent domestic goods for which they have to pay price OP in the domestic market.

It should be noted that the shaded triangle is considerably smaller than the equivalent areas of waste in the situation without exports. The size of the triangle does not depend on the position of the CC' or KK' curve, as long as domestic output is exported at price OQ. It should also be noted that the shaded triangle increases with the margin of dumping on export sales. If the mill-net price for exports were equal to AU or less, private producers would not be interested in exporting, output would remain at OA, and the waste caused by a distorted domestic price of the import-competing product would not be reduced.

As state trading can now be used to intervene on two fronts, the comparison of the various possibilities is more complex, warranting the use of a table. For all cases presented in Table 8.1, it has been assumed that the CC' curve in Figure 8.2 indicates the marginal private cost, and KK' the marginal social cost. The first two cases were discussed in the previous section, when we abstracted from the possibility that an import-competing industry could simultaneously be an exporting industry. In case (1), all imports are wasteful. Substitution of all imports by domestic production saves a value of resources represented by area $RSL'W$ (case (2)). As we recall, optimal import substitution could be achieved either by directing state-controlled purchasers to pay a 'premium' on domestic output when the marginal social cost of imports (LL') exceeds the marginal social cost of domestic production (KK'), or by directing state-controlled sellers to sell at marginal social cost. The outcome would be the same except for effects on domestic income distribution.

For cases (3)–(5) it has been assumed that the import-competing product can be exported at a given mill-net price, OQ. Case (3) is the situation without any intervention, which was discussed earlier in this section. Commercial considerations result in total production being at rate OE, of which AE is for export. In the same situation, private buyers import quantity AD. Compared to the first case, the introduction of exports in case (3) increases the country's welfare by the area $RXZU'$. This area comprises an increase in producers' surplus (area UZU') and an increase in the income (rent) of factors of production (area $RXZU$). Even compared to the second case, the introduction of exports increases the country's welfare (see second column of Table 8.1). But as explained previously, situation (3) still can be improved in

Comparison of situations depicted in Figure 8.2

Case	Gain compared to case (1)	Gain compared to case (2)	Gain compared to case (3)	Gain compared to case (4)	Gain compared to case (5)	Wasteful imports	Total imports	Total exports
(1) No exports No intervention	—	Loss†	Loss	Loss	Loss	AD	AD	Nil
(2) No exports Import intervention	RSL'W	—	Loss	Loss	Loss	Nil	Nil	Nil
(3) Commercial exports No intervention	RXZU'	SXZV'L' minus U'V'W	—	Loss	Loss	AF	AD	AE
(4) Commercial exports Import intervention	RXZV'W	SXZV'L'	U'V'W	—	Loss	Nil	FD	FE
(5) Export intervention Import intervention	RYV'W	SYV'L'	U'V'W plus XYZ	XYZ	—	Nil	FD	FH

* Assuming that *CC'* represents the marginal private cost of domestic production and *KK'* the marginal social cost in all cases, and that *QQ'* represents the mill-net price of exports in cases (3)–(5). For explanation of other curves see section (2) of text.

† Losses in the first row are the negative equivalent to gains in the first column.

two ways, because neither the import margin nor the export margin is optimal under social considerations.

Case (4) shows the effect of state intervention at the import margin. As in case (2), import substitution could take the form of preferential purchasing or of selling at marginal social cost. But in case (4), the marginal social cost of consuming domestic output is represented by the QQ' line. Consequently, state trading should replace only imports AF with domestic output. The substitution does not increase total output, but does reduce exports to FE. In fact, the intervention increases the country's welfare by the amount by which the social cost of imports AF exceeds the social value of the same quantity of exports. That gain, represented by the shaded triangle $U'V'W$ in Figure 8.2, is much smaller than the gain that we found when comparing case (2) to case (1). Similarly, intervention is more moderate in case (4) which, it should be recalled, differs from case (2) only by the assumption of export opportunities. In case (2), state-controlled producers must reduce the domestic price from OP to DL' to eliminate all wasteful imports. In case (4), an equivalent intervention at the import margin requires a domestic price reduction from OP to OQ; and imports are reduced only by AF, rather than by AD.

Case (5), finally, shows the effects of an intervention at the export margin. In order to attain the optimal rate of output and employment, state-controlled producers must be instructed to expand exports to the point at which the marginal social cost of domestic production equals the mill-net export price. In Figure 8.2, this condition is fulfilled at output rate OH. Compared to cases (3) and (4), the intervention at the export margin increases the volume of exports by EH. Consequently, the country's welfare is increased by area XYZ.

(B) CONSIDERING RETALIATION BY FOREIGN COUNTRIES

So far, I have largely disregarded the potential reactions of other countries to an individual country's state-trading actions. Retaliatory actions, in principle, can be triggered by any kind of state intervention that affects trade with other countries. These actions can take many different forms, and may be immediate or delayed. In each case, the expected effects of retaliation must be considered in evaluating the net benefits of an intervention. At this point, I will focus on a small portion of the spectrum of possible retaliatory actions: foreign policies that restrict the exports of a state-controlled industry.

Antidumping action may appear to be the most 'natural' form of foreign retaliation, although, as pointed out above, it is by no means inevitable. Antidumping measures do not necessarily occur more frequently in state trading than in exportation under commercial considerations. Let us now assume that a country A has attained situation (5) in Table 8.1. Intervention at the import margin has reduced imports to *FD* by lowering the domestic price to *OQ*, and intervention at the export margin has expanded exports to *FH*. Let us further assume that another country, B, regards A's exports as dumped imports because the mill-net price, *OQ*, does not cover the 'full' cost of production in A,[21] and that such imports are found to have caused or threatened serious injury to production of like goods in B. As a result of antidumping proceedings, country B imposes a dumping duty on imports from A, or the producers in A, in order to avoid the duty, raise their export price to a level deemed acceptable by the authorities in B. Under our assumptions, buyers in B are unwilling to purchase any of A's exports if their price exceeds the level that they would have paid on the basis of a mill-net *OQ*. Country B's antidumping action thus turns case (5) into case (2). This means that, as a result of antidumping action, country A intervenes more heavily on the import margin, lowering the domestic price to *DL'* and replacing all imports by domestic production. It still suffers a loss equal to area *SYV'L'* in Figure 8.2.[22]

In practice, the effects of B's antidumping action would be less extreme for various reasons: (i) long-standing customers in B continue buying A's exports at a higher price (a case that I have ruled out for the sake of simplicity by drawing a horizontal *QQ'* line); (ii) some producers in A are excused from antidumping action because they can satisfy the authorities in B that price *OQ* covers their full unit cost of production (including 'a reasonable addition for selling cost and profit', or whatever the stipulation may be); or (iii) producers in A 'voluntarily' restrain their exports to a level that authorities in B do not regard as disruptive or injurious. For our purposes, all three possibilities are alike in that the volume of A's exports is restricted to a level that country B finds acceptable. The principle of the matter can thus be illustrated by assuming that country B imposes a mandatory import quota.

Let us assume, for example, that the foreign import quota is equal to *AE* in Figure 8.2. The optimal rate of importing is now determined by comparing the marginal social cost of imports (line *LL'*) to the marginal social cost of domestic production, for output rates beyond *OE*. Graphically, we obtain the desired solution by moving segment

XY of the *KK'* curve to the left by the amount of the foreign quota. The parallel segment intersects the *LL'* line at point *S'*. Imports *AG* are found to be wasteful because their cost (area *AGS'W*) exceeds the cost of producing equivalent products at home (area *AGS'R'*). Country B's import restriction again leads to a more severe import intervention in A. Country A's intervention at the import margin increases when B's quota decreases. Indeed, if we envisage that country B gradually reduced A's exports starting from point *H*, the domestic price of state-controlled producers in A would have to slide along the *KK'* curve, starting from point *Y*.

Largely equivalent results are obtained if we assume that country B, rather than using quantitative restrictions, resorts to measures that reduce the mill-net price for country A's exports. An import surcharge or a domestic price reduction in country B might have such an effect.[23] We saw earlier (in cases (4) and (5) of Table 8.1) that optimal intervention at the import margin requires that state-controlled producers in country A lower the domestic price to the level of the mill-net price of exports. If we assume that country B's actions lower the mill-net price for A's exports, the domestic price in A must comply. This increases the discrepancy between the price that would be maintained under commercial considerations (*OP*) and the socially optimal price. As the mill-net price for exports falls, the socially optimal total output falls (moving along *KK'*). At the same time, more imports are replaced by domestic output (moving along *LL'*), and exports are also shrinking (given by the shrinking horizontal distance between *LL'* and *KK'*).

Producers guided by commercial considerations would quit exporting as soon as the mill-net price falls to *AU* or below (move from case (3) to case (1) in Table 8.1). Producers who are guided by social considerations quit exporting only when the mill-net price falls to *DS* or below. At that point, imports have disappeared (move from situation (5) to situation (2) in Table 8.1).

The upshot of all this is that state trading increases a country's welfare, no matter what other countries do to its exports. Furthermore, retaliatory actions of other countries, if they occur, could be less severe in the case of state trading than with exporting under commercial considerations. Since optimal intervention at the import margin implies that the domestic price is equal to the export price, antidumping action by other countries is less likely, or even impossible, to the extent that antidumping procedures in those countries depend on the exporter's use of price differentiation (rather than a difference between export price and cost of production). Indeed, most complaints about state trading, especially in the European Common Market, result from the fact that other countries are frustrated because they lack the policy tools for safeguarding their own national welfare. This leads into the topic of the following section.

(5) ORGANIZED FREE TRADE IS INEVITABLE IN A MIXED WORLD ECONOMY

The purpose of this paper is to make three principal points. The first point has already been established. When domestic prices are distorted, state trading, guided by social rather than commercial considerations, can improve the welfare of a country. State trading, particularly at times of weak demand, serves the national interest; it is not just a matter of domestic income distribution. The practical implications are that the problem cannot be solved by substituting domestic measures of income re-distribution for trade intervention, and it would be futile to try to prevent state trading by simply preaching the virtues of free enterprise and commercial considerations.

What might sound like heresy is, of course, fully consistent with the 'domestic distortions approach' of the theory of international trade. Indeed, Gottfried Haberler pointed out, as early as 1950, that rigid prices could lead to wasteful imports and judged that domestic price distortions are 'a matter of serious practical concern', at least in the short run (p. 224).[24] It should be added that short-run price distortions are a recurrent problem for all cyclical industries. The principal contribution of the domestic distortions literature has been to demonstrate (from a national point of view) that restrictions on trade such as tariffs and quotas, are not normally the optimal way of correcting domestic distortions.[25] In this paper, it has been shown that state trading can be used to correct domestic distortions and to increase national welfare. The practical problems of implementation and the dangers of abuse do not seem to be greater for state trading than for other types of public policy. The domestic distortions literature generally recommends domestic subsidies as the 'first-best' form of policy intervention. Subsidies, however, are difficult to administer (Corden, op. cit., 1974, pp. 48–50). The difficulties are compounded in the case of cyclical price distortions. State trading also is a 'first-best' form of intervention, in the sense that state-imposed marginal-cost pricing does not create what Corden (1974) has called 'by-product' distortions. Compared to subsidies, state trading has the advantage of being a more direct and flexible policy tool. It might also be a more accurate form of intervention to the extent that government ownership permits access to more accurate cost data than would be available without government control.

The second principal point of this chapter is that state trading, which furthers the national interests of some countries, constitutes a problem for the international trade order only because other countries are unable to correct their own domestic distortions. Differences in political philosophy and institutions make it more difficult for some countries than for others to correct domestic price distortions or to employ domestic measures that compensate for socially unacceptable shifts in income distribution resulting from aggressive international competition. To safeguard their national interests, countries that cannot or will not intervene domestically may find it necessary to employ external measures of protection. In other words: a problem of international coordination arises because we live in a 'mixed' world economy. If all countries used state trading for a certain internationally-traded commodity, or if they all had some mechanism to ensure that domestic prices of the same commodity did not exceed the marginal social opportunity cost of domestic production and an acceptable domestic income distribution could be maintained, grounds for complaints between countries would be eliminated. All remaining imports would benefit any importing country; no one would have to be concerned about dumping, or any kind of 'unfair' export practices. The allocation of resources would also be internationally efficient, in the sense that world output would be produced at the lowest possible total opportunity cost.[26]

In a situation, however, where some countries use state trading guided by social considerations while others depend on free enterprise guided by commercial considerations, the conflict is apparent. A country that tolerates relatively severe domestic price distortions during slump periods not only suffers from relatively large wasteful imports, but also wastes opportunities for off-setting exports to markets where domestic price distortions are less severe. If domestic prices do not reflect the marginal social opportunity cost of production, the total cost of world production cannot be minimized, because countries with relatively large price distortions produce less than their optimal share in the total. More importantly, countries that cannot or will not use state trading or equivalent interventions to remove or reduce domestic price distortions, and which see their markets being taken over by state traders, resort to import restrictions, such as quotas, to safeguard domestic employment. The result could be an explosive chain reaction of protectionism that could eventually hurt all participants.

My third principal point follows from the other two. If state trading is in the interest of individual countries and if an unregulated, mixed, international economy is in danger of sliding into renewed protectionism, some sort of compromise must be found. This means that supposedly 'free' trade has to be organized trade; certain rules must be followed. The purpose of the rules is to safeguard the interests of all participants and the result is not necessarily an efficient allocation of resources. It should be realized that, in practice, we must choose between different forms and different degrees of organized international market sharing.

The market sharing aspect of international trade arrangements is the most obvious, and the most deplored by economists, in the case of so-called 'voluntary' export restraint (VER). The internationally accepted system of national antidumping laws is another, possibly more pervasive, form of market sharing. Antidumping procedures discourage producers from cutting prices in foreign markets when it is not profitable to cut prices at home. Without aggressive price cutting, international market shares will be more stable than they would be in the absence of antidumping laws. Similarly, a code that requires state-controlled enterprise to practice full-cost pricing is a form of international market sharing. If such a code can be enforced, one cannot imagine a more effective form of market sharing at times of weak demand, because in the absence of aggressive price cutting, buyers would simply stay with their traditional suppliers. There is an important difference, however, between VER and codes of conduct that prevent short-run price cutting: buyers still have a choice; they alone decide which suppliers they will favour, on the basis of long-run 'full-cost' considerations.

The dilemma is, of course, familiar from the context of domestic competition policy: how much 'unfair' or 'ruinous' price cutting should be permitted in the short run, in order to stimulate competition as a process? In the context of domestic markets, policy makers are not normally concerned when producers, who hold the price umbrella, lose sales to aggressive rivals. In the world of international trade, however, a reduction in a country's market share generally implies a reduction of national welfare, if domestic prices are distorted. As a consequence, restricting competition from abroad may be in the interest of the country. The hope remains that rules which slow down interpenetration of national markets in the short run may permit us to attain a desired, more secure level of international integration in the long run.

NOTES AND REFERENCES

The author gratefully acknowledges valuable comments by Martin Prachowny and Dev Misir.

1. A comprehensive survey of the extent, form and purpose of public sector enterprise in western mixed economies was published by *The Economist* in its issue of 30 December 1978, pp. 37–58. For the case of the EEC, see also CEEP, *Die öffentliche Wirtschaft in der europäischen Gemeinschaft*, (Brussels, 1978), and W. Keyser, *Public Enterprise in the EEC* (Alphen: Sijthoff and Nordhoff, 1978). Concerning the relevant provisions of the GATT (Article XVII) and the EEC Treaty (Articles 37 and 90), see K. Dam, *The GATT*, (University of Chicago Press, 1970), see especially Chapter 18, pp. 331–2.
2. The international market power aspect of state trading is covered by several chapters in this volume, notably the contributions by McCalla and Schmitz (Chapter 3), Labys, (Chapter 4), Kostecki (Chapter 2) and Denis (Chapter 11). See also recent proposals for oil-import policies of the industrialized countries, such as the scheme proposed for the United States by Professor M. A. Adelman, *Challenge* (July-August 1979) p. 45.
3. For a survey of different aspects of state trading, see the recent article by M. M. Kostecki, 'State Trading in Industrialized and Developing Countries', *Journal of World Trade Law*, vol. 12, (1978) pp. 187–207.
4. For an example and a more detailed explanation, see K. Stegemann, *Price Competition and Output Adjustment in the European Steel Market*, chapters 2 and 3. (Tubingen: J. C. B. Mohr, 1977), and K. Stegemann, 'The Rationale of Antidumping Protection for the Steel Industry', section 2, Discussion Paper no. 321, Institute for Economic Research, Queen's University, Kingston, Ontario (1978).
5. The diagrammatical exposition follows largely Stegemann, ibid. section 3.
6. In the present context, it does not matter why domestic producers set their price(s) at this particular level, how and whether the industry manages to achieve complete adherence to this price, or in what circumstances they might decide to change their price(s). The essential requirement is that the domestic-producers' price(s) exceed their marginal private short-run opportunity cost and/or the marginal social opportunity cost, at times of slack demand. Assuming complete rigidity and uniformity of the domestic producers' prices merely serves to simplify the presentation.
7. Stegemann, op. cit. (1978), section 2, and K. Stegemann 'Domestic Monopoly as a Domestic Distortion under Free Trade Conditions', Discussion Paper no. 379, Institute for Economic Research, Queen's University, Kingston, Ontario, 1980.
8. Strictly speaking, the horizontal summation concept applies only for a perfectly competitive industry. As the present argument is built on the

assumption that domestic producers practice some form of market sharing, the CC' curve might be more complex. See D. Patinkin, 'Multiple Plant Firms, Cartels, and Imperfect Competition', *Quarterly Journal of Economics* vol. 61 (1947) pp. 173–205.

9. The remaining imports, ED, benefit the country if CC' applies; the total benefit is given by the area $VL'Z$.

10. If domestic demand were larger than GG', and domestic producers maintained the price OP, there would be two possible outcomes:
    (i) either producers are unwilling to increase output beyond OH because it is unprofitable to do so; in this case, imports would fill the gap; some of these imports would be more costly than additional domestic production;
    (ii) alternatively, domestic producers could exceed output OH and supply as much as buyers demand at price OP. In this case, some of the additional domestic output would be more expensive than additional imports.

11. Incidentally, state purchasing under my assumptions does not result in any 'by-product distortions', such as loss of consumers' surplus. On the concept of by-product distortions, see W. M. Corden, *Trade Policy and Economic Welfare* (Oxford: Clarendon Press, 1974).

12. For a further discussion of the feasibility of protective government procurement in a mixed economy, under different assumptions, see B. Hindley, *Britain's Position on Non-Tariff Protection*, Thames Essay no. 4 (London: Trade Policy Research Centre, 1972) and J. David Richardson, 'The Subsidy Aspects of a "Buy American" Policy in Government Purchasing', *The Economics of Federal Subsidy Programs*, a compendium of papers submitted to the Joint Economic Committee, United States Congress, Part 2 (Washington, DC: US Government Printing Office, 1972), pp. 220–42.

13. A reduction to DL' would be sufficient to assure the optimal result because KK' intersects the vertical segment of the residual demand curve for the domestic product.

14. If the domestic price were reduced below OP, but remained above the marginal social cost of domestic production, there would still be savings, although they would be smaller. If foreign suppliers cut their export prices, in response to domestic price reductions in the importing country, the optimal solution would be different, as the LL' curve would not represent the marginal social cost of imports. This case has been ruled out by assuming that foreign suppliers' prices are given (small country assumption).

15. See O. E. Williamson, 'Peak-Load Pricing and Optimal Capacity under Indivisibility Constraints', *American Economic Review*, vol. 56 (1966) pp. 810–27.

16. It might also be interesting to pursue the problem of 'bilateral' government control, i.e., the case in which the government has a choice between state-controlled buying and state-controlled selling in the domestic market.

17. See H. G. Grubel, and P. J. Lloyd, *Intra-Industry Trade* (London: Macmillan Press, 1975).

18. See P. Lloyd, *Antidumping and the GATT System*, Thames Essay no. 9 (London: Trade Policy Research Centre, 1977).

19. Eliminating the distortions by expansion of exports at price OP would

clearly be more advantageous than any form of intervention discussed in the previous section. As can be seen in Figure 8.1, the exporting country would gain the full area of producers' rent for volume AH, represented by the areas above the relevant marginal cost curve, and not just areas UVW or $RSL'W$.

20. The KK' curve has been drawn less steeply in Figure 8.2 than in Figure 8.1 for graphical reasons only.

21. The 'cost-of-production' definition of dumping, contained in paragraph (1) (b) (ii) of Article VI of the GATT has, of late, been used more widely. See Stegemann, op. cit. (1978), section 2. As an alternative to antidumping measures, Country B might apply a national countervailing duty law to counteract the subsidization of state-controlled firms in A. This would not change the principle of the argument in the text.

22. The imports replaced in country A could have been B's exports. It is not possible, in this framework, to show the gains or losses in the other countries. The effects of antidumping measures on the importing country were discussed in a previous paper (Stegemann, op. cit., 1978, section 4).

23. Country A has been assumed to be a price taker in the world market (small country), but Country B (rest of the world) might possess price-making power. The gist of the argument would be the same, though the presentation would be more complicated, if we assumed that Country A had some market power too.

24. See Gottfried Haberler, 'Some Problems in the Pure Theory of International Trade', originally printed in *Economic Journal*, (June 1950); re-printed in R. E. Caves and H. G. Johnson (eds.), *Readings in International Economics*, (Homewood, Ill.: Irwin, 1968), pp. 213–29.

25. A concise and lucid outline of the principles and conventional assumptions of the domestic distortions approach, also referred to as the 'theory of optimal trade intervention', is contained in Chapter 2 and 3 of Corden (1974), with a survey of the literature on pp. 40–1.

26. It should be noted that the cyclical price flexibility assumed in the text would not entail wasteful adjustment processes. For one, marginal social cost pricing would not necessarily result in drastic changes of relative prices and, secondly, the buyers' choice between domestic and imported products includes a consideration of the costs of changing sources of supply (see definition of import sales curve in section 3 above).

9 Income Taxation of State-Trading Enterprises

Robert H. Floyd

(1) INTRODUCTION

In the strict sense state trading may be defined to exist when the government 'establishes or maintains a state enterprise, . . . or grants to any enterprises, formally or in effect, exclusive or special privileges . . . in its purchases or sales involving either imports or exports . . . '[1] In a broader context state-trading enterprises are merely one form of public enterprise if the latter are defined to include any government-owned and/or controlled unit that produces and sells industrial, commercial, or financial goods and services to the public.[2] There is no necessity in either context that the government actually own the trading enterprise so long as it has control over its operations, and state-trading enterprises would appear to differ from other public enterprises only because they are primarily concerned with internationally traded goods or services.[3]

This paper reviews certain aspects of state-trading enterprises and addresses the question of whether their profits should be taxed. The structure of the paper is as follows: section 2 asks whether state-trading enterprises should only be viewed as quasi-taxing authorities and establishes an alternative viewpoint. Section 3 reviews various arguments for and against income taxation of public enterprises in general and assesses their relevance in the particular case of state-trading enterprises that are not quasi-taxing authorities. Section 4 analyses the economic effects that might result from income taxation, particularly on the equity of income distribution and the efficiency of resource allocation. Some concluding remarks are drawn in section 5.

189

(2) TAXONOMY OF STATE-TRADING ENTERPRISES

It is useful to categorize somewhat taxonomically the various forms that state-trading enterprises may take by their economic objectives, type of economic activity, organizational form, and market status.[4] The following categories would appear to be meaningful and useful:[5]

(1) Economic objective
    (*a*) revenue generation
    (*b*) regulatory
(2) Economic
    (*a*) production
    (*b*) distribution
(3) Organizational form
    (*a*) departmental
    (*b*) corporate and quasi-corporate
    (*c*) private concession
(4) Market status
    (*a*) monopoly
    (*b*) oligopoly
    (*c*) competitive

State-trading enterprises can represent essentially any combination of the preceding categories, although some combinations seem less likely than others. For example, the enterprise is more likely to be a monopolist but there is certainly no requirement that the trading enterprise have either monopoly or monopsony power. Furthermore, the monopoly power may be restricted to only the international trading stage while other distribution stages (e.g., wholesale and retail) and production stages may not be monopolized. Thus, there could be competition for state-traded goods from freely-traded goods and from domestically-produced non-traded goods, and freely-traded inputs may substitute for state-traded finished goods.[6] Similarly, within the economic objectives and activities categories, it is conceivable that the state-trading enterprise can be characterized by more than one subcategory. For example, the enterprise may be involved in both the distribution and production of traded goods. This would be fairly common among mineral resource extractive industries. The National Iranian Oil Company and the Abu Dhabi National Oil Company are involved in both the production and distribution operations in their nationalized oil industries. Similarly, a regulatory trading enterprise might also generate substantial revenues even though that were not its primary objective.

Beban has also listed at least several possible objectives of state-trading enterprises. These include efforts to accomplish any of the following:[7]

(*a*) Protect domestic production from imports;

(*b*) Stabilize certain domestic incomes or prices;

(*c*) Discriminate in favour of certain trading partners;

(*d*) Aim at improving the terms of trade by raising export prices relative to import prices;

(*e*) Improve the balance of payments by directly determining the trade components;

(*f*) Control domestic access to and consumption of certain items such as drugs or alcoholic beverages;

(*g*) Promote national defence and security by monopolizing trade in related commodities;

(*h*) Serve fiscal objectives by channeling profits from trade to the state.

Perhaps the most interesting aspect of this enumeration is that seven objectives would fall into the regulatory category of the previous taxonomy and only one into the revenue-raising category.

(3) STATE-TRADING ENTERPRISES AND TAXATION

The use of a trading enterprise solely for the objective of raising revenue is most likely when the enterprise acts only as a monopolistic intermediary in the trade process with the sole function of purchasing goods in domestic (international) markets for resale in international (domestic) markets. In such a situation the state-trading enterprise is in part little more than a quasi-taxing authority, and it would appear unnecessary to subject the surplus or profits of the enterprise to income or profits taxation.[8] Its position as a monopoly seller or buyer in domestic markets enables it, as the government so wishes and directs, either to maximize or to earn a target level of surplus on its monopolistic trading activities. After deducting its operating expenses, these surpluses may be transferred entirely to the central treasury. In terms of the preceding taxonomy such a trading enterprise would represent a combination of a revenue raising enterprise with a monopoly in distribution at the stage of exportation or importation.

By their very nature such surpluses are more akin economically to receipts from export taxes levied on private producers or import duties levied on private consumers than they are akin to profits in the sense of a return to invested capital. So long as they are transferred to the treasury, the application of a profits tax to what are in effect tax receipts would appear to be pointless. Although in this case the arguments in favour of a profits tax are not strong, the practice does exist.

In Togo, the Office of Agricultural Products (Office des Produits Agricoles du Togo, or OPAT) which is responsible for the marketing of agricultural exports and for guaranteeing minimum prices at levels fixed annually by the government, is subject, as an autonomous public enterprise, to the tax on commercial and industrial profits. In addition to its payment of export duties and taxes, the enterprise pays the profits tax on its surplus from operations and then transfers either partially or completely its remaining disposable reserves to the budget.[9]

If there is little logic to taxing profits that are economically equivalent to excise tax receipts, then what other considerations would suggest that state-trading enterprises should be subject to income taxation? In this connection, it is worth noting that there is a fundamental case for separating the taxing and trading functions of all state-trading enterprises including those intended primarily to raise revenue. That is, a trading enterprise often serves dual objectives of facilitating efficient trade in the commodities for which it is responsible as well as some other function, such as raising revenue. Obviously, these two objectives are not necessarily consistent since the exercise of monopoly pricing power could hardly be expected to induce efficient resource allocation in commodity markets. For example, the trading enterprise might attempt to maximize its surplus by holding down the prices it pays to producers. However, this action effectively drives a wedge between producer and consumer prices and domestic and international prices that would distort efficient resource allocation. Thus, ignoring the administrative advantages that are likely to result from the use of trading enterprises as a quasi-taxing authority, there seems to be a conceptual case on efficiency grounds for separating the trading function from the taxing function by having the tax expressed as an export or import duty explicitly as the government so desires. In the simplest case, the pursuit of two objectives requires at least two instruments and the pricing policy of trading enterprises may be insufficient.

Although this suggests that in theory trading enterprises are not necessarily an adequate instrument for undertaking a taxing function, they will in practice almost certainly continue to perform this function, and the question remains as to whether and when an income tax might be appropriate.

If the trading enterprise is owned by private interests, and some of the trading surplus is not transferred as revenue to the treasury and is left with the enterprise as a return to capital, then there is a strong presumption that the portion remaining with the enterprise should be taxed in the same manner as profits of other privately-owned enterprises. Even if the prices charged by the private enterprise were controlled by the government, failure to tax these remaining profits could create at least the impression that the enterprise was being given an unfair competitive advantage relative to other private enterprises that may be in competition for factor inputs or close substitutes in output markets. This would seem especially important if the trading enterprise were involved in domestic markets. This suggests that the distribution of the enterprise's surplus should be carefully weighed. It should also be borne in mind that if the commodity procurement and sales prices are controlled by the government, and if an income tax is applied to the profits retained by the enterprise, the possibilities for shifting by the private owners are limited to non-capital factor markets. Consequently, the tax's effects may differ from its effects in the cases of other privately-owned enterprises.

Even for trading enterprises that are wholly owned by the government and are used solely for raising revenue a distinction can be made between profits that arise from their exercise of monopoly power as a quasi-taxing authority and those that arise from their role in performing a trading function. There are conceptually two components to a state-trading enterprise's profits: a rent element arising from monopolistic international trading activities, and returns to capital arising from its productive trading activities in foreign and domestic markets. Whereas it would seem reasonable for all of the rent element to be transferred to the central treasury, either as a dividend or a special excise receipt, the remaining profit elements might conceptually be left with the enterprise and treated as potentially taxable income. However, in practice such a distinction could probably be made only if an explicit export or import tax were levied so that the trading enterprises' profits could be isolated.

For government-owned trading enterprises that are not used essentially as quasi-taxing authorities the question as to whether their profits should be taxed ought to be analysed in terms of more general consideration. If any tax is to apply to government-owned enterprises, including state-owned trading enterprises, it ought to be designed to promote the same objectives as private enterprises, that is, inter-personal horizontal and vertical equity, efficient allocation and use of resources and a stable, growing economy. However, special character-istics of trading enterprises may alter equity and efficiency considera-tions and revenue requirements and, consequently, affect the decision as to whether to tax their profits. For example, the relevance of the equity, efficiency, as well as macroeconomic stabilization, goals of taxation is affected by the extent of government ownership of trading capacity. Our present concern is primarily with mixed economies rather than the largely centrally-planned economy.

The actual effects of an income tax on equity and efficiency will depend on the managerial response and may, therefore, differ between trading and other enterprises if the behavioural patterns of their managers differ. Unless otherwise noted, for the remainder of this chapter it is assumed that the managers of trading enterprises attempt to operate as profitably as possible, even though their efforts may be constrained by a variety of external decisions imposed by the government. Thus, they are assumed to behave rationally and similar-ly to managers of private enterprises, insofar as external constraints do not limit such behaviour. For example, managers of state-trading enterprises would neither give away their output nor pay more than necessary for their inputs other than the one in which they have a trading monopoly.[10,11]

STABILIZATION

The more important are government-owned trading enterprises in the overall economy, the greater would be the potential implications for macroeconomic stabilization policy of excluding their profits from taxation. Where government ownership of trading and other enter-prises is quite limited, whether or not a tax were levied on the profits of the public enterprises is likely to have little impact on macro-economic variables. However, if the government's concern is with stabilization in the narrower sense of stabilizing the income or prices of producers, in a particular industry or the prices of particular commodities, then a tax on such a trading enterprise's profits may be clearly undesirable. Since the profits of such an enterprise would be used over the cycle to stabilize incomes or prices, the government would need to recognize that the imposition of a profits tax would impair the trading enterprise's ability to achieve its purposes unless the government were willing to provide operating grants as necessary.

Regardless of extent of ownership, macroeconomic stabilization effects may be avoided for the remainder of the analysis by employing a differential incidence analysis so that an equal yield dividend is assumed, *ceteris paribus*, to substitute for the yield of an income tax on public trading enterprises. Any of several dividend policies could produce equal revenue for the government. The dividend could be stated as a percentage of profits, which would be identical to an income tax at the stated percentage. Alternatively, the dividend could be stated as a percentage of the value of an enterprise's capital, but this implies that the percentage of capital's value would have to vary in order to obtain an equal yield over the business cycle. Consequently, it is convenient to assume that, as an alternative to an income tax on public trading enterprises, a flexible dividend policy could be adopted to accomplish the same macroeconomic impact, with payments negotiated between the government and individual public enterprises.

For stabilization purposes the equal-yield requirement need hold only in the aggregate, and there is no need to have equality between potential tax bills and dividend payments of individual public enterprises. However, even though there would be no aggregate stabilization effects, the exemption of public enterprises could, in some circumstances, give rise to inequities and inefficiencies in both individual enterprises and the economy as a whole. The question of profits taxation of public enterprises, therefore, may be viewed mainly as one of tax structure rather than tax levels.[12]

EQUITY

Tax equity is inherently a matter of interpersonal comparisons, not of interenterprise or intercorporate comparisons, and thus is affected only when real income distribution in the private sector is affected by differential income taxation of trading enterprises. Private-sector income distribution is likely to be affected directly only when there is at least partial private ownership of the enterprise. For enterprises that are fully owned by the government, it makes little sense to speak of equity unless it is assumed that the tax is shifted, since the tax burden would otherwise fall solely on the enterprise's profits, and hence on the government, with priavte-sector incomes remaining unaffected.[13] If the tax is shifted it would indirectly affect private incomes, but the question of whether the profits tax is or is not shifted has produced a controversy with few conclusions. Furthermore, even assuming that shifting occurs, a thorough analysis of vertical and horizontal equity would require a knowledge or presumption of the relative income position of various income recipients, as well as of the consumption patterns of all income groups, that is beyond the scope of this chapter. Consequently, this analysis is restricted to a general statement of when equity may be affected, rather than a determination of actual effects.

In the short run, forward shifting into product prices would be borne by relatively heavy consumers of the traded commodities, and the tax would be proportional, progressive, or regressive depending on the relative values of the income and price elasticities of demand for the output. Forward shifting seems most likely when unutilized monopoly power is available to the trading enterprise.[14] Short-run backward shifting to recipients of non-capital factor payments seems more likely when an industry is monopolized by the trading enterprise, which as a consequence would be less likely to be a price-taker in factor markets. When the trading enterprise faces competition in the industry, shifting of the tax by either the public or private enterprise may lead to shifting by the other and consequently to a substantially different pattern of real income distribution than would probably have emerged if the tax had not been applied to public enterprises.

In the longer run, shifting through interindustry or interenterprise factor movements may occur if the tax does not apply uniformly to all profits and if there is capital mobility between taxed and untaxed industries. In this case, capital in the untaxed sector may be forced to share the burden of the tax as capital shifts from the taxed to the untaxed sector, thus lowering the net rate of return in the latter.

RESOURCE ALLOCATION

Perhaps the strongest case for taxing the profits of trading enterprises in the same manner as other public and private enterprises is based on the implications for efficient resource allocation. Any public use of resources involves an opportunity cost in terms of foregone resources for alternative private and public uses. Although the evaluation of opportunity costs may be somewhat arbitrary when resources are used to provide traditional public goods, it should be more precise, and consequently even more useful, when resources are employed by the public sector to provide goods and services, such as most traded goods, that could be provided efficiently by the private sector.

Differences in taxation between trading and other enterprises that result in differences between opportunity cost pricing of inputs and outputs may distort decisions on resource usage unless they are taken into account. For example, the exclusion of a trading enterprise from a profits tax may lead to a relative overstatement of its profits; conversely, it may lead to an understatement of the opportunity cost of capital employed by trading enterprises relative to capital employed by other enterprises, and, consequently, to an over-allocation of capital resources to the trading enterprises and perhaps to overly capital-intensive production or excessive employment of working capital. Furthermore, if a trading monopoly is not desired by the government, the use of a profits-tax exclusion by public enterprises to keep output prices at an artificially low level could constitute a permanent barrier to entry of private firms that are subject to tax.

The efficiency arguments for equal taxation retain validity even if there is no direct competition in commodity markets between the trading and other enterprises since there is always competition for resource inputs and factors of production.[15]

NON-MARKET CONSTRAINTS

Special characteristics associated with government ownership of trading enterprises may undermine the efficiency case for equal taxation or affect the ability to achieve traditional goals by taxation, and, consequently, suggest that public and private enterprises should be taxed differently.

Non-market constraints on managerial behaviour resulting from other government policies are among the more important of these special characteristics. There is probably an almost endless variety of such constraints imposed in attempts to achieve various objectives, but the more important are likely to be government-imposed decisions on investment, prices, wages, employment, and perhaps output levels. Some constraints may be explicitly articulated while others may be implicit or informal. In many cases, they may reflect nothing more formal than a conversation between the enterprise's managing director and a cabinet minister.[16] From a practical point of view, the existence and extent of non-market constraints is likely to be directly related to the relative political power of individual enterprise managers and government ministers and perhaps even the stability of the government.[17]

The nature and existence of non-market constraints may be difficult to ascertain, but their economic significance is clear. They may be expected to close ordinarily available avenues of adjustment and to impede the ability of managers of enterprises to respond to market signals or taxes in making their input and output decisions. Input and output prices may not reflect opportunity costs, with the results that an inefficient use of resources may result.

Non-market constraints are likely to be particularly important to trading enterprises. For example, when the objective of the enterprise is to generate government revenue or to stabilize certain domestic prices and incomes, the primary means of achieving the objective is likely to be a non-market contraint on traded commodities' prices. In such cases the impact of a profits tax may be inconsequential.

ACCOUNTING PROCEDURES

Especially when there are non-market constraints or other external influences, it is important for trading enterprises to maintain economically meaningful accounts. Failure to account for such constraints could lead to a misallocation of resources or at least to a lack of sufficient information to evaluate the cost of the constraint. In this connection, the application to trading enterprises of any profits tax may serve another useful function. Tax laws often specify the method of accounting to be used for the determination of taxable profits. To the extent that the law forces enterprises to take into account deviations from opportunity costing and pricing, such as through proper allowances for depreciation, then the tendency to misallocate resources may be reduced. However, even though uniform accounting practices are generally desirable, one should not expect too much. When externalities are involved, accounting profits may bear little resemblance to social return, and the appropriate income-tax base for trading and other public enterprises is not obvious.

INCENTIVES TO EFFICIENCY

The uniform application of a profits tax to trading enterprises has the advantage, especially when contrasted with the potential use of dividends, of providing both managers of enterprises and the government with a greater degree of certainty as to the distribution of profits. The certainty of control over a portion of profits is likely to provide an incentive to managers of enterprises to improve the efficiency of their operations and, at the same time, to provide them with increased flexibility in their investment planning and operations. Furthermore, except for enterprises with non-market constraints on prices, a profits tax ensures that relatively more funds for investment will be available automatically to firms or industries than the market may signal, through relatively higher profits, as desirable areas for investment.[18]

The certainty provided by a tax can also be advantageous to the government. The tax automatically provides the government with funds for general purposes as well as for investment in areas of high public priority where market forces alone would not necessarily indicate the need for investment. The tax also provides a strong built-in stabilizer whose effects would not necessarily be duplicated by an arbitrary dividend. Furthermore, the imposition of a profits tax does not preclude the use of dividends to transfer additional funds to the government when desirable; for example, profits of enterprises exploiting scarce natural resources or profits of enterprises in sectors with low investment priorities.

(4) ANALYSIS OF ECONOMIC EFFECTS

In determining the expected effects of taxing trading enterprises' profits, the market structure in which they operate should be taken into account. The market structure also suggests the appropriate analytical technique. For example, a monopolized industry might be studied with partial equilibrium techniques, but a firm operating in competitive markets should be studied in a general equilibrium context.

MONOPOLIZED INDUSTRY

If the trading enterprise has a monopoly in its commodity market, and if there are neither monopoly nor monopsony elements in the markets for factors of production other than capital, the short-run effects of a profits tax are obvious.[19] Since the imposition of the tax would not affect the maximum profit solution for the industry, the tax would fall in the short-run on monopoly profits and the normal returns to equity capital.[20] Price and output decisions would not be affected, and the tax itself would have no direct effect on the equity of private income distributions or the efficiency of resource allocation. The sole effect of the tax would be to transfer automatically to the government a certain portion of the monopoly profits and the normal return to equity.

However, any trading enterprise that prices to maximize monopoly profits is probably a quasi-taxing authority for which a profits tax would be unnecessary.

These observations would be altered, of course, if imposition of a profits tax induced monopolistic behaviour in an enterprise that had not previously been characterized by such behaviour. If the trading enterprise were to adopt monopolistic pricing in order to restore its net profits to a pretax level, then the tax might in the short run be shifted forward to consumers or backward to non-capital factors, thus altering the distribution of private real income and probably leading to an underallocation of resources.[21] To the extent that the tax induced monopolistic behaviour where none had been practised, it would also probably result in a longer-run misallocation of resources and in increased barriers to entry.

Monopolistic pricing behaviour could be either mitigated or enhanced if prices or wages are determined by the government, either arbitrarily or under various rules. So long as the tax does not affect the arbitrarily imposed price, it will have neither equity nor efficiency effects, although the pricing decision has both effects. However, if wages or payments to other factors of production are not constrained by market conditions, backward shifting could occur through changes in the administered price. Furthermore, if the commodity price is administered and is set by a fixed markup over cost including the tax or is set to achieve a fixed net rate of return, then the price would increase with the imposition of the tax, and some of the tax burden would be shifted to consumers.

Thus, the imposition of a profits tax on a trading monopoly is not likely, in itself, to lead either to a deterioration or improvement in resource allocation, and it would have no direct effect on income distribution in the private sector, if the imposition of the tax were to induce monopolistic behaviour or changes in administered prices. Even though traditional considerations of efficiency and equity offer no direct implications for whether or not to tax, there are certainly no grounds for exempting a monopolistic trading enterprise that is not essentially a quasi-taxing authority from a general profits tax. Furthermore, owing to its automatic and compulsory nature, the tax could circumvent any tendency by some enterprises to retain their profits and thereby to enhance their ability to pursue objectives that might be inconsistent with those of the government. In summary, it might be said that neither the arguments for nor the arguments against taxing the profits of monopoly trading enterprises are strong.

OLIGOPOLISTIC INDUSTRY

Behaviour in an oligopolistic industry can be quite varied, and the effects of profits taxation in general will turn on the assumptions one makes about the interdependent behaviour of the firms in the industry. Furthermore, in the case of trading enterprises in oligopolistic markets the effects of a profits tax cannot be ascertained without additional knowledge of the price and output policies of these firms, the non-market constraints imposed on them, and the ways in which these would be altered by the tax. It is obvious that in an oligopolistic market the trading enterprise could not function as a quasi-taxing authority, and it is therefore assumed that any revenue raising objective would be secondary to some other primary objective.

One variant of oligopolistic behaviour, joint maximization of the profits, is intuitively unappealing when at least one of the firms in the industry is a state-trading enterprise. Indeed, a prime motivation for establishing a trading enterprise might be to introduce competition into oligopolistic industries by facilitating the flow of competing imports subject to certain constraints, such as availabilty of foreign exchange or the need for domestic employment. It is possible for the trading enterprise to take such a leading role in the industry by promoting higher output and lower prices than would obtain if the private firms jointly maximized profits and at the same time retain some domestic production and employment.[22]

So long as the trading enterprise follows objectives other than profit maximization, the application of the tax to its profits is not likely to affect its behaviour or its impact on the allocation of resources.[23] However, if profits are an objective of the trading enterprise, the decision to tax may well affect equity. Such a possibility is illustrated in Figure 9.1. Suppose the trading firm does not collude with private firms, imports a limited amount of the commodity in which it trades, and accepts a price that yields only a normal return to equity capital. Before the trading enterprise enters the market, a few constant-cost private firms face supply curve *AS* and demand curve *dd*. Through collusion the private firms maximize profits by selling an amount equal to *OE* at the price equal to *OC*. So long as the world price of imports exceeds the domestic cost of production *OA* and is less than the monopoly selling price *OC*, it would be to the advantage of the private oligopolists to collude in order to prevent imports from entering the market. However, if a state-owned trading enterprise enters the market by importing an amount equal to *DF* and selling it at a price

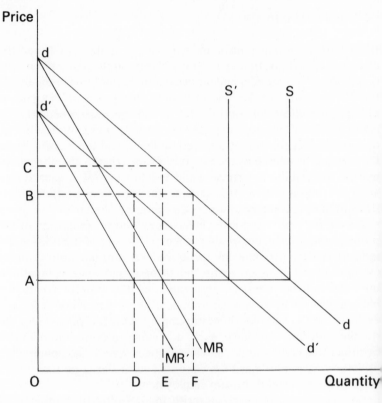

FIGURE 9.1
State trading and profit taxation

equal to *OA*, the private firms will face a residual demand curve *d'd'*, and will sell an amount equal to *OD* at a price *OB*. The trading enterprise's imports would have forced an increase in consumption equal *EF*, a decrease of *BC* in the prices charged for private output, and a decrease of *DE* in private output, thus improving the efficiency of resource usage, even though private firms continued to collude. However, the trading enterprise could have achieved the same results *vis-à-vis* its private competitors while charging a price as *OB* and earning some monopoly profits. Thus, if the trading enterprise were subject not only to a constraint on the level of imports, but also had as an objective a targeted amount of internally generated funds for investment or revenue purposes, then imposition of the tax could induce (or increase) oligopolistic behaviour and forward shifting of the tax in the short run without any worsening of the efficiency of resource usage resulting from the import constraint. In this case, imposition of the tax on the trading enterprise could result in:

(*a*) the automatic transfer of some existing returns to equity and monopoly profits, if any, to the government, or
(*b*) forward shifting, or
(*c*) both.

However, profit-maximizing private firms could not shift the tax, and· it would fall in the short run on their monopoly profits.

In the longer run, efficiency (and perhaps income distribution) could only be improved in the industry by a reduction of barriers to the entry of additional resources. Exemption of the trading enterprise from the tax might result in higher net profits that the trading enterprise could use to finance additional imports, but this outcome could also be achieved through taxation and budgetary allocation. On the other hand, equal taxation of its profits might improve the leadership behaviour of the trading enterprise, enhance its efficiency, and reduce barriers to entry into the industry by other private competitors.

On the whole, traditional considerations of equity and efficiency appear to offer little reason for preferring a profit tax to a dividend for trading enterprises in oligopolistic markets; similarly they offer little reason to exclude such enterprises from a profits tax. The tax is not likely to have a significant long-run or short-run impact unless it results in changes in other public sector policies that would alter efficiency and income distribution. There is no obvious reason this might be expected. However, as is true for a monopoly, a reasonable case for taxing trading enterprises lies with the argument that the compulsory nature of a profits tax is more likely to ensure that any profits are automatically made available for public purposes, and that exemption could, under some circumstances, constitute a barrier to the entry of private enterprises and perhaps lead to inefficient complacency on the part of trading-enterprise managers.

COMPETITION BETWEEN STATE- AND PRIVATE-TRADING ENTERPRISES

Even when there is no direct competition for a government-owned trading enterprise, there may be strong indirect competition between near-substitutes. Furthermore, even if there is no competition in product markets, there is always competition in the markets for factors of production. In the face of competition from freely-traded goods, domestically produced non-traded goods and freely-traded inputs, a profits tax could not be shifted in the short run and would fall on the return to equity capital. However, in the longer run tax shifting of the profits tax may occur. An analysis of longer-run shifting under conditions of either direct or indirect competition between private- and public-trading enterprises in commodity markets can be conducted in the context of a Harberger-like neoclassical, competitive economy. In this framework, two factors of production, capital and labour, are fixed in total supply, but are fully employed in producing two goods, X and Y.[24]

The effects of differential taxation of competing enterprises' profits in this context depends crucially on the assumption that it made concerning the mobility of capital resources, or, more importantly, the responsiveness to the rate of return that the assumption represents. So long as the government's investment decision is based on any considerations other than those affected by tax changes, capital invested in the trading enterprises in each industry may be assumed to be fixed exogenously. Thus, if the government has no profit objective for its trading enterprise, whether or not the enterprises profits are taxed will not affect factor allocation or private-income distribution. The sole effect of the exclusion would be that the net retained earnings of public enterprises would be higher, by the amount of the tax, than they would be if the tax were applied to these earnings.

If capital invested in the government-owned trading enterprise sector is mobile and responsive to the rate of return, the results are different. However, even with mobility the exemption of the state-trading enterprise from the profits tax will affect equity and resource allocation only when there are tax-induced shifts of resources resulting from partial taxation within the private sector. For example, if the tax applied only to private corporations, private enterprises would be induced to shift resources to non-corporate uses, and the tax would be shifted as the net rate of return to all private capital would fall.[25] This would lead to a rise in the price of corporate goods relative to the price of both non-corporate and state-traded goods and to an increase in the gross return to corporate capital. If the state-trading enterprises were exempt from the tax and capital mobile, there would be a tendency to shift resources to production of corporate goods, which would offset, at least somewhat, the tax-induced shifts in the private sector and their consequent effects on equity and efficiency. Exemption of the trading enterprise could, under these circumstances, result in relatively more concentrated government participation in taxed industries than in untaxed industries.

The conclusion that only under certain circumstances would the exemption of a trading enterprise from the profits tax affect income distribution in the private sector is restricted to the Harberger 'fixed resource endowment' context. It ignores, for example, the various incentives to efficiency that may result from equal taxation. In a longer-run growth context trading enterprises' investment decisions would almost certainly be influenced by their own net rates of return if the enterprises were allowed to retain a substantial part of their profits for net investment. The exclusion of its earnings from taxation could result in higher investment expenditures than might be justified on the basis of opportunity costs. This suggests that, if the government does not retain control over trading enterprises' investment in the long run, the profits of these enterprises should be taxed in the same manner as private enterprises, simply to preclude the possibility of unproductive investment.

(5) SUMMARY AND CONCLUSIONS

The cases for and against the taxation of the profits of a state-trading enterprise seem to be less than conclusive. If the trading enterprise is a monopolistic intermediary in the trade process with the sole objective of purchasing and reselling commodities in order to raise revenue for the government there would seem to be little logic to taxing its profits. Such an enterprise is itself little more than a quasi-taxing authority. However, if the trading enterprise were privately owned and perhaps operated under some form of government licence, there is a strong presumption that the profits accruing to the private owners should be taxed in the same manner as profits from other privately owned enterprises.

For government-owned trading enterprises that are not used essentially as quasi-taxing authorities the case for taxing their profits depends on a variety of factors. The objectives of taxing public trading enterprises should be essentially the same as those for taxing private enterprise, that is, efficient resource usage, equitable distribution of the tax burden, and a stable and growing economy. However, even though the goals of taxation should not differ for trading enterprises, they may have special characteristics, such as the existence of other government policies and social objectives, that may significantly alter the effects of taxation of public enterprises. For example, while a case could be made for the tax on the grounds of allocation efficiency, various non-market constraints often applying particularly to state-trading enterprises may neutralize the ordinarily expected impact of the tax.

Simple analysis of the effects of profits taxes imposed on a trading enterprise under monopolistic conditions indicate that, so long as the enterprise maximizes profits, the tax would have no effect on resource allocation or income distribution. However, if profits have not been maximized but the trading enterprise operates with some positive profit objective, then the tax may be shifted, with various possible implications for resource allocation and income distribution. For trading enterprises facing some direct or indirect competition with private firms, the effects of taxing the trading enterprise's profits depend upon the importance of the profit motive to public enterprises. If it is not a quasi-taxing authority but still exhibits behavioural responses similar to those of competitive firms – as might be indicated, for example, by the enterprise channeling investment into areas with high rates of return – then there would be a strong suggestion that the trading enterprise should be taxed in the same manner as private enterprise in order to prevent tax-induced distortions in the allocations of resources. However, if investment, pricing, and output policies of trading enterprises were not affected by rates of return, then it would be of no importance to efficiency or equity whether or not profits were taxed.

The economic effects resulting from a tax on trading-enterprises' profits depend greatly on managerial behavioural patterns. Nevertheless, some tenuous observations may be drawn. First, the potential for short-run shifting of a tax on public-enterprises' profits and the consequent effects on the economy are greatest when market imperfections or non-market constraints have prevented the attainment of maximum profits. In this case the tax could constitute an additional distortion in the economy and may not have undesirable effects. In general, however, non-market constraints on public enterprises appear just as likely to insulate the economy from any short-run effects of taxing on trading enterprises' profits as to provide new channels for transmission of such effects. In the longer run, when resources are mobile and when the extent of state ownership of trading enterprise is sufficient to affect resource allocation, application of a profits tax will have no effect on the economy if investment in trading enterprises is unresponsive to rates of return, but exemption from the tax may distort resource allocation and alter private-income distribution if investment is responsive to rates of return.

In general, the greater are non-market constraints on trading enterprises, the more limited will be the effects of the tax. But the less important are market incentives, the greater will be the effects on the economy of exempting trading enterprises from the tax. Consequently, while imposition of the profits tax under many circumstances might have neither bad nor good implications, the exemption of trading enterprises from this tax could have either no effects or only bad effects. The stronger case, therefore, rests with taxing state-owned trading enterprises that are not operated as quasi-taxing authorities in the same manner as private enterprises are taxed.

NOTES AND REFERENCES

1. The Contracting Parties to the General Agreement on Tariffs and Trade, *The General Agreement on Tariffs and Trade*, Vol. III: Basic Instruments and Selected Documents (Geneva: The Contracting Parties to the General Agreement on Tariffs and Trade, 1958), Article XVII, para. 1.
2. A more rigid definition of public enterprises seems both elusive and undesirable in view of the variety of legal and organizational forms encountered in various countries. However, to distinguish them more clearly from bodies providing governmental and quasi-governmental administrative services, such as school districts and charitable organizations, it is useful to require that the the the revenues of public enterprises should be more or less related to their output and that at least some day-to-day operational autonomy should be in the hands of the managers of the enterprise rather than the ministerial authoities. Such a definition obviously leaves possible borderline cases that would have to be classified by individual characteristics.
3. For a similar definition see P. J. Lloyd, Chapter 6 in this volume.
4. For a discussion of possible political objectives of state-trading enterprises see chapters 1 and 5 in this volume.
5. For a similar categorization of fiscal monopolies, see Sijbren Crossen, *Excise Systems: A Global Study of the Selective Taxation of Goods and Services* (Baltimore: Johns Hopkins University Press, 1977), pp. 84–98.
6. See Roy Beban, 'State Trading and the GATT', *Journal of World Trade Law*, vol. 11, no. 4 (July/August 1977), p. 336.
7. Roy Beban, ibid, p. 3.
8. For a more detailed discussion see P. J. Lloyd Chapter 6 in this volume.
9. Ubadigbo Okonkwo, 'Export Taxes on Primary Products in Developing Countries: The Taxation of Cocoa Exports in West Africa', IMF (unpublished), November 29, 1978.
10. Unless otherwise noted, in the remainder of the paper it is assumed that trading enterprises are owned by the government since it is assumed that privately-owned trading enterprises would be fully liable to income taxation.

11. This assumption is not necessarily inconsistent with other behavioural assumptions that could be made about trading-enterprises' managers, such as output maximization or the generation of a targeted amount of internal funds. For example, output maximization could qualitatively affect profits in the same way as a government requirement to operate at plant capacity. A targeted level of internal funds may have a similar effect on profits to government-imposed prices or output levels. Of course, an assumption of optimal behaviour of any sort by managers of trading enterprises suggests that the important, but separate problem of incentives to managerial behaviour is only considered insofar as it may be affected by taxation. Also, although the analysis is largely restricted to the likely response of trading enterprises, the possibility of interreactions in the response of publicly- and privately-owned competitors is also considered when appropriate.

12. This ignores both the built-in stabilizer aspect of a profits tax and the possible implications for investment and growth.

13. If the purpose of the trading enterprise were to stabilize countercyclically the prices of incomes received by producers, then the imposition of a tax on its profits would reduce the ability of the enterprise to accomplish its purpose and producer incomes would thereby be directly affected.

14. Even in the absence of monopoly power, it is not uncommon in developing countries for government-owned enterprises to charge different (often lower) prices for outputs or pay different (often higher) wages to non-capital factors than their privately-owned competitors, often because of government-imposed constraints. This, of course, necessitates the use of some type of rationing mechanism. For example, rationing may take the form of long lines and empty shelves in government shops.

15. It appears that Albert H. Hanson oversimplified when he concluded that taxation of public enterprise is necessary for 'an equal footing' only when it is in direct competition with private enterprise. See Albert H. Hanson, *Organization and Administration or Public Enterprises* (New York: United Nations, Economic and Social Council, 1968), p. 110.

16. For a more detailed discussion, see Albert H. Hanson, ibid, pp. 28–51.

17. Shepherd depicts the relationship between the government and a public enterprise as a bilateral monopoly in which each side possesses certain advantages that enhance its ability to control the enterprise. See William G. Shepherd, 'Objectives, Types, and Accountability', in William G. Shepherd (ed.) *Public Enterprise: Economic Analysis of Theory and Practice*, (Lexington: D. C. Heath and Company, 1976), pp. 44–5.

18. This ignores the case of a firm or industry earning economic rents in which additional investment may not be desirable. Furthermore, in the case of monopoly, there may be need for more variable, but not more fixed, inputs.

19. It is assumed that the monopolist attempts to maximize profits even when subject to externally-imposed constraints.

20. Quasi-rents accruing in the short run to factors temporarily in limited supply, such as capital or specialized managerial talents, may in the longer run be forced to absorb some part of the tax.

21. In this case the results are quite similar to the analysis of oligopolistic market structures.

22. See the discussion of the purposes of Italian public enterprises in

Giuseppino Treves, 'Public and Private Enterprise in Italy', in Wolfgang G. Friedmann (ed.), *Public and Private Enterprise in Mixed Economies*, (New York: Columbia University Press, 1974), pp. 47–50. See also John B. Sheahan, 'Public Enterprise in Developing Countries,' in William G. Shepherd (ed.), op. cit., chapter 9, p. 212. Pricing guidelines to Indian public enterprises in semimonopolistic or oligopolistic industries also indicate the government's intention that these firms should operate as industry leaders.

23. The price, wage, output, and investment decisions of the public enterprise obviously have important implications for both the allocation of resources and the equity of private-income distribution. However, in this situation they should be regarded as independent of the profits tax.

24. The following discussion is intuitively obvious, but it can be substantiated, by modifying the standard Harberger model to include public ownership of some capital and some public production of at least one good. The basic model on which this discussion is founded can be found in Arnold C. Harberger, 'The Incidence of the Corporation Income Tax', *Journal of Political Economy*, vol. 70, no. 3 (June 1962), pp. 215–40. Since factors of production are both mobile and fixed in supply, the context of the Harberger model is neither strictly short run nor long but rather somewhere in between. Thus, while it can depict the effects of taxes on factor allocation, the model can be used only to infer their long-run effects on such variables as the growth rates of capital and labour.

25. This is essentially the original Harberger result.

10 Co-operation Among State-Trading Organizations of Developing Countries

Klaus Netter [1,2]

In the literature on economic integration, and also in general international trade theory, the subject of state trading has been treated as an aberration from the rules of the game, rather than one of its integral parts. This orientation is particularly misplaced in dealing with economic integration among developing countries, in which state trading usually plays an important – and often a dominant – role in the country's overall international trade.[3]

The trade-policy instruments which have been chosen to promote economic integration among developing countries, primarily preferential tariffs, have relied almost exclusively on manipulations of the market mechanism. Consequently, state trading was seen as a special case, requiring administrative rules designed to produce non-discriminatory patterns of operational behaviour *vis-à-vis* partner countries in integration groupings.[4] State-trading organizations (STOs), moreover, were enjoined to include preferential customs rates into their cost calculations, so as not to nullify the incentives which their own governments had devised to stimulate trade with integration partners.[5]

It is the purpose of this paper to move one step further in the direction of treating state trading as an institution which is not only capable of reacting to market-type policy instruments designed to promote trade with particular countries, but is also a potentially active agent in the implementation of a much broader range of trade policies that two or more developing countries might wish to pursue in common. Although the foremost consideration of ensuing policies would be the promotion of mutual trade, they could well comprise a pooling of resources among the developing countries which would serve:

(*a*) to increase their bargaining power so as to secure better terms of trade *vis-à-vis* their common trading partners, including transnational corporations operating within their own countries;

(*b*) to diversify their import sources of supply and their exports towards new markets;

(*c*) to effect an extension of the transformation process of raw materials, so as to achieve a larger value-added content in the exported product; and

(*d*) to improve their efficiency, resulting in higher returns (or lower costs) for their economies at large, and larger revenues (or lower subsidy payments) for their respective treasuries, to the extent that the latter hold equity in the STOs concerned.

Apart from these intrinsic benefits that might be derived from closer mutual co-operation, STOs are especially suited to elicit closer economic and technical cooperation among developing countries (ECDC and TCDC); a desire often expressed by their respective governments. The evolution of this kind of co-operation is an idea that has become increasingly important in these countries' concept of factors that should constitute the 'New International Economic Order'.

In contrast to most other proposals, which have been advanced to breathe life into the concepts of ECDC and TCDC, co-operation among developing countries' STOs does not necessarily require the creation of new national or multi-national institutions – a slow and uncertain process absorbing scarce human and financial resources – nor does it pre-suppose cumbersome intergovernmental negotiations, whose cost could surpass the actual accrued benefits, in terms of new trade flows generated by them. In view of the existence of STOs and analogous institutions in many developing countries (particularly in Asia and Africa), and given the importance of government procurement and international trading activities of major state-owned production enterprises (particularly in Latin America), policies designed to intensify mutual trade and to bring about selected measures of co-operation can be instituted by administrative sanction. These policies would be within the limits of (a) effective governmental prerogatives in the conduct of the STOs' operations,[6] and (b) the cost-benefit ratio, calculated for the economy as a whole (as distinct from such a calculation limited to the executing STO itself).

A further contrast between trade expansion measures instituted among STOs and negotiated preferential trade policies affecting the private sector, lies in the direct and active impact of the former as opposed to the indirect and permissive role of the latter. State trading expands the role of the state from that of a policy-formulating body to that of an executor of such policies in foreign- or domestic-trading activities.[7] In trade conducted by the private sector, the state can do little more than stimulate and facilitate a re-orientation of trade flows, since the success of such measures depends ultimately on decisions made by private traders. These decisions are necessarily affected by business links with traditional suppliers in the developed countries (e.g., profitable exclusive franchises bolstered by consumers' brand preferences built up over long years of costly advertising), and may well be at variance with governments' desire for geographical diversification and minimization of foreign-exchange costs of imports.

For purposes of this paper, the term 'state-trading organization' (STO) is to be understood as any firm or agency engaged in international trade, in which the government directly influences the internal decision-making process in a manner different from the external controls and regulations that affect all other firms trading in similar goods. Under this definition, a wholly state-owned trading firm which operates exclusively according to commercial criteria would not be covered, while a privately-owned trading firm whose commercial decisions are subject to governmental control or guidance, for whatever reason (e.g., exclusive trading privileges with certain countries), is covered.[8] Similarly, it matters little whether international trade constitutes the primary area of operation of the firm or whether such trade is ancillary to the firm's production or domestic distribution or procurement activities. This choice of a functional, rather than the conventional legal approach, is closely related to the purpose of this paper, as mentioned above. This approach seeks to identify joint actions that might be undertaken by the governments of two or more developing countries attempting to implement general development policies and particular trade policies through the use of trading enterprises subject to their influence.

No attempt will be made here to discuss the factors obstructing trade among developing countries in general, such as the similarity of exportable goods, insufficient transportation and communication links, historical business and consumer orientation towards the former metropoles, tied aid, privileged monetary links with a reserve currency, and excessive protection of domestic industries, since these have been repeatedly discussed in the literature.[9] At this point, only those problems which are peculiar or particularly relevant to the pattern of operations of STOs will be analysed.

Outright protectionism – both overt and covert – against imports from all sources, is a widespread policy underlying the operations of many STOs. Its existence is difficult to prove and its quantitative impact is virtually impossible to measure, the more so if the company enjoys monopoly rights.[10] While the characteristics of state trading may render the offending country immune to retaliation, a real or perceived protectionistic attitude by any STO is likely to deter potential counterpart institutions in other developing countries from serious trade expansion initiatives. To the extent that protectionist policies are adopted by STOs, their *prima facie* effects may appear to be non-discriminatory between foreign suppliers. In fact, the full burden of these effects is likely to be borne unequally by the potential suppliers from other developing countries, since the qualities and models of any item offered by another developing country are likely to compete most directly with the domestically-produced good whose protection is sought. By way of illustration, if a STO enjoying a monopoly on tobacco imports is instructed to protect the nascent cigarette industry geared to the mass low-income market, the STO is likely to continue importing the far more expensive internationally-known cigarette brands from the developed countries, catering to an entirely different clientale.

STOs are frequently considered to be the most efficient instrument for rationing foreign exchange in situations where severe exchange shortages have created pressures for maximizing imports involving no exchange outlays in the short run. This may lead to an unintended bias in favour of procurement from traditional suppliers in developed countries, because the latter can offer subsidized export credits for capital goods and turn-key projects. Those credits often become the determining factor favouring the choice of capital-intensive equipment appropriate for high labour-cost economies. This type of equipment is preferred over that which is offered by other developing countries incorporating a less sophisticated technology, even though theirs is likely to be more economical in terms of foreign-exchange outlays in the long run.

Certain factors impeding closer co-operation among developing countries' STOs are rooted in the very origins of these institutions. Only rarely were STOs created for the explicit purpose of stimulating trade with other developing countries.[11] More often, the *raison d'être* of these enterprises is either neutral or sometimes even hostile towards the prospect of trade with other developing countries. Thus, countries that generally rely on the private sector to conduct their foreign trade have established or appointed STOs to act as sole counterparts for the centralized trading agencies of the socialist countries of eastern Europe and Asia. They have not, however, created or designated other institutions to perform similar roles in promoting trade with other developing countries. Illustrations of this phenomenon are the Philippines International Trading Company, Pernas National Trading Corporation Ltd. (Malaysia), SORESMA (Morocco) during the initial phase of its operations, and the National Trading Company Ltd. (Nepal).

In a broader sense, these institutional shortcomings attest to a lack of coherence between broadly-stated economic policy objectives, among which obeisance to ECDC is *de rigueur*, on the one hand, and specific trade-policy decisions, which ignore these precepts, on the other.[12]

State trading is often linked to monopoly privileges, particularly in socialist countries wedded to the concept of central planning. These STOs typically rely on open or (for major equipment orders) limited tenders, or instruct their overseas offices (mostly located in developed countries) to bid on the major international commodity exchanges for the procurement of basic foodstuff and raw material requirements. In both cases, such procurement procedures imply a bias against direct links with developing-country suppliers, for it is only the rare developing-country STO which is directly represented in another developing country in a manner equivalent to that of the trans-national corporations (TNCs). Rarely, too, is their diplomatic representation equipped to transmit timely and complete information on outstanding tenders and their specifications. Similarly, only the largest among developing-country STOs are directly represented on the international commodity exchanges.

Whereas the monopoly position of STOs is designed, in part, to secure concentration of buying power (often through long-term contracts), and consequently better terms of trade on the part of the importer, this position – unless mitigated by specific countervailing policies – will create a bias towards establishing trade with large-scale trading partners who are able to make long-term supply commitments, requirements which TNCs are ideally suited to fulfill.

All too often, STOs are denied the power to make important business decisions without first referring to a responsible Ministry, or worse yet, to an inter-Ministerial committee. Even in cases where the STO enjoys sufficient formal autonomy, there is a tendency to shift the decision-making burden upwards,[13] relieving the STO from the responsibility for possible errors of judgment. This spreading and shifting of the decision-making process is designed, in part, to prevent abuses of power and outright corruption on the part of STO managerial personnel. Experience has shown, however, that integrity in the conduct of STO operations cannot be ensured by such measures, but depends ultimately on the choice and appropriate remuneration of qualified managerial staff. Nevertheless, what this type of decision-making does ensure is a lengthening of the reaction time, which is frequently a crucial element in securing a sales contract or obtaining optimum conditions in a major purchase. Faced with inordinate delays which are intensified by communication difficulties, it is not surprising that STOs prefer to retain their tested business links with the TNCs.

Perhaps the single most important obstacle, serving to compound all the others, is the dearth of the most elementary information available to developing countries' STOs about the locations, activities, supply capabilities, importing requirements, personnel and organizational structures, of other STOs, even if located in the same geographical region.[14] This information gap forms part of a vicious circle, leading to sporadic business contacts (if any develop at all), insufficient incentive for the punctilious performance of contract specifications and delivery dates, lack of mutual confidence and lack of interest to seek mutual information.

The brief elaboration of the numerous and weighty obstacles preventing or retarding mutual contacts must be set against the numerous and real potential advantages that STOs (and through them, their respective economies) can expect to derive from an expansion of mutual trade and other forms of co-operation.

By virtue of their size and financial resources, STOs are better placed than domestically-based private traders to assume the risks and the costs of opening up new trade channels and distribution systems. They are also better able to mobilize the productive resources required to fulfill major contracts and to extend credit terms that are competitive with the subsidized export credits available in developed countries.

The fact that most STOs enjoy the explicit or implicit financial guarantee of their respective governments removes the purely commercial risks attaching to private-trade partners in little-known countries.

Some of the major commodity trade flows among developing countries are largely dominated by powerful international trading concerns, e.g., in the fields of petroleum, cereals, edible oilseeds and oils, sugar, cocoa, tea, copper and bananas, because they control all or part of the production, processing, transportation and distribution cycle. To the extent that developing countries wish to acquire the knowhow and control over the trade of their staple exports, only the concentrated power of STOs operating at both ends of the trade channel can provide the countervailing force required to unseat vested interest. The direct contracts signed by nationalized petroleum companies in exporting and importing countries (e.g., Iran-India, Iraq-Brazil, Libya-Argentina, Algeria-Brazil) offer illustrations of practical achievements in a sector particularly tightly controlled by the TNCs.

World trade trends during the 1960s and early 1970s were marked by a greater dynamism in the developed market economies' trade, but this dynamism was not so prevalent in the trade of developing countries.[15] The radically changed constellation in the world economy since 1973 has made the developing countries, as a group, the most dynamic markets, making mutual trade expansion among developing countries in general, and among their STOs in particular, not only a political slogan to which lip service is due, but a commercially rational option. Although these recent trends may again be reversed, developing countries have a long-term interest in diversifying their markets and sources of supply, namely, to spread the inherent economic risks of demand fluctuations in their principal markets and the political risks of excessive dependence on a limited number of suppliers of strategic commodities.

For several strategic commodities such as grains, vegetables oils, sugar and fertilizers, developing countries' STOs are the single-channel buyers in their respective countries. As such, the efficiency and the timing of their procurement decisions weigh heavily on their countries' balance of payments.[16] In addition, some developing countries hold prominent positions in the world markets for certain commodities.[17] As such, STOs can bid up world market prices by unco-ordinated decisions, a process which works to their mutual detriment. Conversely, through advance co-ordination of import requirements, co-operating STOs can time their purchases so as to take maximum advantage of seasonal price fluctuations.

The sharing of market intelligence would be an important ingredient serving to strengthen the STOs' negotiating positions and could well be the first step towards operational import co-operation in the form of pooled orders,[18] where concentrated market power can make itself felt. Ultimately, a joint procurement agency with representation on the leading commodity exchanges can be envisaged.

The savings to be achieved through freight pooling and common packing are significant. It has been estimated that the shipping costs incurred by India, Pakistan, Bangladesh and Indonesia for the importation of their cereals and edible oil requirements amount to $200 million.[19] This outlay provides a wide scope for more advantageous jointly-negotiated charter terms, accompanied by bulk shipping and commonly-operated facilities located at a mutually convenient transit point for breaking down and re-packing bulk orders. These facilities could also serve as warehousing centres, permitting participating STOs to make optimal spot purchases without singly having to bear year-round rents of the peak-period warehousing capacity. Joint warehousing facilities can also produce economies through the stocking of commonly-required high unit-value spare parts for major capital equipment, such as turbines and civil engineering equipment.

The utilization of the potential for mutual trade expansion requires deliberate national policy decisions at the government level, with appropriate implementation measures at the STO level. Such action is the *sine qua non* condition for any meaningful inter-governmental initiative, whether bilateral or multilateral. Beyond general expressions of intent, governments of centrally planned developing countries might set realistic medium- and long-term goals for individual STOs' trade with other developing countries, in a manner akin to the overall targets set for that trade. In countries where STOs operate more in accordance with market principles, rules governing access to government credit and equity capital, as well as top management remuneration schedules, could be amended to stimulate trade with other developing countries.

The constraints on a rapid decision-making process could be lessened (a) by co-opting governmental representation to the full-time managerial staff of STOs and to their boards of directors,[20] and (b) in countries practising foreign-exchange control, by removing the requirement for approvals of individual import transaction in favour of blanket foreign-exchange allocations given to each STO for a given period, with possible sub-allocations for major product categories.

Since trade with other developing countries poses special problems,

STOs need to create specialized departments, or to appoint particular officials in each commodity department charged with promoting such trade, who should be equipped to overcome the peculiar problems which might ensue. In order to be effective, these departments or officials must either be represented in the top decision-making body or must have ready access to the general manager.

A number of intergovernmental initiatives have been proposed[20] in support of national actions. They can be broadly grouped into three categories:

(a) regular regional and inter-regional meetings;
(b) information centres; and
(c) training courses.

Regional and inter-regional meetings of developing countries' STOs who specialize in similar lines can bring about structured organizations parallel to those long in existence among private traders (regional and international chambers of commerce). These would provide the framework for contacts, which could lead, in turn, to the signing of contracts, to the discussion of mutual problems and to the launching of certain joint import or export endeavours.

The information gap, which obstructs mutual trade and weakens the efficiency of STO procurement and marketing efforts in the developed countries, could be overcome by the creation of information offices located in major trading centres, staffed by specialists for each major commodity group of export and import of interest to participating STOs. These offices should be able to provide the same services as those provided by the major international trading companies to their branch offices throughout the world. While existing overseas subsidiaries of major developing country STOs could assume such functions for other STOs, with respect to major imports of joint interest, such an arrangement would, at best, be feasible for a small group of STOs which have already established mutual bonds of trust. On the other hand, only a neutral body could be expected to serve potential competitors without provoking fears of deliberate omissions or misinformation in the area of export co-operation.

The avowed lack of expertise in management and trading techniques on the part of STO officials calls for intensive efforts at the international level to fill this shortcoming. While the required training could be given at the national level, both the difficulty of finding highly specialized lecturers, and the advantages of establishing contacts among participants work in favour of organizing training programmes at the regional level. In the achievement of this objective, the developed countries' private sector is in a position to make a contribution towards a better-functioning world trading system, for it is in their own enlightened self-interest to deal with counterparts who are thoroughly familiar with the wide spectrum of international trading practices.

Beyond any support that the international trading houses might be able to render, this is an area in which the concept of technical co-operation among developing countries can find full expression, because the STOs of certain major developing countries have built up world-wide trading networks, permitting them to negotiate with the international trading houses on a level of equality. These STOs are well placed to share their experience with others facing problems similar to those which the former have overcome. But, by virtue of differences of economic size, solutions that are feasible on a national scale for countries such as India and Brazil, may only be relevant to others if implemented on a joint basis. Herein lies one of the main justifications for the concept of co-operation among STOs of developing countries.

NOTES AND REFERENCES

1. Although the author of this article is a staff member of the UNCTAD secretariat, this article was written in his personal capacity and the views expressed therein should not be construed as representing those of the institution to which he is affiliated.
2. In the preparation of this article the author has drawn heavily on the following regional studies undertaken on behalf of UNCTAD by consultants who gathered information on the spot in thirty-one developing countries. J. B. Esteves and F. Sanchez, *Co-operation between State trading organizations in Latin America* (TD/B/C.7/16); B. R. Bhandari, *Co-operation among State Trading Organizations in Asian Developing Countries* (TD/B/C.7/17); S. B. Rutega, *Co-operation among State-trading organizations in developing countries in English-speaking Africa* (TD/B/C.7/18/Add. 1); I. Sy *Co-operation among State-trading Organizations in French-speaking Africa South of the Sahara* (TD/B/C.7/18/Add. 2); M. K. Anous, *Co-operation among State trading organizations of Arab countries* (TD/B/C.7/37). All are documents of the UNCTAD Secretariat (Geneva, 1979).
3. M. M. Kostecki, 'State-trading in Industrialized and Developing Countries', *Journal of World Trade Law*, vol. 12, no. 3 (May–June 1978), p. 201.
4. East African Community, *Rules for the Operation of State-Trading Confinements* (unpublished internal document, 1972).

5. Dharam Ghai, *State Trading and Regional Economic Integration among Developing Countries* (New York: United Nations, 1973) TD/B/436, Sales no. E.73.II.D.17, Part I, para. 49; Part II, paras. 71 and 84(c).

6. See p.217 below.

7. B. R. Bhandari, op. cit., para 29.

8. Article XVII of GATT also recognizes privileges and immunities granted to a private enterprise by governmental fiat as manifestations of state trading, but excludes government procurement for its own needs, a gap filled in the agreements resulting from the Tokyo Round.

9. UNCTAD, *Trade Expansion and Economic Integration Among Developing Countries* (TD/B/85/Rev. 1) 1967, and the series of papers entitled *Current Problems of Economic Integration*.

10. See Ghai, op. cit., para. 24.

11. Among exception that 'prove' this rule, the following may be cited: (a) Intra-Africa Trade (Uganda) Ltd., was established to promote inter-African trade; (b) The Arab Foreign Trade Company (Egypt) exercised leadership in trade with other Arab countries between 1967 and 1975, while three other 'public-trading companies' were given similar monopolies for African, Asian and Latin American countries.

12. Although African economic integration is one of the declared policies of the United Republic of Tanzania, as set out in the Arusha Declaration of 1967, the practical effect of that country's trade agreement with China was to weaken its trade links with its partners in the now-defunct East African Community (See Ghai, op. cit., Part II, para. 71).

13. See Bhandari, op. cit., paras. 54–9.

14. These information problems are in addition to the more familiar ones plaguing trade among developing countries generally, such as lack of familiarity with administrative customs and payments rules and procedures.

15. The share of the developed market economies in world imports grew from 65.9 per cent in 1960 to 72.7 per cent in 1973, but had fallen to 68.0 per cent in 1978. This decline cannot be explained exclusively by the enormous growth of the imports into the petroleum-exporting countries, for the other developing countries also raised their share from 12.9 per cent in 1973 to 14.1 per cent in 1978.

16. For example, cereal imports comprised 11 per cent of Egypt's total imports in 1978, 22 per cent of Bangladesh's and 33 per cent of Sri Lanka's in 1977.

17. Between them, the three countries of the Indian subcontinent import about 1.5 million tons of vegetable oils and seeds, accounting for about 10 per cent of world trade in this group of items.

18. See UNCTAD, *Import Co-operation Among Developing Countries* (TD/B/AC.19/R.4)1975.

19. Bhandari, op. cit., para. 133(h).

20. This procedure is currently being successfully followed in Morocco.

21. See documents cited in note 1.

11 Export Performance of the Marketing Boards in LDC's – the Case of Cocoa and Coffee in West Africa

Jean-Emile Denis [1]

Marketing boards have long attracted the interest of researchers. Although much has been published on the subject, the research has focussed on a few specific themes:[2]

The description and classification of marketing boards according to their functions,[3] and extensive evaluation of marketing boards' contribution to the economic advancement of developing countries. The research has attempted to answer such questions as: Do marketing boards effectively improve or stimulate production? Do they stabilize or increase farm revenue and help to meet the needs of local consumers?

Many developing countries depend strongly on a few commodities and, most often, these products are sold on foreign markets through more or less explicit state-trading arrangements, usually in the form of boards. Given the prevalence of these arrangements, one would expect that researchers would be more inclined to analyse them as a major aspect of international marketing, especially propounding the effectiveness of boards. Paradoxically, the main function of these boards has not been studied extensively; in fact, the performance of these boards, on foreign markets, has been treated in only a few texts.[4]

METHODOLOGY

The purpose of this chapter is to consider the marketing performance of third-world marketing boards, using the prices obtained in export markets as a sole parameter for that performance.[5]

The study deals only with boards located in sub-Saharan countries, and only with two raw products: cocoa and coffee. The period studied varies by product and depends on the availability of statistical data, but, on the average, it covers a fifteen-year period. A comparative approach will be adopted: board performance will be compared to that of other currently-used marketing arrangements which are primarily guided by private interests.

Two aspects will be touched upon:

(1) Performance of countries, in terms of price levels obtained.
(2) Performance of countries, in terms of their ability to adjust to world price variations.

For each of the aspects, the performance of countries using marketing boards will be compared to the performance of countries using other arrangements.

MEASURING PRICE-LEVEL PERFORMANCE

To measure the price-level performance in exports one would need a detailed knowledge of sales contracts or, at least, a schedule of sales for the various markets. Unfortunately, statistics of this sort – compiled for private use by the various commodity exchanges – are not available. In the absence of this data, the price performance of producing countries can still be evaluated by using the export unit value, which measures the average price obtained by a country for its annual exports.

Let Y_{ij} stand for the value of exports from country i for year j; X_{ij} for the quantities exported; $\bar{Y}_{ij}$ for the average unit value of these exports, and $\bar{Y}_j$ for the average unit export price from all countries studied for year j. One could then calculate the price-level performance index as follows:

$$P_{ij} = (\bar{Y}_{ij} - \bar{Y}_j)/\bar{Y}_j$$

P_{ij} would thus give the relative deviation between the average unit-value price obtained by country i for year j, as compared with that for the whole set of countries studied.

For each country, over the period studied, we will derive $\bar{P}_{ij}$ which is the average deviation for P_{ij}. X^2 analysis of P_{ij} frequency distribution for each country will allow us to test how marketing-board countries compare to non-marketing-board countries in their behaviour, as expressed by their P_{ij} frequency distribution.

Quite aside from the intrinsic effectiveness of boards, one must take into account a certain number of factors affecting their performance:

the relative importance of the traders: one might expect the size of each country's market share to affect its performance;

external dependence: excessive reliance on a single commodity for export revenue may induce a country to accept lower prices than more fortunate competitors would be willing to accept;

international commodity agreements: agreements were signed for both commodities during the period under study. They may have been of unequal benefit to the various countries.

In order to assess the relative impact of these arrangements, least-square multiple-regression analysis of P_{ij} on each of them will be performed for each country.[6]

MEASURING PERFORMANCE IN ADJUSTING TO WORLD-PRICE VARIATIONS

Good price administration is reflected not only in price levels obtained, but also in the ability to react advantageously to market-price variations. Nerlove's partial adjustment test[7] will be applied to each country's data. The underlying model is the following:

$$P_t^* = \alpha + \beta\,SPOT_t \qquad t = 1, n \qquad (1)$$

where P_t^* is the optimal price for year t, $SPOT$ the New York average spot price for year t. It is further hypothesized that the variations in the price obtained from $t-1$ to t are in proportion to the gap between the optimal price for year t and the price obtained for year $t-1$:

$$(P_t - P_{t-1}) = \lambda \; (P_t^* - P_{t-1}) + \epsilon_t \tag{2}$$

or

$$P_t = \lambda \, P_t^* + (1 - \lambda) \, P_{t-1} + \epsilon_t \tag{3}$$

and by substitution (1) into (3)

$$P_t = \lambda \, (\alpha + \beta) \, SPOT_t \; (1 - \lambda) \, P_{t-1} + \epsilon_t$$

$$P_t = \lambda \, \alpha + \lambda \, \beta \, SPOT_t + (1 - \lambda) \, P_{t-1} + \epsilon_t$$

Therefore, λ measures the speed with which a country reduces the gap between the price it obtained the previous year and the price it wants to obtain in the current year, given the current world-price situation.

CHARACTERISTICS OF THE COCOA TRADE

The production of cocoa is limited to the subtropical regions of Africa and South America. In African countries, the seasonal production stretches over five months, from October to February. The Brazilian harvest is just beginning as the African harvest ends.

Cocoa is not a perfectly homogeneous product and price differs among the various grades. The two basic grades are Accra (Ghana) and Bahia (Brazil). The other beans sell at the going price for one or the base grades; this base price is raised or lowered as the case requires.[8]

Because of climatic conditions and difficulty of controlling plant diseases, production fluctuates widely from one year to the next. Since 1951, it has increased only slightly.

The demand for cocoa (or its complements or substitutues) has very little short-term price elasticity. The demand for raw cocoa depends on the demand for manufactured products derived from cocoa. Over a long period, however, an increase in the price for raw cocoa beans can lead to substitution. As a matter of fact, one notices that the use of cocoa substitutes in lower-quality confectionary is becoming general practice.[9]

The main importers of raw cocoa are Western Europe, the United States, and the countries of Eastern Europe. These are all zones where consumption markets for chocolate-base products are concentrated. The United States are far and away the major cocoa consumer, absorbing some 20% of the world production.

Most cocoa (about 85%) is exported as raw beans; it is then refined and transformed into cocoa mass or liquor, in consuming countries. In its raw form, cocoa deteriorates quickly in producing countries with humid climates – keeping for a maximum of nine months, as compared to three years in western countries.

Shipping is handled primarily by large shipping lines from Western countries. Recently, however, producing countries have demonstrated the desire to take over their own shipping needs.

One observes a slight difference among shipping rates, depending on the itinerary used. In 1972, the percentage of shipping costs in the CIF value of exports stood at 3.8 per cent between Ghana and the United Kingdom, 3 per cent between Nigeria and the United Kingdom, 5.8 per cent between West Africa and Continental Europe and 5 per cent between Ivory Coast and France.[10]

Because of tremendously unstable export revenues resulting primarily from price instability,[11] producing countries were led to work out an international agreement in 1972. That agreement provided, among other things, for quotas and a buffer stock which was to hold prices between a bottom and ceiling price.[12] The agreement caused prices to rise well beyond the price-ceiling set, thus rendering it inoperative. A second agreement was ratified in 1975.

Trading in cocoa takes place mainly on the New York, London and Paris exchanges. Since 1970, London has taken the lead, followed by New York and Paris. Most of the business transactions involving cocoa beans are made on five markets: London and New York are the two most important. Paris, Amsterdam and Hamburg are secondary markets, with Paris as the main target for cocoa from Ivory Coast and other French-speaking African countries.

The development of exchange arbitration led to the growth of a large terminal market on the three exchanges where the volume of terminal operations can be ten or twelve times that of actual transactions. Unfortunately, the growth of terminal markets has encourged speculative activity which, according to an UNCTAD study,[13] has noticeably disrupted normal market operations.

Six countries are responsible for 80 per cent of world production (see Table 11.1); of these six, the performance of Ghana, Nigeria, Ivory Coast, Cameroon and Togo will be studied. Ghana, with a yearly production of 400,000 tons for the 1959–75 period, is by far the major producer, but its share in world production has shown a significant drop: 35 per cent for the 1960–5 period against 28 per cent for the 1970–5 period (see Table 11.1). Ghana's loss has essentially been Ivory Coast's gain. This last country has doubled its production in fifteen years to become the world's second producer, on a par with Nigeria (whose world production share remained stable over the period studied). As for the other three producers, moderate production growth has allowed them to keep their share of the market. Brazil has kept her position as the world's fourth-largest producer, despite considerable fluctuations from year to year. With the exception of Brazil (which manufactures a large portion of its raw cocoa production into intermediate products), the market share of the principal exporters reflects the position they hold as producers (see Table 11.2)

The leading world producer, Ghana, is also the one whose export receipts depend most heavily on cocoa. For Ghana, the average ratio between cocoa exports and total exports, for the period studied, reaches 60 per cent, compared with a maximum of 30 per cent for the other countries: Nigeria, less than 20 per cent; Ivory Coast, 20 per cent; Togo 30 per cent; Cameroon, around 25 per cent. A fifth of the world's cocoa-bean production is manufactured locally. The remaining four-fifths are exported under three principal arrangements: state-marketing boards, stabilization funds, private-marketing firms.

State-marketing boards came into being at the end of the Second World War in the two largest producing countries, Ghana and Nigeria (responsible for 49 per cent of total exports for 1971–4 period).[14] These boards took definitive form at the beginning of the fifties and began to operate according to the following principles: guaranteed production price; purchase monopoly for agents registered with the board; export monopoly for registered sales agents. These boards also find themselves charged with development objectives, for cocoa and for the economy in general. Until 1972, the boards made no direct interventions on the London and New York markets. Since 1972, Ghana has been assigning agents to London, where they make massive market interventions.

Stabilization funds, in operation since the end of the 1950s in Ivory Coast, Cameroon and Togo (22.6 per cent of world exports in 1971–4), also guarantee production prices but are responsible for neither the buying nor the selling of cocoa on foreign markets. The funds do set an export, FOB reference price which actually guarantees the export

Leading producers of cocoa beans (in percentage of world production)

	Ghana	Nigeria	Ivory Coast	Cameroon	Togo	Brazil	All countries
1959–62	35.4	16.0	7.5	6.4	1.0	12.5	78.8
1963–6	34.0	18.3	9.6	6.4	1.2	11.0	80.6
1967–70	28.3	17.3	11.7	7.5	1.6	13.6	79.9
1971–4	27.4	16.0	14.3	7.8	1.6	13.3	80.4
1975	26.2	14.6	14.9	7.4	1.0	17.2	81.3

Source: FAO, *Annuaire de la production et du commerce*, various issues.

TABLE 11.2

Leading exporters of cocoa beans (in percentage of world exports)

	Ghana	Nigeria	Ivory Coast	Cameroon	Togo	Brazil	All countries
1959–62	37.1	18.2	8.4	6.1	1.1	9.7	80.5
1963–6	37.5	19.3	10.5	6.6	1.3	7.7	82.8
1967–70	30.0	19.2	11.4	6.5	1.9	10.0	78.9
1971–4	29.8	19.2	13.8	7.0	1.8	9.1	80.7
1975	27.6	16.9	14.5	6.1	1.5	15.1	81.6

Source: FAO, *Annuaire de la production et du commerce*, various issues.

price to be received by private exporters. When the exporter receives less than the reference price, the fund makes up the difference. In the reverse case, the exporter returns the excess to the fund, to be used for future compensation and also to finance its outlays for research and development.

Brazil (9.1 per cent of world exports for the 1971–4 period) has adopted a formula which sets a minimum export price, but no guaranteed production price; the purchase and exporting of the new cocoa are left to the initiative of private firms.

PERFORMANCE OF BOARD IN COCOA MARKET

Table 11.3 contains the relative deviations for each of the countries studied. Notably, Nigeria's performance has almost consistently been

TABLE 11.3

Cocoa: P_{ij} for each country (1959–75)

			P_{ij}		
Years	Ghana	Nigeria	Ivory Coast	Cameroon	Togo
1959	2.7	–0.3	–7.8	–3.1	1.4
1960	0.4	4.4	–7.7	–7.0	10.8
1961	–0.7	6.6	–4.1	–9.1	–4.1
1962	–1.3	5.6	-4.3	–2.6	2.2
1963	–2.0	8.4	–3.0	–5.1	5.4
1964	–2.8	10.6	–6.0	–6.3	6.3
1965	–5.2	14.8	–13.0	–4.2	2.6
1966	–6.6	5.7	10.4	1.4	6.3
1967	–7.7	12.2	–3.0	–1.2	–3.7
1968	–12.2	13.5	6.8	6.5	5.1
1969	–17.7	12.2	9.3	13.0	11.8
1970	–1.9	18.1	–16.4	–4.9	–4.6
1971	–10.6	13.3	1.7	–7.3	1.7
1972	–7.5	17.6	–3.6	–0.7	–10.1
1973	–4.4	–3.1	6.0	15.5	7.8
1974	–0.4	–1.5	–2.7	9.9	5.9
1975	1.3	2.4	–10.4	7.8	18.7
$\bar{P}_{ij}$	–4.53	8.26	–2.81	0.15	3.74

Sources: P_{ij} are calculated with data obtained from FAO, *Annuaire de la Production et du Commerce*, various issues.

superior to that of its competitors (except in 1959, 1972 and 1974). Ghana rarely performed well (except in 1959, 1960 and 1975). The performance of the three other countries has varied from year to year. Generally, Nigeria's performance has been the best ($\bar{P}_{ij}$ = 8.26), followed by that of Togo ($\bar{P}_{ij}$ = 3.75), Cameroon ($\bar{P}_{ij}$ = 0.15), Ivory Coast ($\bar{P}_{ij}$ = −2.81) and, finally, Ghana ($\bar{P}_{ij}$ = −4.53).

The frequency distribution of P_{ij} is presented in Table 11.4). According to Table 11.5, the hypothesis that the two marketing-board countries have similar behaviour is not supported. Two-countries' tests also indicate that the hypothesized comparability or lack of comparability appears statistically significant only between Nigeria and Cameroon, and between Nigeria and Ivory Coast.

Regression analysis of P_{ij} on international agreements, market share, and export-revenue dependency on cocoa yields better results for Ghana and Nigeria (R^2 = 0.87 and 0.72, respectively) than for the only two non-marketing-board countries – Cameroon and Togo – for which such analysis proved to be feasible (see Table 11.6). Marketing-board countries, therefore, seem to be more sensitive to these variables than non-marketing-board countries. This, in turn, leads to the deduction that the performance of Ghana and Nigeria is not likely to be strongly affected by their reliance on a marketing-board system for export.

With regard to the impact of individual explanatory variables on price performance, it is worth noting that the four countries, especially Ghana, are unfavourably affected by their dependency on cocoa-export revenue. International agreements have also had an unfavourable influence on Ghana and Nigeria, but have possibly benefitted Cameroon.

The results of the partial adjustment model are summarized in Table 11.7. They show that Ghana and Nigeria are slower to adjust to world price variations than are Ivory coast and Cameroon. Togo's coefficient is closer to that of the marketing-board countries than to that of non-marketing-board countries. This may reflect the impact of the notorious illicit cocoa trade between Togo and neighbouring Ghana.

PRINCIPAL CHARACTERISTICS OF THE COFFEE TRADE

Coffee, unlike cocoa, is produced and marketed in several different varieties:[15]

TABLE 11.4

P_{ij} Frequency distribution – cocoa

P_{ij} classes	Ghana	Nigeria	Ivory Coast	Cameroon	Togo	Marketing-board countries	Total Non-marketing-board countries
⩽ 20.0							
−19.9 to −15.0	1		1			1	1
−14.9 to −10.00	2		2			2	2
− 9.9 to − 5.0	4		4	5	2	4	11
− 4.9 to 0.0	7	2	5	6	8	9	19
0.0 to 4.9	3	3	1	1	2	6	4
5.0 to 9.9		4	3	3	3	4	9
10.0 to 14.9		6	1	1	1	6	3
15.0 to 19.9		2		1	1	2	2
⩾ 20.0							

TABLE 11.5

X^2 test on P_{ij} frequency distribution – cocoa

	Marketing-board countries		Non-marketing-board countries			Total marketing-board countries
	Ghana	Nigeria	Ivory Coast	Cameroon	Togo	
Ghana	—					
Nigeria	21.78	—				
Ivory Coast	5.33	15.00*	—			
Cameroon	9.19	13.71†	4.20	—		
Togo	8.93	9.85	5.69	1.90	—	
Total Marketing Board countries						7.04

* Results conform to expectations at the 0.05 level
† Results conform to expectations at the 0.10 level

TABLE 11.6

Regression of P_{ij} for cocoa – values of coefficients, F and R^2

Countries	Independent variables				
	Value of coefficients				
	International agreements	Market share	Export dependency	F	R^2
Ghana	13.66*	—	0.93*	54.21*	0.87
Nigeria	−11.50*	1.88*	−0.34*	13.67*	0.72
Cameroon	6.77†	3.71*	−0.76†	4.94*	0.44
Togo	—	5.60†	−0.80†	4.76*	0.42

* Significant at the 0.05 level
† Significant at the 0.10 level

TABLE 11.7

Partial adjustment model – cocoa

Countries		R^2	F
Ghana	0.39*	0.96	194.99†
Nigeria	0.33*	0.91	75.93†
Ivory Coast	0.56*	0.97	299.47†
Cameroon	0.45*	0.96	207.43†
Togo	0.32*	0.97	224.43†

* Significant at the 0.05 level
† Significant at the 0.01 level

(1) robustas, grown mainly in Africa and Indonesia, making up 30 per cent of basic world production over the 1968–72 period;

(2) unwashed Arabicas, representing another 30 per cent of world production, coming from Brazil and Ethiopia;

(3) Colombian milds, 15 per cent of world production, grown in Columbia, Tanzania and Kenya;

(4) other milds (20 per cent of the world production), originating in Central America, South America and India.

Consumers prefer Arabicas, and they sell at higher prices than robustas. Since the end of the Second World War, however, robustas have increased their market share from 10 per cent to 30 per cent, and the price difference between the two varieties has shrunk noticeably.

Coffee is an easily stored commodity; this quality has been used to advantage, especially by Brazil, to control the market price.

World coffee production increased rather rapidly in the post-war period, but this growth came to a virtual halt at the end of the 1950s (7 per cent total increase from 1959 to 1975). This production slow-down is largely the result of Brazil's policy of production cut-backs.

Most of the coffee produced is sold raw (green coffee beans). Brazil is the only coffee producing country to have set up an industry to refine its coffee for export.

For any given country, the long-term price elasticity of supply is especially influenced by the degree to which its economy relies on coffee exports. This elasticity will thus be relatively higher in Africa than in Colombia or Central American countries.[16] The short-term elasticities are weaker than long-term ones, and vary from one country to the other, for the same reason.

The goal of the first international coffee agreement (signed in 1963) was to assure price stability and to maintain reasonable price levels. Despite this attempt, the 1964–9 period was marked by mounting stocks and falling prices. Under the new agreement, in effect from 1968 to 1972, prices improved noticeably, an improvement in which adverse climatic conditions doubtlessly played a part. The last agreement ended in 1972 and was not renewed, since producing and consuming countries were unable to settle their differences.[17]

According to Nyssens,[18] evolution of the coffee demand depends on the real revenue in consuming countries, the prices of the current year, and on speculation. For the United States and Western Europe, income elasticity is weak and tends to decrease. On the other hand, while price elasticity at high prices may be very strong in the United States, it may be viewed as stable for the other importing countries.[19] Interference by the New York, London and Bremen exchanges between highly centralized producers and coffee roasters contributes to disruptive speculation.

Considering the heterogeneity of the product, we can only compare the performance of boards with that of other marketing mechanisms for a single category of coffee. Our analysis will thus be limited to robusta coffee from African countries exporting only this type of coffee and – among these countries – those for which separate data on robusta exports are available. Six countries fit these criteria: Nigeria, Ghana, Togo, Angola, Ivory Coast and the Central African Empire.

As Table 11.8 indicates, these six countries play a minor role on the world coffee market. The analysis of their comparative positions as exporters of robusta reveals wide disparities (see Table 11.9); Ivory Coast and Angola are by far the leading suppliers, compared with the other four countries.

The degree to which each of these countries depends on coffee export receipts is highly variable. Except for the Central African Empire and Nigeria, this dependence has been on the decrease since the beginning of the 1960s, up to 1975. For the 1971–5 period, the ratio coffee exports/total exports stood at 27 per cent for Angola, 24 per cent for the Central African Empire, 12.4 per cent for Togo, 25.6 per cent for Ivory Coast and less than 1 per cent for Nigeria and Ghana.

Nigerian and Ghanaian exports are directly controlled by marketing boards, while those of Togo and Ivory Coast rely on stabilization

TABLE 11.8

Share in world coffee exports

	Angola*	CAE	Togo	Ghana	Ivory Coast	Nigeria	Total six countries
1959–61	3.6	0.2	0.3	0.1	5.1	—	9.4
1962–4	5.0	0.3	0.4	0.2	6.1	0.1	12.1
1965–7	5.4	0.3	0.3	0.2	5.7	0.1	12.2
1968–70	5.5	0.3	0.3	0.2	5.8	0.1	12.2
1971–3	5.4	0.2	0.3	0.1	5.5	0.1	11.7
1974–5	5.5	0.3	0.3	0.1	7.5	—	13.6

* Includes a small portion of Arabica.
Source: FAO, *Annuaire de la production et du commerce,* various issues.

TABLE 11.9

Share in robusta exports

	Angola*	CAE	Togo	Ghana	Ivory Coast	Nigeria	Total
1959–61	38.8	2.5	3.5	0.8	53.8	0.6	100
1962–4	41.5	2.5	3.2	1.3	50.8	0.7	100
1965–7	44.3	2.5	2.6	1.3	46.5	0.9	100
1968–70	45.0	2.1	2.8	1.4	47.9	0.8	100
1971–3	46.3	2.1	2.7	1.2	47.0	0.8	100
1974–5	40.3	2.0	2.0	0.5	54.9	0.1	100

Source: Derived from FAO, *Annuaire de la production et du commerce*, various issues.

funds. For the period under study, Angola and the Central African Empire marketed their coffee without the intervention of boards or funds.

PERFORMANCE OF BOARDS IN COFFEE MARKETS

The P_{ij} analysis (see Table 11.10) shows that the Central African Empire and Ivory Coast obtained the best results ($\bar{P}_{ij} = 3.0$ for the Central African Empire and 2.9 for Ivory Coast). Then, by decreasing order, follow Angola, Togo, Nigeria and Ghana (-1.9, -2.6, -5.7 and -33.8 respectively). Obviously, boards are ineffective for this purpose.

TABLE 11.10

Robusta coffee:
P_{ij} for each country (1959–75)

			P_{ij}			
Year	Ghana	Nigeria	Ivory Coast	Togo	CAE	Angola
1959	−14.6	−13.9	5.8	−0.3	13.9	7.8
1960	−2.8	—	−0.1	−45.9	−2.8	−1.6
1961	3.9	—	9.9	3.9	18.7	−13.7
1962	−46.6	—	15.0	6.9	6.9	−12.9
1963	−35.1	−2.6	6.0	−2.6	−2.6	−6.8
1964	−56.2	−23.4	−3.1	−4.2	−5.7	9.1
1965	−12.2	—	−0.9	−4.2	−12.2	2.7
1966	−49.8	−13.9	1.8	−7.3	−4.2	2.3
1967	−61.3	−22.6	7.0	−22.6	3.2	−3.3
1968	−24.2	−24.2	2.7	−9.0	−5.3	−1.3
1969	−36.7	−5.0	4.1	0.7	−12.1	−2.3
1970	−62.5	−12.5	4.3	0.9	2.0	−2.2
1971	−49.9	−6.1	2.9	−6.1	11.3	−1.6
1972	−36.2	27.5	−2.9	15.9	13.3	1.6
1973	−46.5	−28.5	−1.0	−22.2	18.9	2.6
1974	−5.4	—	−5.1	−31.2	15.6	7.1
1975	−38.7	83.8	3.4	−8.1	−8.1	−4.2
$\bar{P}_{ij}$	−33.8	−5.7	2.9	−2.6	3.0	−1.9

Sources: FAO, *Annuaire de la production et du commerce*, various issues.

The X^2 tests performed on the P_{ij} frequency distribution (see Table 11.11), summarized in Table 11.12, indicate that, on the whole, marketing-board countries behave significantly differently from non-marketing-board countries ($X^2 y = 65.82$ significant at the 0.01 level). Inter-country comparisons generally support this hypothesis.

Regression analysis of P_{ij} on international agreements, market share, and export-revenue dependency, yields satisfactory results only for Ghana, and to some extent, for the CAE. The regression is not statistically significant for Nigeria, Angola and Ivory Coast. As for cocoa, Ghana seems to be the most sensitive to dependency on export revenue and market share. International agreements appear to have had a statistically significant effect only in the case of Ghana (favourable) and Ivory Coast (unfavourable). (See Table 11.13.)

The R^2 suggest that it is unlikely that the type of marketing organization may have affected the performance of Ghana. It is not possible to draw such an inference in the case of the other countries.

λ coefficients, estimating the speed at which countries adjust to world-price variations, are presented in Table 11.14. Non-marketing-board countries tend to have higher coefficients than marketing-board countries, implying that the former do not adjust as quickly to world-price variations as the latter. Furthermore, the greatest λ, obtained for Angola (although not statistically significant), is consistent with the fact that this country relies on private agents who are probably more flexible than stabilization funds.

CONCLUDING REMARKS

In the final analysis, how does the performance of boards compare with that of stabilization funds or private agents? We observed that Ghana's board exhibited the worst price-level performance, compared with its competitors, for both cocoa and coffee. Nigeria's performance was best for cocoa, and last but one for coffee. As for the stabilization funds of Togo, Cameroon and Ivory Coast, their performance fell between the two extremes.

From the present analysis one cannot conclude that Ghana's price-level performance was poor on cocoa and coffee or that Nigeria's performance was good on cocoa simply because they relied on a marketing-board system. Indeed, in these cases, certain independent variables – international agreements, market share, export-revenue dependency – clearly had a definite impact on the relative price-level

TABLE 11.11

P_{ij} frequency distribution – coffee

P_{ij} classes	Ghana	Nigeria	Angola	CAE	Togo	Ivory Coast	Total Marketing-board countries	Total non-marketing-board countries
≪ −30.0	12	2			1		14	1
−29.9 to −25.0	1				1		1	1
−24.9 to −20.00	2	1					3	
−19.9 to −15.0	1	3					4	
−14.9 to −10.0	1	2	2				3	2
−9.9 to −5.0		5	2	2	5	1	5	10
−4.9 to −0.0			7	5	4	3		19
0.0 to −4.9		1	4	2	2	8	1	16
5.0 to −9.0		1	2	2	2	3	1	9
10.0 to −14.9		1		3	1	2	1	6
15.0 to −19.9					1			1
20.0 to −24.9				2				2
25.0 to −29.9				1				1
≫ 30.0		1					1	

TABLE 11.12

χ^2 test on P_{ij} frequency distribution – coffee

| | Marketing-board countries | | Non-marketing-board countries | | | | Total marketing-board countries |
	Ghana	Nigeria	Angola	CAE	Togo	Ivory Coast	
Ghana	—						
Nigeria	18.81†	—					
Angola	31.33*	21.62‡	—				
CAE	34.00*	22.62†	9.00†	—			
Togo	29.33*	15.33	8.77†	8.40	—		
Ivory Coast	34.00*	25.00†	7.46†	7.83†	9.95†	—	
Total non-marketing-board countries							65.82*

* Results conform to expectations at the 0.01 level
† Results conform to expectations at the 0.05 level
‡ Results conform to expectations at the 0.10 level

TABLE 11.13

Regression of P_{ij} on the independent variables – coffee – values of coefficients, F and R^2

	International agreements	Value of coefficients		Export dependency	F	R^2
		Market share				
Ghana		−25.74*		34.71*	206.44*	0.98
CAE		−20.91*		1.73*	17.25*	0.68
Togo		−12.76*		1.58*	4.51*	0.32
Ivory Coast	−4.20†	−0.65*		0.34*	2.94	0.28

* Significant at the 0.05 level
† Significant at the 0.10 level

TABLE 11.14

Partial adjustment model – coffee –
values of λ, R^2 and F

Countries	λ	R^2	F
Ghana	0.46*	0.88	57.24‡
Nigeria	0.20	0.47	7.68‡
Angola	0.64	0.85	42.89‡
CAE	0.50*	0.66	15.43‡
Togo	0.52†	0.85	44.79‡
Ivory Coast	0.40†	0.96	205.37‡

* Significant at the 0.10 level
† Significant at the 0.05 level
‡ Significant at the 0.01 level

performance. For the remaining countries, other factors may have contributed, including the prevailing type of marketing organization.

If one is of the opinion that boards generally exert a deeper, more concerted and more beneficial influence on a country's economic development than do funds (which rely more heavily on private and foreign agents), then this evaluation need not be substantially modified by the comparative results of board performance on foreign markets.

However, the analysis of performance in adjusting to world-price fluctuations does permit certain important observations. One does in fact notice that funds tend to adjust more quickly than boards to these variations. (Rapid adjustment is more profitable with rising than with falling prices). The price rigidity observed for Nigeria and Ghana probably proved beneficial when cocoa prices made sharp turns during the 1959–75 period. From this point of view, the rigidity associated with long-term sales agreements turned to their advantage. The same rigidity has been observed for coffee, and had opposite results since world coffee prices showed a rather steady increase over the period studied. Less rigidity would have been beneficial to boards. As a matter of fact, it turns out that their price-level performance for coffee proves worse than that of the funds.

NOTES AND REFERENCES

1. The author is indebted to Denyse Dagenais and Simon Dahan for valuable advice and to Daniel Depelteau for research assistance and computer work.
2. A. Onitrim and D. Olatunbosun (eds.), *The Marketing Board System, a Bibliography*. Proceedings of an International Conference, March 1971. (Ibadan: Nigerian Institute for Social and Economic Research, 1974).
3. J. C. Abbott, and H. Creupelandt, *Les Offices de Commercialisation Agricole: Leur Création et Leur Fonctionnement* (Rome: FAO, 1966). E. P. Hibbert, 'Statutory Marketing in a Developing Economy', *European Journal of Marketing*, vol. 6, no. 3 (Autumn 1972), pp. 155–69. E. H. Whitham, *Agricultural Marketing in Africa* (London: Oxford University Press, 1972). W. Lamade, 'Policies of Marketing Boards in East Africa', *Studies in Production and Trade in East Africa* (München: Weltforum Humanities Press, 1970), pp. 281–433.
4. J. C. Abbott, and H. Creupelandt, 'Les Offices de Commercialisation Agricole dans les Pays en Voie de Développement: Problèmes d'Evaluation du Degré d'Efficacité', *Bulletin Mensuel, Economies et Statistique Agricoles*, vol. 16, no. 9 (September 1967). H. Kriesel, *Cocoa Marketing in Nigeria* (East Lansing: Michigan State University, 1969). D. Israeli, and J. Zib, *Societal Marketing Boards* (New York: John Wiley & Sons, 1977). In particular, see Chapter II. Sidney Hoos, (ed.), *Agricultural Marketing Boards – an International Perspective* (Cambridge Mass.: Ballinger Publishing Co., 1979). In particular Chapter 6, David Blandford, *West African Export Marketing Boards*
5. The reader interested in a broader discussion of the marketing role of the boards should refer to Blandford in Hoos (ed.), ibid., pp. 129–34.
6. At an earlier stage, various tests were performed with regard to the impact of political events and the direction of trade on P_{ij}. They did not yield any statistically significant relationships and were therefore deleted in the remainder of the study.
7. M. Nerlove, *Distributed Lags and Demand Analysis for Agricultural and other Commodities*, Department of Agriculture Handbook no. 141 (Washington, DC: US Government Printing Office, 1958).
8. P. Van der Hagen, 'Le Marché Mondial du Cacao', *Etudes et Expansion*, vol. 77, no. 277 (July, August, September 1978), pp. 519–35.
9. J. R. Behrman, 'Monopolistic Cocoa Pricing', *American Journal of Agriculture Economics* (August 1968), pp. 702–19.
10. *Cocoa Market Report* (London: Gill and Duffus) various issues.
11. See, for example, J. K. Olayide Olayemi, 'Measurements of Instability in Nigeria's Agricultural Export Trade', *Journal of Rural Economics and Development*, vol. 10, no. 1 (1976) pp. 3–14; also J. R. Behrman, and F. G. Adams, *Econometric Models of World Agricultural Commodity Markets* (Cambridge, Mass: Ballinger Publishing Co., 1976), pp. 18–22. It must also be pointed out that this instability is increased by the unpredictability of harvests. This unpredictability, in turn, blocks the effectiveness of terminal markets in stabilizing prices. On this subject, see: T. A. Kofi, 'A Framework for Comparing the Efficiency of Futures Markets', *American Journal of Agricultural Economics*, vol. 55, no. 4, (November 1973), pp. 584–94.

12. Carmine Nappi, *Commodity Market Controls* (Lexington, Mass: Lexington Books, 1979) (Montréal: Centre d'Etudes en Administration Internationale, 1978), pp. 79–81.

13. CNUCED, *Système de Commercialisation et de Distribution du Cacao, Commission des Produits de Base, Huitième Session* (Genève: Nations Unies. 1975).

14. For a general discussion of the history, role, and functioning of marketing boards in West Africa, see Blandford in Hoos (ed.), op. cit.

15. See A. Nyssens, 'Le Marché Mondial du Café', *Etudes et Expansion*, no. 277 (July, April 1978), pp. 539–52.

16. J. De Vries, *Structure and Prospects of the World Coffee Economy*, International Bank for Reconstruction and Development, World Bank Staff Working Paper, no. 208 (June 1975), pp. 8–12.

17. See Alton D. Law, *International Commodity Agreements* (Lexington, Mass: Lexington Books, 1975), p. 44 and Nappi, op. cit., pp. 54–60.

18. Nyssens, op. cit., pp. 545–6.

19. De Vries. op. cit., pp. 28–31.

12 State Trading and the GATT

Ivan Bernier

In June 1947, during the second session of the Preparatory Committee of the United Nations Conference on Trade and Employment, the delegate of New Zealand declared:

We should beware of attempting to legislate too precisely to meet the case of State enterprises, not out of any feeling that State enterprises should be put in a privileged position, but rather from the feeling that the first essential of sound legislation is that we should be thoroughly familiar with what we are legislating about.[1]

Unfortunately, this precious advice, it seems, has been lost in the discussions. More than thirty years later, one must admit that the present GATT measures dealing with state trading remain, to a large extent, an exercise in futility, based on a misunderstanding of the real nature of state enterprises and monopolies. Suffice it to mention, at this stage, that the main obligation imposed by the GATT on state-trading enterprises is to act as if they were private enterprises: but how can this be done, when state enterprises and monopolies are created precisely to fulfil roles not normally assumed by private enterprises?

In 1969, some of the ambiguities surrounding the present GATT measures on state trading were brought forward in the Committee in Industrial Products; after taking notice of various notifications having to do with state trading, the Committee then made the following remarks, very much to the point:

Further light might be shed on the notifications by a study to determine to what degree the problems involved in the notifications

245

had been caused by governmental restriction of quantity purchased rather than by the nature of state trading as such. This should narrow the problem somewhat by showing separately the degree to which, and ways in which, state trading as such created problems as distinct from the effects of other objectives which might also be involved, such as the protection of particular sources of supply, revenue consideration, or social policy.[2]

Since then, not much has been done on the subject and the ambiguities remain, to a large extent, amplified by the accession to GATT of contracting parties with centrally planned economies. In view of this, and as a modest contribution to a better understanding of state enterprises, it shall be the purpose of this paper to present, in a critical perspective, the overall approach of GATT towards state enterprises.

Basically, the GATT deals with state trading:

(1) by identifying the enterprises considered as state trading;

(2) by extending to such enterprises the nondiscriminatory treatment of Article I;

(3) by imposing upon them a duty to act according to commercial considerations only, barring in particular the use of quantitative restrictions;

(4) by providing for regular reports by the contracting parties on their state-trading enterprises including, if required by other contracting parties, the import mark-up in the case of state-trading monopolies and

(5) by excluding nullification of tariff concessions through import mark-ups in the case of import monopolies.[3]

As we shall see, however, the only measure that appears practicable and corresponds approximately to the actual practice of the contracting parties is the obligation to grant to foreign products the most-favoured nation treatment; and this measure, to a large extent was already covered by Article I of GATT.

THE IDENTIFICATION OF STATE-TRADING ENTERPRISES

In Article XVII, paragraph 1, of GATT, state trading is deemed to exist when a contracting party 'establishes or maintains a state enterprise, wherever located, or grants to any enterprise, formally or in effect, exclusive or special privileges . . . '. This is a rather curious formulation. First, it begs the question insofar as it presents state trading as the result of the creation or maintenance of state enterprises. This would be acceptable if there were a definition of state enterprises; but there is no such definition. Secondly, by equating state enterprises with private enterprises that enjoy 'exclusive or special privileges', it clearly implies that the criterion of state trading is not so much state property or even state control as state-induced distortions in the functioning of trading enterprises. This again would be an acceptable proposition if a distinction was established between state regulation of enterprises and state participation in trade. But no such distinction exists and, as it is, one is left to wonder when, for example, a subsidized industry becomes a state enterprise for the purpose of GATT. To make matters worse, the vagueness of the expression 'exclusive or special privileges' leaves the door open for the contracting parties to interpret according to their own canons when an enterprise,[4] state controlled or not, is possessed of 'exclusive or special privileges'.

Curiously, the Contracting Parties, while admitting the existence of a link between this ambiguous definition of the entities covered by Article XVII and the lack of success of the reporting obligation to be found in that article, have consistently refused to review the problem from that perspective.[5] The difficulty is similar, to a large extent, to that encountered in the regulation of subsidies where, lacking a clear definition of what constitutes a subsidy, the Contracting Parties have had to face various problems, including non-compliance with the reporting requirement of Article XVI.[6] But if, in 1962, it was considered 'neither necessary nor feasible to seek an agreed interpretation of what constitutes a subsidy',[7] the Contracting Parties now appear to have come to terms, in the Tokyo round of negotiations, with the idea of providing at least an illustrative list, of the practices covered by Article XVI.[8] A parallel evolution, concerning state-trading enterprises, has yet to take place. In 1959, a special working group set up to examine the problem of state-trading concluded, as in the case of subsidies, that the text of Article XVII, together with the interpretative notes, give sufficiently clear indications to permit the identification of the entities covered by that article.[9] In 1960, the problem was again dealt with briefly by the same working group, only to be quickly put aside. Since then, the incertitude concerning the exact scope of Article XVII has increased with the apparent tendency of developing countries to consider that article as applying essentially to state-trading enterprises in developed market economies[10] and the apparent acceptance by the GATT of the non-pertinence of Article XVII to countries with centrally planned economies.[11] In these circumstances, it does not appear exaggerated to state that the effectiveness of Article XVII will depend, in the last analysis, upon a better description of the entities to be covered by that article, or at least the enunciation of a test sufficiently explicit to provide a clearer idea of what the GATT is 'legislating about' when it deals with state-trading enterprises.

The problem, it must be stressed, is not simply one of semantics. The fundamental difficulty is that the GATT just does not reflect a clearly articulated position concerning state-trading enterprises. Thus, in Article XVII, paragraph 3, one finds a general statement that appears to reflect GATT's fundamental attitude on the subject:

> The contracting parties recognize that enterprises of the kind described in paragraph 1(a) of this Article might be operated so as to create serious obstacles to trade; thus negotiations on a reciprocal and mutually advantageous basis designed to limit or reduce such obstacles are of importance to the expansion of international trade.

However, this 'yellow light' approach concerning state-trading entities, comparable in a way to that used in Article XVI regarding subsidies, is not devoid of ambiguity in its formulation. While the first part of the sentence implies that the entities described in paragraph 1(a) of Article XVII, in certain circumstances, do not create obstacles to trade, the second part of the sentence appears to assume that such obstacles are more or less inherent to the kind of entities described. Indeed, the simple reference to the technique of negotiation for the limitation or reduction of such obstacles, in the GATT philosophy, indirectly assimilates them to tariff barriers rather than non-tariff barriers, normally dealt with through sheer prohibition, national treatment obligation or, in most recent practice, through supplementary codes.[12]

Further evidence of the ambivalence of GATT concerning state-trading enterprises may be found in Article XVII, paragraph 1(b) and in Article XX (d). When state-trading enterprises, including monopolies, are requested to act according to commercial considerations only, as is the case in Article XVII 1(b), what is implicitly suggested is a rejection of the essence of state trading. But is it really the case? Article XX (d) of GATT provides a general exception for measures:

. . . necessary to secure compliance with laws or regulations which are not inconsistent with the provisions of this Agreement, including those relative to customs enforcement, the enforcement of monopolies operated under paragraph 4 of Article II and Article XVII, the protection of patents, trademarks and copyrights, and the prevention of deceptive practices.

There is a clear indication here that even a state enterprise that constitutes a trading monopoly is acceptable if it respects certain rules in its operation. In addition to that, by associating the enforcement of such monopolies with the protection of patents, trademarks and copyrights, or the prevention of deceptive practices, it is somehow implied that those monopolies may, as a matter of fact, play a positive role. But is a monopoly 'operated under Article XVII', that is according to commercials considerations only, possible?[13] In the end, one is left to wonder what GATT's exact position is on the subject of state-trading enterprises in general, and state monopolies in particular.

Contrasting with this ambiguous attitude regarding state-trading enterprises, Article XI of GATT makes it fairly clear that quantitative restrictions are not to be tolerated in principle, while Article XVI, in paragraph 2, is quite explicit about the danger of export subsidies, and in paragraph 4 attempts to prohibit them altogether. Domestic subsidies, on the contrary, are overtly accepted in Article III, paragraph 8(b), despite the fact that they may cause serious prejudice to international trade as is recognized in Article XVI (l).

Now, if state-trading enterprises in general, and state monopolies in particular, are to be considered as some kind of evil to be discouraged, if not absolutely prohibited, the fact should be stated more clearly. This view appears to be held by the United States[14] and is shared by various writers.[15] In such a case, however, the problem of definition is bound to remain of foremost importance, as one will necessarily have to distinguish between what is allowed and what is prohibited. But if, on the contrary, one considers that state-trading enterprises and monopolies are there to remain, and one accepts them, notwithstanding their potentially disruptive effect on international trade, it would appear that an approach based upon the idea of prejudice has a better chance to succeed, and requires less in terms of precision of definition. From that point of view, there is something to learn, as we shall see later, from the recently concluded Protocol on Subsidies and Countervailing Duties.

THE NON-DISCRIMINATORY TREATMENT OBLIGATION

The basic obligation of state enterprises, as they are described in Article XVII, paragraph 1(a), is 'to act in a manner consistent with the general principles of non-discriminatory treatment prescribed . . . for governmental measures affecting imports or export by private traders'. Some doubts have been expressed as to whether this entails a most-favoured nation treatment obligation, that is an obligation to treat foreign states equally, or, instead, a national treatment obligation, obliging that foreign competitors be placed on an equal footing with national enterprises.[16] The better view, considering the preparatory documents, appears to be the interpretation that favours a most-favoured nation obligation.[17] One could add that, in practice, it is certainly easier to establish the existence of discriminatory practices between foreign states than to prove that a specific state-trading enterprise favours, in its various operations, the local producers. The difficulty lies in the fact that, unless some insight is gained into the internal working of state-trading enterprises, it is nearly impossible to establish to what extent a specific practice is justified by protectionist motives. Yet it is precisely here that state-trading enterprises have had to do with alleged protectionist practices rather than with violations of the most-favoured nation treatment. In answer to this problem, the GATT draftsmen have added, to the fundamental obligation of state-trading enterprises to operate on a non-discriminatory basis, a further obligation to act, in their sales and purchases, according to commercial considerations only. In practical terms, this amounted to an attempt to square the circle.

THE DUTY TO ACT ACCORDING TO COMMERCIAL CONSIDERATIONS ONLY

Quite apart from the problem of whether a state-trading enterprise can truly act according to commercial considerations only, to which we shall revert later, it may be useful to inquire first what is meant exactly by 'commercial considerations' and, above all, whether this is a useful tool to discourage discriminatory practices in general. As for the meaning of the expression 'commercial considerations', Article XVII, paragraph 1(b) gives what appears to be, at first glance, a straightforward interpretation: such considerations include '. . . price, quality, availability, marketability, transportation and other conditions of purchase or sale, and . . . adequate opportunity, in accordance with customary business practice, to compete for participation in such purchases or sales'. But when one looks at this measure in the light of the preparatory documents and the interpretative note added to paragraph 1(b) of Article XVII, the meaning of the expression 'commercial considerations' becomes less clear. In 1946–7, during the discussions on what was to become Article XVII, paragraph 1(b), various delegations expressed views to the effect that the 'commercial consideration' clause did not imply a national treatment obligation, which can only be interpreted to mean that state-trading enterprises can legitimately discriminate between domestic and foreign products in their purchases and sales.[18] Similarly, '[i]n discussing whether or not a long-term contract was a "commercial consideration" the delegates refused to chance rigid interpretation, arguing that specific cases would provide the specific law'.[19] Finally, in the interpretative note added to Article XVII, paragraph 1(b), the contracting parties have accepted that 'a country receiving a "tied loan" is free to take this loan into account as a "commercial consideration" when purchasing requirements abroad'. Judging by these interpretations, one would be justified to consider that the expression 'commercial considerations' is at least as problematic as the expression 'in the ordinary course of trade under fully competitive conditions', to be found in Article VII of GATT. The latter expression refers to one of the most important problems that the contracting parties have had to face in their effort to eliminate distortions, and to harmonize national systems of valuation for customs purposes, namely that of 'associated homes' transactions or transactions between connected firms.[20]

The difficulty with a 'commercial considerations' clause is that it can easily be used in order to protect vested interests. Thus, in the case of the provincial monopolies on alcohol in Canada, complaints to the effect that they restrict the import and sale of foreign products have been answered with the argument that such products are simply not in demand. Of course, they can hardly be in demand if they are not offered on sale; but at the same time, the provincial monopolies on alcohol are under no duty to promote the sale of foreign alcoholic beverages.[21] In such a situation, the 'commercial considerations' test obviously plays a very limited role. Yet, particularly in the case of developing countries, it presents serious dangers, because it tends to exclude them as newcomers on the national market. The situation, in a way, has much in common with that considered in Article XIII of the

GATT, which deals with the problem of non-discriminatory administration of quantitative restrictions. As a matter of fact, an interpretative note added to this article as well as to Articles XI, XII, XIV and XVIII of the GATT, specifies that the terms 'import restrictions' or 'export restrictions' used in those articles 'includes restrictions made effective through state-trading operations'. But curiously, another interpretative note added to Article XIII explains that 'no mention was made of commercial considerations, as a rule, for the allocation of quotas because it was considered that its application by governmental authorities might not always be practicable'. This is probably as close to the truth as the GATT draftsmen could come.

The real problem, in final consideration, is whether state-trading enterprises can truly act according to commercial considerations only. In answer to this question, a distinction is sometimes made between state-trading enterprises that operate in a monopoly situation and those that do not. In a monopoly situation, it is more easily accepted that the absence of competition makes it academic to speak of a duty to act according to commercial considerations only.[22] But where a state enterprise is in a competitive situation, it does make sense at first sight to speak in such terms: it implies then that the enterprise, in its buying or selling policy, is not supposed to act according to governmental instruction or, if it is a private enterprise, to benefit from special or privileged situations. Yet, this is a rather dubious proposition. Either the enterprise is state owned or controlled, and then its buying or selling decisions, backed as they are by the resources of the state, simply cannot have the same meaning as those of a purely private enterprise; or else the enterprise is private, but enjoys a special or privileged position as far as buying or selling is concerned, in which case it cannot act according to commercial considerations only without renouncing its special or privileged position. In either case, the duty to act according to commercial considerations only is bound to remain, as in the case of state monopolies, largely academic.

THE NOTIFICATION REQUIREMENT

It has already been mentioned that the notification requirement of Article XVII (4) has not met with much success since the enactment of that provision in 1955, and it has been suggested that this was partly due to the lack of a satisfactory definition of what constitutes a state-trading enterprise for the purposes of GATT. However, it must be admitted that the very idea of requesting that contracting parties notify the GATT of their state-trading enterprises suffered inherently from the common defect of all self-incriminating procedure, that is the natural lack of goodwill of those immediately concerned. To make matters worse, the questionnaire eventually devised in order to give effect to Article XVII, paragraph 4, reflected the typical bureaucratic approach which seeks to cover all petty details.[23] As a matter of fact, this questionnaire, because it typifies so well the GATT approach to state-trading enterprises, merits to be quoted *in extenso*.

NEW QUESTIONNAIRE ON STATE TRADING
I. *Enumeration of state-trading enterprises*
Does your country maintain enterprises covered by the provisions of Article XVII? If so, list the products or groups of products for which a state enterprise is maintained or for which an enterprise has exclusive or special privileges.

II. *Reason and purpose for introducing and maintaining state-trading enterprises*
State, for each product, the reason and purpose for introducing and maintaining the enterprise (it should be indicated, for example, whether the purpose or the effect of the enterprise is to prevent prices to consumers from exceeding certain maximum limits, or to protect domestic producers by the control of imports and/or the purchase of domestic supplies at above world price levels, or to facilitate export sales, or to make it possible to establish or administer a stabilization arrangement). A description of the legal provisions should be included insofar as this has not been submitted in earlier notifications.

III. *Description of the functioning of the state-trading enterprises*
Describe, item by item, the functioning of such enterprises and state in particular:

Whether the enterprise deals with exports or with imports, or both.

Whether private traders are allowed to import or export and, if so, on what conditions. Whether there is free competition between private traders and the state-trading enterprise.

The criteria used for determining the quantities to be exported and imported.

How export prices are determined. How the mark-up on imported products is determined. How export prices and the re-sale prices of imports compare with domestic prices.

Whether long-term contracts are negotiated by the state-trading enterprise. Whether state-trading methods are used to fulfill contractual obligations entered into by the government.

IV. *Statistical information*

Furnish statistics (where possible by quantity and value) on imports, exports and national production on the products notified, on the following lines:

(*a*) the figures should cover the last three available years;

(*b*) the figures for the three groups (imports, exports and national production) should be given, where possible, in a comparable form;

(*c*) the figures should be broken down so as to show:

 (i) trade by the enterprise;

(ii) other trade.

V. *Reason why no foreign trade had taken place (if this is the case) in products affected*

In cases where no foreign trade has taken place in the products affected, state the reasons.

VI. *Additional information*

Provide any additional information that may be appropriate.

Unfortunately, the general approach of the GATT towards state-trading enterprises, as manifested in this questionnaire, appears to take for granted what it seeks to achieve. There are few state-trading enterprises sufficiently concerned by the maintenance of a system of undistorted competition to divulge willingly the essence of their workings. Indeed, there are good reasons to believe that in many instances, the governments maintaining state-trading enterprises simply do not receive the information requested. More fundamentally, one must admit that invisibility or lack of transparency, from the government's point of view, is one of the advantages of a state-trading enterprise. As a matter of fact, the importance of this consideration is such that the contracting parties, when enacting paragraph 4 of Article XVII in 1955, found it necessary to qualify their obligation to provide information with the proviso that it 'shall not require any contracting party to disclose confidential information which would impede law enforcement or otherwise be contrary to the public interest or would prejudice the legitimate commercial interests of particular enterprises'.[24] What remains of the original obligation, in this context, is an open question.

In practice, it is symptomatic that, notwithstanding all efforts made, the situation, as far as notifications are concerned, remains basically unchanged. Indeed, as recently as 1977, the problem of notification was still being discussed within the GATT, as a general problem that needed to be solved in order to facilitate the implementation of the GATT.[25] In the specific case of state-trading enterprises, the most recent notifications obtained from the contracting parties, in answer to the lengthy questionnaire mentioned previously, remain limited in number, and although more detailed in appearance, do not reveal much more about the functioning of such enterprises.[26] The situation is such that the suggestion has been made, in various quarters, that the self-incriminating procedure now in existence should be dropped in favour of the more shocking and effective 'complaint procedure' that was used for the GATT inventory of non-tariff barriers.[27] A better solution would be that which was recently adopted in the Code on Subsidies and Countervailing Duties, which provides, in its Article 7, for a 'request for information' procedure that is less distressing but just as effective as a complaint procedure.[28]

THE PROHIBITION AGAINST NULLIFICATION OF TARIFF CONCESSIONS THROUGH IMPORT MARK-UPS

Article II, paragraph 4, of the GATT, states:

> If any contracting party establishes, maintains or authorizes, formally or in effect, a monopoly of the importation of any product described in the appropriate Schedule annexed to this Agreement, such monopoly shall not, except as provided for in that Schedule or as otherwise agreed between the parties which initially negotiated the concession, operate so as to afford protection on the average in excess of the amount of protection provided for in that Schedule.

This provision, which exclusively concerns import monopolies, implies two things that are not immediately apparent. It means, in the first place, that the mark-up of an import monopoly is considered by the GATT as essentially similar to a tariff; such import mark-up is defined, in an interpretative note added to Article XVII, as 'the margin by which the price charged by the import monopoly for the imported product (exclusive or internal taxes . . . , transportation, distribution, and other expenses incidental to the purchase, sale or further processing, and a reasonable margin of profit) exceeds the landed cost'. The second implication is that the contracting parties may, if they wish, negotiate the binding of their import mark-ups. Few nations, however, have availed themselves of this opportunity; not because products subject to import monopolies have not been made the object of tariff concessions, but rather because few states apparently have considered import mark-ups equivalent to tariff duties.[29] The result is that Article II (4) has remained largely ineffective.

The case of the provincial monopolies on alcohol in Canada is particularly interesting in that respect. During the Kennedy Round, Canada had bound itself concerning the rate of duties applicable to various alcoholic products, without specifying that monopoly margins were excluded.[30] If one takes into account the monopoly margins practised by the provinces, one concludes that Canada does not, in fact, respect its obligation under Article II (4) of the GATT. Fortunately, what appears to be a misinterpretation of that provision by Canada has never given rise to any complaint by the other contracting parties, which would seem to indicate that the error is common to all contracting parties.[31] Finland, which also maintains a state monopoly on alcohol, appears to be in the same situation as Canada.[32]

Behind the inefficiency of Article II (4), there is more than an error of interpretation. The truth is that Article II (4) exceeds the limit of credibility when it claims that all monopoly margins are globally equivalent to customs duties. This ignores the fact that monopoly margins, considered as a fiscal measure, may also affect similar or directly-competing domestic products. In that case, only the difference between the mark-up of domestic products and foreign products should be considered as equivalent to an import duty.[33] As it is now, Article II (4) simply does not take into consideration the fiscal character of a state-trading monopoly. An amendment to correct that situation was proposed in 1954 but failed to receive sufficient support.[34] In such circumstances, it is not suprising to find that few contracting parties have availed themselves of the possibility to negotiate concessions on their import mark-ups, since, in practice, this may imply the binding of an internal tax.

CONCLUSION

On the whole, thus, it does not appear exaggerated to claim that the existing provisions of the GATT concerning state-trading enterprises have remained so far insignificant. A first serious defect, which may be

explained by historical reasons but needs, nevertheless, to be corrected, has to do with the limited scope of those provisions: they are
presently considered to apply essentially to state-trading enterprises
operating in developed countries. If this is a valid approach, then there
should be other provisions to deal with state-trading enterprises
operating in a different environment. Secondly, even in the case of
enterprises that operate in the context of a market economy, the
GATT does not make it clear why and when they must be considered
as state-trading enterprises and thereby distinguished from other
enterprises. Furthermore, the very idea of requesting such enterprises
to act as if they were not state-trading enterprises, that is, according to
commercial considerations only, appears illusory. The use of a self-
incriminating procedure in order to get information from contracting
parties that maintain such entities has not served the situation any
better; in fact, it has rarely given any satisfaction. Finally, the attempt
to present monopoly margins as essentially equivalent to custom
duties has simply not given the results expected. Obviously, the time
has come to undertake a review of these provisions.

It is not our purpose here to suggest a new approach to the subject.
This should come as a result of multi-faceted studies dealing with all
aspects of the problem. However, it may be useful to emphasize, in
conclusion, that if state-trading is accepted as an alternative method of
intervention of states in economic matters,[35] its treatment should
remain basically consistent with that granted by the GATT to other
methods of intervention. In that perspective, it may be queried why
the concept of injury, as used in the case of subsidies,[36] does not play
any meaningful role in the case of state-trading enterprises. In many
respects, the two problems are largely similar; and a solution along the
lines of that adopted recently in the Code on Subsidies and Countervailing Duties,[37] as previously suggested, would appear logical.

What do we find in this code? At the outset, the preamble gives the
tone: it states, in a forthright manner:

> Recognizing that subsidies are used by governments to promote
> important objectives of national policy;
>
> Recognizing also that subsidies may have harmful effects on trade
> and production;
>
> Recognizing that the emphasis of this Arrangement should be on
> the effects of subsidies and that these effects are to be assessed in
> giving due account to the internal economic situation of the signa-

tories concerned as well as to the state of international economic and monetary relations. . . .

As if the preamble was not enough, Article 8 picks up the same idea in the following terms:

> Signatories recognize that subsidies are used by governments to promote important objectives of social and economic policy. Signatories also recognize that subsidies can cause adverse effects on the interests of other signatories.

Finally, the same view is expressed again in Article 11, which concerns subsidies other than export subsidies. One can see, in those repetitive statements, the expression of a decisive choice between two approaches: rather than to try to discourage more or less openly the use of subsidies, the contracting parties have opted in favour of a realistic attitude whereby subsidies, notwithstanding their danger, are accepted as a fact of life, but are simultaneously subjected to fairly strict control, as far as their impact is concerned. Now, if the same reality persists in state-trading enterprises, why not adopt the same attitude in examining their case and pay greater attention, not so much to what they are, but to the prejudice that they cause?

NOTES AND REFERENCES

1. GATT, document E/PC/T/A/PV/14, p. 152.
2. GATT, document L/3496, p. 28.
3. These norms are to be found essentially in Articles XVII and II (4) of the GATT, to which must be added an interpretative note to Articles XI–XIV and XVIII.
4. For a more detailed analysis of the concept of 'state-trading enterprises', as found in Article XVII, see in particular J. H. Jackson, *World Trade and the Law of GATT* (New York: Bobbs-Merrill, 1969), pp. 339–45.
5. GATT, 8th Supp. BISD 142; 9th Supp. BISD 179; document L/3496, p. 27.
6. There is a wealth of research on this subject. For a short study undertaken in a Canadian perspective, see Caroline Pestieau, *Subsidies and Countervailing Duties: The Negotiating Issues* (C. D. Howe Research Institute: The Canadian Economic Policy Committee, 1976). For a more detailed and recent study, see John J. Barcello III, 'Subsidies and Countervailing Duties – Analysis and a Proposal', *Law and Policy in International Business*, vol. 9 (1977), p. 779. For a study that takes specifically into account the problems of developing countries, see M. Rom, 'GATT Export subsidies and Developing Countries', *Journal of World Trade Law*, vol. II, (1968), p. 544.

7. GATT, 10th Supp. BISD 208.

8. GATT, *Agreement on Interpretation and Application of Articles VI, XVI and XXIII of the General Agreement on Tariffs and Trade*, document MTN/NTM/W 236, Articles 9 and 11, and Annex I.

9. GATT, 9th Supp. BISD 179.

10. See, for an expression of this view, GATT, document L/3496, p. 27.

11. See, on this subject, J. M. Reuland, 'GATT and State-Trading Countries', *Journal of World Trade Law*, vol. 9, no. 3 (May/June 1975) p. 318; R. Baban, 'State Trading and the GATT', *Journal of World Trade Law*, vol. 11, no. 4 (July/August 1977) p. 334, and 344. See also GATT, document MTN/38/1–94.

12. See K. W. Dam, *The GATT – Law and International Economic Organization*, (University of Chicago Press, 1970), p. 19.

13. See, for instance, E. Mestmäcker, 'State-Trading Monopolies in the European Economic Community', *Vanderbilt Law Journal*, vol. 20 (1967), pp. 321 and 333. See also below, p. 252 and Frieder Roessler, 'State Trading and Trade Liberalization', Chapter 13 in this volume.

14. See, for instance, GATT document MTN/3B/1, Section E, general comment by the United States.

15. Although rarely expressed in explicit terms, this view nevertheless is implicit in the writings of these authors; see for instance, in this volume, such authors as F. Roessler (Chapter 13) and P. Lloyd (Chapter 6).

16. For the two opposite views, see Jackson, op. cit., pp. 346–7 and Dam, op. cit. p. 322.

17. See in particular GATT, *Contracting Parties*, 9th Session, document W/9/99, p. 4.

18. See Jackson, *supra*, note 4, pp. 345–6.

19. Ibid. p. 348.

20. Article VII of GATT, which deals with the problem of valuation for customs purposes, is now completed by a customs valuation code.

21. See I. Bernier, 'Le GATT et le problème du commerce d'état dans les pays à économie de marché: Le cas des monopoles provinciaux des alcools au Canada', *Canadian Yearbook of International Law XIII*, (1975), p. 98.

22. See, for instance, E. Mestmäcker, op. cit., pp. 342–3. See also J. E. S. Fawcett, 'State Trading and International Organization', *Law and Contemporary Problems*, 24, (Spring 1959), pp. 341–5.

23. See GATT, 9th Supp. BISD 184.

24. Article XVII, paragraph 4 (d).

25. GATT, 24th Supp. BISD, pp. 59–60.

26. GATT, document L/4623 and addenda.

27. See, for instance, GATT document L/3496, p. 27. See also R. Baban, op. cit., p. 344, on the relative efficiency of the two types of procedure.

28. *GATT*, document MTN/NTM/W 236.

29. See Jackson, op. cit., p. 336, Dam op. cit., and F. Roessler, Chapter 13 in this volume.

30. See Bernier, op. cit., pp. 132–3.

31. Canada could also have argued that the provincial monopolies were covered by the federal clause of Article XXIV (12); but considering the interpretative note to Article III, paragraph 1, the validity of the argument is at least open to doubt: Bernier, op. cit., pp. 144–5.

32. Bernier, op. cit., p. 133, note 109.
33. The problem could easily be solved by considering the mark-up of a fiscal monopoly as an internal tax coming under Article III of GATT.
34. See GATT, document W/9/99 p. 3.
35. See H. Matejka, Chapter 7 in this volume.
36. The fundamental importance of the concept of injury in the GATT is particularly obvious in Article XXIII which deals with nullification or impairment, and in Article XIX which concerns emergency measures.
37. See GATT, document MTN/NTM/W 236.

13 State Trading and Trade Liberalization

Frieder Roessler [1]

(1) INTRODUCTION

The past three decades have been marked by an unprecedented liberalization of trade among the western industrialized countries. The liberalization efforts have primarily focussed on discriminatory or protective rules which governments apply to regulate the trade of private enterprises. Some attention, however, has also been paid to discriminatory or protective measures implemented through state-trading enterprises. The purpose of this paper is to examine and evaluate the approaches to the liberalization of the trade conducted by such enterprises under the General Agreement on Tariffs and Trade (GATT), the Convention establishing the European Free Trade Association (EFTA) and the Treaty establishing the European Economic Communities (EEC).

The following section of the chapter establishes a taxonomy of trade controls and state-trading enterprises. A distinction is made between *rules*, which are abstract and of general applicability, and *measures*, which are applied in concrete circumstances to achieve predetermined results. Three types of enterprises are distinguished: government-owned enterprises, privileged enterprises and government monopolies. With this taxonomical and analytical framework established, the chapter briefly describes the main provisions on state-controlled enterprises contained in the GATT, the EFTA Convention and the EEC Treaty. Various approaches to the liberalization of trade by state-controlled enterprises can be found in these agreements: first, a *normative approach*, under which governments are obliged to follow certain rules in exercising control over enterprises; secondly, a *result-oriented approach*, which provides for commitments to achieve agreed targets through state-controlled enterprises; thirdly a *structural approach*, under which the parties to the agreement are required to eliminate, through structural adjustments, the possibility of governmental control over the enterprise. The paper examines each of these approaches in detail and discusses their relative merits.

The analysis of the different approaches to the liberalization of the trade conducted by state-controlled enterprises raises the question of whether it is meaningful, in the context of present economic policies, to subject certain categories of enterprises to special rules and procedures in the international economic agreements. The distinction between private and state-controlled enterprises was primarily made in these agreements because it was assumed that private enterprises respond only to general rules (which are necessarily public and known in advance), while state-controlled enterprises can also be directed through specific measures (which can be secret and verifiable only *ex post*). Today, however, governments in the western industrialized world have such broad discretionary powers to intervene in the economy – in particular, under industrial aid schemes – enabling the government to subsidize any enterprise in any sector for any purpose – that they can subject all enterprises to specific measures. If all enterprises can be the object of direct state control, is it meaningful to distinguish between private and state-controlled enterprises? Should the international economic treaties not be primarily concerned with the various laws, schemes and arrangements enabling governments to exercise discretionary power rather than with the enterprises that are the objects of the discretionary power? In the last section of the chapter an attempt will be made to answer these questions. The results of the enquiry are summarized in the conclusions.

(2) TAXONOMY OF TRADE CONTROLS AND STATE-CONTROLLED ENTERPRISES

In the mixed economies of the western industrialized countries, governments intervene in the economy both through general rules and through specific measures. Rules are abstract; they regulate an unknown number of future instances and the acts of an unknown number of persons. They influence, but also preserve, the spontaneous order of the market. They are generally set by parliament and are therefore subject to effective democratic control. Rules can only implement 'historical' principles of distributive justice, that is, principles which state how a distribution originated and came to be considered just.[2]

Measures, by contrast, aim at particular results; they determine the actions of particular persons in known circumstances and impair the spontaneous order of the market. Individuals are unable to pursue their goals within the framework of rules set by the government with the amount of knowledge available to them but are obliged to serve particular goals of the government which can only be determined on the basis of knowledge available to the government itself.[3] In many instances, measures are taken by the executive branch, enabling it to escape parliamentary control. Unlike rules, they can be used to realize 'end-result' principles of distributional justice; that is, principles which state to which distributional result transactions must lead in order to be considered just.

From the perspective of the international trade order, the main differences between rules and measures are the following: a rule, being addressed to an unknown number of enterprises, necessarily has to be made public before it can become effective. A measure, being addressed to one or several specific enterprises, need not be made public. Access to information on measures depends, therefore, on the co-operation of the authority taking them or of the enterprise subject to them. The conformity of a rule with an internationally agreed standard can, for these reasons, be verified *ex ante*; that is, before it has any effects. Whether a measure conforms with an internationally agreed standard can only be verified *ex post*, by examining its result. A country using rules to intervene in the economy cannot promise specific results in trade negotiations; it can only promise to create conditions favouring developments toward certain results. A government that can take measures can commit itself to the realization of more concrete objectives.

The economic orders of the western industrialized countries represent comprises between the idea of a 'nomocratic' society, in which the citizens can pursue their own goals within a set of abstract rules; and the ideal 'teleocratic' society, in which citizens have to serve specific ends determined by the government.[4] As the idea of the welfare state spread, the teleocratic element in the economic orders of the industrialized countries became more and more important. To an increasingly large extent, governments do not limit themselves to the creation of a trade order but intervene to achieve specific trade results.

If the government wishes to produce specific trade results, it must have discretionary powers to influence specific trading operations of enterprises. There are essentially three ways in which a government can gain such power over enterprises in a market economy. First, the government can acquire control with ownership. Secondly, it can grant a privilege to the enterprise on the condition that it accepts certain government instructions. The privilege may be in the form of fiscal advantages, direct financial aid, the sale of land or premises below the market value, loan guarantees, export credit guarantees, the acquisition and resale of equity at a loss, preferential government procurement, the grant of a licence to exploit natural resources, and so forth. Finally, it might confer on the enterprise an exclusive right, that is, a monopoly in the production, consumption or trade of certain goods, and make the exercise of this subject to government instructions. In a market economy, an enterprise that is privately owned and enjoys neither a privilege nor a monopoly right is not likely to accept specific government instructions. Having to compete on equal terms, it can generally only abide by rules applicable both to itself and to its competitors.

The scope of government intervention depends on whether the control is based on ownership, grant of privilege or grant of monopoly rights. Government control based on ownership or grant of privilege can only be used to subsidize economic activities; control based on monopoly rights can also be used to tax or to restrict activities. If, for instance, the government controls a wheat importing firm that competes with private importers, it can only give it instructions that lower the price of imported wheat since any instructions aimed at raising import prices would result in the displacement of wheat importation from the government-controlled importer to uncontrolled importers and would be, therefore, without practical effect. If the government granted the firm an exclusive right to import wheat, it could also instruct it to raise the price of imported wheat or to limit the quantity of wheat imports.

If the government control of an enterprise in a competitive position is based solely on ownership, the scope for subsidization through instructions to the enterprise is normally determined by the profit margin of the entity. Any instructions entailing costs higher than the profit margin would necessitate the granting of an off-setting privilege, such as government financial aid. If the government control is based on the grant of privilege, the scope for subsidization is determined by the value of that privilege. For instance, if the government offers an enterprise a preference margin in the procurement of goods for governmental purposes on the condition that it delays a planned dismissal of workers, the enterprise will obviously weigh the value of the preference against the cost of retaining unneeded workers.

The scope of government control obviously depends not only on the type of enterprise, but also on the activities of the enterprise. Depending on whether the enterprise is engaged in the production, sale, purchase, import or export of goods, the government can give it instructions that have an effect equivalent to a taxation or subsidization of production, consumption, imports or exports.

Table 13.1 summarizes the above considerations. It indicates the scope for tax- and subsidy-equivalent instructions that can be given to state-controlled enterprises, depending on their status and activity. The table has been devised on the assumption that state-owned and privileged enterprises have to compete with uncontrolled enterprises and that the monopoly enterprises are legally protected from competition. It has also been assumed that the government instructions compel the enterprise either to:

(1) continue its operations despite losses or below-normal profits;

(2) or refrain from expanding operations despite above-normal profits;

(3) or charge or pay prices that are higher or lower than the market price,

(4) or discriminate in its purchases or sales between foreign and domestic producers or consumers.

(3) STATE-CONTROLLED ENTERPRISES IN INTERNATIONAL ECONOMIC AGREEMENTS

(A) THE GENERAL AGREEMENT ON TARIFFS AND TRADE (GATT)

Article XVII, paragraph 1 of the General Agreement contains special rules for three types of enterprises:

(1) state enterprises;

(2) enterprises that have been granted a special privilege, and

(3) enterprises that have been granted an exclusive privilege.

TABLE 13.1

Scope for tax and subsidy-equivalent instructions to state-controlled enterprises

Activity of enterprise	State-owned enterprise	Privileged enterprise	Monopoly enterprise
Production	Production subsidy limited to profit margin	Production subsidy limited to value of privilege	Production tax
Sale	Export or consumption subsidy limited to profit margin	Export or consumption subsidy limited to value of privilege	Export or consumption tax
Purchase	Production, consumption or import subsidy limited to profit margin	Production, consumption or import subsidy limited to value of privilege	Consumption or import tax
Import	Import subsidy limited to profit margin	Import subsidy limited to value of privilege	Import tax
Export	Export subsidy limited to profit margin	Export subsidy limited to value of privilege	Export tax

The General Agreement does not define these enterprises and a clear definition has not evolved in GATT practice.[5] The notifications contracting parties make to GATT on their state-trading activities indicate a wide range of interpretations. Most of the notifications comprised only the activities of import monopolies. The United Kingdom also reported those of its National Coal Board, which is state-owned but enjoys no monopoly rights.[6] Poland notified the GATT that it does not operate state-trading enterprises within the meaning of Article XVII,[7] while Czechoslovakia transmitted lists of firms that export or import.[8] In general, the notifications cover only the activities of enterprises with a commercial character. The United States, however, also notified the stockpiling of strategic and critical materials, an activity undertaken by the General Services Administration for the sole purpose of ensuring sufficient materials to fulfill national requirements in an emergency.[9]

The interpretative notes to Article XVII give some idications as to what is meant by state-trading enterprise. Thus, the note to paragraph 1(a) declares that privileges granted for the exploitation of national natural resources do not constitute 'exclusive or special privileges', if they do not also allow the government to exercise control over the trading activities of the enterprise in question. One could possibly extract from this interpretative note the general idea that the Article covers only those enterprises whose trading activities are controlled by the government; and that state ownership or granting of special or exclusive privilege does not, in itself, turn an enterprise into a state-trading enterprise.

The pattern of obligations of contracting parties, with respect to state-trading enterprises, closely follows the pattern of obligations which apply to private traders. For private traders, the basic obligations of the contracting parties to the General Agreement are to avoid discrimination among other contracting parties and the imposition of quantitative restrictions. They are free to levy import duties unless they have bound them, usually after reciprocity negotiations, in their schedule of concessions. As to state-trading enterprises, the basic obligations of the contracting parties are to ensure that they follow the principles of non-discriminatory treatment applicable to private traders (which means that they are to conduct their foreign trade solely in accordance with commercial considerations, as is assumed private traders do) and to avoid quantitative restrictions made effective through state-trading operations.[10] The contracting parties are free to levy duties made effective through state-trading operations, for instance in the form of an import mark-up by an import monopoly.[11] According to Article II, paragraph 4, the mark-up must, however, not be such 'as to afford protection on the average in excess of the amount of protection provided for in the relevant schedule of concessions'. This provision is to be applied in the light of Article 31 of the Havana Charter,[12] which states that an import duty bound in a schedule 'shall represent the maximum margin by which the price charged by the import monopoly for the imported product (exclusive of internal taxes . . . transportation, distribution and other expenses incident to the purchase, sale or further processing, and a reasonable margin of profit) may exceed the landed cost: provided that regard may be had to average landed costs and selling prices over recent periods . . . '. An import tariff concession thus implies a commitment regarding the maximum mark-up of any import monopoly that exists at the time the concession is made, or that may subsequently be established.

In Article XXVIII *bis*, the contracting parties recognize that customs duties often constitute serious obstacles to trade and that tariff negotiations based on reciprocity are of great importance to the expansion of international trade. Under Article XVII, paragraph 3, the contracting parties recognize that state-trading enterprises may be operated in a manner that creates serious obstacles to trade and that negotiations, conducted on a reciprocal and mutually advantageous basis and designed to limit or reduce such obstacles, are of importance to the expansion of international trade. While there have been extensive tariff negotiations in GATT, commitments regarding state-trading operations in market economies have been exchanged only in a few instances. Thus, in 1952, Italy committed itself to a maximum mark-up of 15 per cent on wheat and rye imported by the Italian government or its agencies.[13] In the same year, France made an identical commitment regarding wheat imports by its 'Office National Interprofessionel des Céréales'. France also included in its schedule a commitment that its national tobacco monopoly, subject to certain provisos, would import 15,000 tons of lead tobacco and 1400 tons of cigarettes annually from countries other than those in the French Union.[14] It further undertook a complex commitment regarding the relationship between the selling prices of foreign and domestically produced cigarettes. The Italian and French concessions lapsed with the formation of the EEC and the creation of a common schedule for all EEC countries.

(B) CONVENTION ESTABLISHING THE EUROPEAN FREE TRADE
ASSOCIATION (EFTA CONVENTION)

Article 14 of the EFTA Convention obliges the Member States to
ensure the elimination,

in the practice of public undertakings, of:

(*a*) measures the effect of which is to afford protection to
domestic production which would be inconsistent with the Convention if achieved by means of a duty or charge with equivalent effect,
quantitative restrictions or government aid, or

(*b*) trade discrimination on grounds of nationality insofar as it
frustrates the benefits expected from the removal or absence of
duties and quantitative restrictions on trade between Member
States.

The term 'public undertakings' comprises, according to Article 14 (6)
of the Convention, 'central, regional, or local government authorities,
public enterprises and any other organization by means of which a
Member State, by law or in practice, controls or appreciably influences imports from, or exports to, the territory of a Member State'.
The definition makes it clear that Article 14 applies to both the public
procurement of goods for governmental use and to state-trading
activities, in contrast to GATT, which regulates the two issues
differently.[15]

In a series of meetings in 1964–6, a sub-committee of the EFTA
Committee of Trade Experts studied the implications of Article 14.[16]
It extended its investigation to

both undertakings controlled by statutory public boards and
companies on which the state otherwise exercises influence by
means of public law (e.g. conditions attached to concessions,
licences, privileges, etc.) and privately operated companies on
which state influence may be exercised on the basis of private law
through shareholding, board membership, etc.[17]

Based on the sub-committee's report, EFTA ministers reached an
agreement in 1966 in Lisbon on the interpretation of Article 14.

Among the salient points of the Lisbon Agreement are the
following:

> Article 14 does not prevent Member States from having any state-trading organizations they wish, provided the practices of these undertakings do not lead to protection or discrimination in the sense of the Article. . . . Any influence exerted by Member States, whether as shareholders, through board membership or in any other way on the procurement activities of the state-owned or state-controlled organizations or enterprises is subject to the provisions of Article 14. . . . Conditions imposed by the state or privately-operated enterprises or industries shall, even where no direct state interest exists, comply with the obligations of Article 14.

The Lisbon Agreement confirmed that the EFTA 'Member States are free to have any procurement system they wish, provided that it has no discriminatory or protective effects'. The Ministers agreed however on certain minimum standards for tendering procedures to be 'borne in mind together with the objectives of Article 14'.[18]

(C) TREATY ESTABLISHING THE EUROPEAN ECONOMIC COMMUNITY (EEC TREATY)

The EEC Treaty distinguishes between 'state monopolies of a commercial character', which are regulated in Article 37, and public enterprises, including enterprises with special or exclusive rights, which are dealt with in Article 90. The Member States' systems of property are referred to in Article 222. The main features of these three Articles and their principal implications will be briefly described below.

State monopolies. Article 37 (1) stipulates that 'Member States shall progressively adjust any state monopolies of a commercial character in such a manner as will ensure the exclusion . . . of all discrimination between the nationals of Member States in regard to conditions of supply or marketing of goods'. The adjustment is to be made progressively and to be completed at the end of the transitional period, that is on 31 December 1969. The provision applies to 'any body by means of which a Member State shall *de jure* or *de facto* either directly or indirectly control, direct or appreciably influence importation or exportation between Member States' and to 'monopolies assigned by the State'. Article 37 (6) gives the Commission the power to 'make recommendations as to the particulars and the timing according to which the adjustments referred to in this Article shall be carried out'.

What is meant by the requirement that the monopolies be 'adjusted' to ensure the exclusion of all discrimination? Two schools of thought developed on this issue. The 'normative' school interpreted Article 37 to mean that Member States have to ensure, through appropriate rules and procedures, that their monopolies do not discriminate.[19] It was opposed by a 'structural' school, which argued that the aim of Article 37, namely the elimination of the *possibility* of discrimination, could not be attained through rules and procedures. The decisions of the monopolies were essentially of an entrepreneurial nature, and could not be sufficiently regulated to avoid discrimination without taking from them the discretion necessary for their effecient management. In effect, no conceivable set of rules could prevent a monopoly from discriminating against imports in its sales-promotion efforts, maintenance of stocks, handling of import formalities and after sales services.[20] Article 37 should therefore be interpreted to require that the monopolies' exclusive trading rights be eliminated since only this could eliminate all possibilities of discrimination.[21]

The EEC Commission did not take a clear position on this interpretative question when, in 1969, it addressed to France, Germany and Italy a total of twelve recommendations, indicating the measures that these countries should take to fulfil their obligations under Article 37.[22] The Commission suggested, in all recommendations, that 'the best solution to achieve the purpose of Article 37 would be to eliminate the exclusive rights because the effectiveness of this solution is already now certain'.[23] This wording suggested that normative solutions, albeit not optimal, would also be possible under Article 37. The specific measures recommended by the Commission, however, seemed to be based on the assumption that structural adjustments were the only way to implement Article 37, because in all recommendations the Member States were asked to remove the monopolies' exclusive trading rights. Thus, in the case of the French potash import monopoly, the Commission recommended that the free importation of all quantities and qualities of products originating in other Member States be permitted, and that all operations necessary for the marketing of potash products from other Member States be liberalized (by granting suppliers from other Member States the right to maintain stocks in France, to establish their own distribution networks, to advertise and to contract prices freely).[24]

In the early 1970s, many European monopolies were restructured in response to the Commission's recommendation and lost their exclusive trading rights. Where the restructuring was slow or incomplete, the Commission initiated infringement proceedings.[25] Its efforts were supported by the European Court of Justice. In a case concerning an Italian-manufactured tobacco monopoly, the Court ruled that Article 37 required the abolition of the exclusive right of a state monopoly of a commercial character to import from other Member States.[26] The structural approach to the interpretation of Article 37, on which the legal literature had been divided, and for which the Commission had indicated its preference, was thus declared to be the correct one. The Commission's political and legal efforts gradually bore fruit. In 1977, it reported that: 'As a result of the Commission's action, almost all monopolies have been eliminated throughout the Community'.[27]

Public Enterprises. According to Article 90 of the Treaty of Rome, 'Member States shall, in respect of public enterprises and enterprises to which they grant special or exclusive rights, neither enact nor maintain in force any measure contrary to the rules contained in this Treaty . . . '. The main purpose of the provision is to ensure that the EEC Member States do not use their control over public or privileged enterprises for the purpose of circumventing the Treaty's rules on non-discrimination and competition, and that the enterprises themselves do not abuse their special position.[28] The Commission has not yet clearly indicated how it interprets the term 'public enterprise'. According to some authors, an enterprise is to be considered 'public', within the meaning of Article 90, if the Member State can influence the management decisions of the enterprise without having to resort to its official powers.[29] The term 'enterprise' comprises all bodies that produce, trade or distribute goods or services, but not public entities that merely purchase goods or services for governmental purposes.[30] Article 90 (2) exempts enterprises that are charged with the management of services of general economic interest or that have the character of a fiscal monopoly from the rules of the Treaty to the extent that the application of such rules would obstruct the *de jure* or *de facto* fulfilment of the specific tasks entrusted to the enterprise. However, this exception is subject to the proviso that 'the development of trade may not be affected to such a degree as would be contrary to the interests of the Community'. The meaning of this rather mysterious provision still needs clarification.[31]

According to Article 90 (3) the EEC Commission shall, where necessary, issue appropriate directives or decisions to Member States to ensure the application of Article 90. In 1975, in response to wishes expressed in the European Parliament, the Commission started to work on a directive based on Article 90 (3). The Commission's aim was to clarify the obligations under Article 90, to put itself in a better position to check compliance, and to make the financial links between governments and public undertakings more transparent.[32] The Commission found that its work on the directive was hampered by one of the problems it intended to solve: namely 'the lack of transparency in the financial links between governments and undertakings whose conduct may be influenced by governments'.[33] In its Eighth Report on Competition Policy (1979), the Commission indicated that a draft of the directive was being discussed with the parties concerned.[34]

Systems of property. Article 222 of the EEC Treaty declares that 'this Treaty shall in no way prejudice the system existing in Member States in respect of property'. The Commission has taken the view that this provision establishes a 'principle of neutrality with regard to ownership arrangements' which prevents the Member States 'from using their power to intervene in the ownership of production facilities to take measures which, if other intervention techniques were used, would be incompatible with [the EEC Treaty]'.[35] While the wording of Article 222 would suggest that it merely reserves the right of Member States to choose their ownership systems, the Commission interpreted this provision as comprising the obligation to refrain from changing ownership patterns for the purpose of circumventing EEC Treaty rules.

The Commission reached this conclusion when it reviewed the activities of a number of government-backed financial companies authorized to acquire holdings, such as the Italian 'Gestione e Participazioni Industriali' (GEPI), which was set up to put industrial undertakings facing temporary financial or management difficulties on a sound footing and to help reorganize or convert enterprises. For these purposes, GEPI was empowered to acquire, under the instructions of the Interministerial Committee for Economic Planning, temporary holdings in companies.[36] The Commission stressed, in evaluating this and similar cases, that public ownership as such, even if it was dictated – as was inherently the case – by exigencies going beyond the profit motive, would not justify bringing into play the Treaty rules on aid. This was only the case if the concrete circumstances of acquiring ownership brought out aid effects. This could be the case if:

(1) the acquisitions of holdings are used as an alternative to or a factor strengthening, traditional forms of aid;

(2) acquisitions are made of firms in liquidation which would disappear from the market without such assistance; or

(3) the purchases of holdings do not ensure normal remuneration of the capital committed or they are eventually resold to the partners at a price lower than the acquisition price.[37]

The Commission recognized that the aid effect of purchases of holdings by public agencies could rarely be determined in advance. 'Only *post facto* knowledge of the actual work of the agencies can therefore enable the Commission to determine whether the acquisitions do in fact have the effect of aid.' The Commission therefore requested regular reports on the activities of the public-holding companies.[38]

(4) COMPARATIVE ANALYSIS OF THE GATT, EFTA AND EEC PROVISIONS ON STATE-CONTROLLED ENTERPRISES

The three agreements examined in the previous section are neutral as to the systems of ownerships. Whether enterprises are owned by the state, private capital holders, workers, consumers (as in the retail co-operative shop) is, in itself, legally irrelevant.[39] The agreements are also neutral as to the maximands of enterprises. They make no distinction between the profit-seeking firm and the non-profit foundation, the small family enterprise and the low-dividend high-capital-gain corporation, the undertaking managed by representatives of shareholders and that (co-)managed by workers, even though all these entities have different aspirations and, therefore, respond differently to market signals and economic policy instruments.[40]

While the agreements are indifferent as to the ownership and maximands of enterprises, they make important distinctions as to the modes of government control over enterprises. The agreements assume that governments control the operations of enterprises mainly through general rules, that is, policy instruments of wide applicability, in particular, taxes and subsidies, and hence regulate primarily the use of such instruments. They recognize, however, that governments control trade also through specific measures made effective through state-owned enterprises, privileged enterprises or state monopolies. The agreements, therefore, subject these three types of enterprises to special requirements designed to ensure that they are not used for the purpose of circumventing the rules on general policy instruments.

Three approaches are applied in the agreements to ensure government neutrality with state-controlled enterprises. First, a 'normative' approach under which governments are to follow certain rules with regard to these enterprises. Second, a 'result-oriented' approach which provides for commitments on specific trade targets. And, third, a 'structural' approach, aiming at institutional reforms eliminating the possibility of state control. The advantages and drawbacks of each of these three approaches will be examined below.

(A) NORMATIVE APPROACH

All the agreements examined in the previous section contain rules regulating the parties' conduct towards state-controlled enterprises. In essence, these rules declare that the parties must not induce or tolerate practices of state-controlled enterprises that have effects which, if brought about by tariffs, quantitative restrictions or subsidies,[41] would be violation of commitments under the agreements.

Such international rules on state trading can effectively prevent discriminatory or protective domestic *rules* on state trading, such as laws obliging state-owned enterprises to give a margin of preference to domestic suppliers. International rules, however, are not an efficient instrument to prevent specific governmental *measures* of a discriminatory or protective nature, made effective through state-controlled enterprises. The decisions of enterprises involve many incalculable elements, such as the assessment of market opportunities, the reliabilty of suppliers, the quality of machinery, future developments of raw-material prices and so forth. It is impossible, then, to regulate in detail how an enterprise's decisions are to be taken. The international rules can only state basic standards to be observed, such as the commercial considerations standard in GATT. Because of the large element of individual judgement in entrepreneurial decision-making, deviations from an internationally agreed standard can rarely be detected. An enterprise can systematically discriminate against foreign suppliers in its decisions about what to buy, how much to stock, which goods to advertise, where to sell and so forth, and still remain within the broad range of discretion that must be granted to an enterprise.[42] Moreover, the information necessary to survey the application of the internationally agreed standard is often not publicly available since measures made effective through state-controlled enterprises can be taken secretly.[43] In short, international rules of state trading are not an

efficient means to achieve trade liberalization because they address a
process that escapes detailed regulation and close surveillance.

This approach has been applied only in GATT and there, only once, in
its early history, when France committed itself to purchase, through its
national tobacco monopoly, 15,000 tons of leaf tobacco and 1400 tons
of cigarettes annually from countries other than those in the French
Union.[44] The difficulties to which the normative approach gives rise
can be avoided through such target commitments. The obligation is
clear and compliance with its can be easily verified. There are, however, a number of legal limitations and practical shortcomings that
undermine this approach.

Under GATT, governments may not, in principle, use state-
controlled enterprises for the purpose of discriminating among contracting parties or imposing quantitative restrictions. A GATT
schedule commitment to purchase, from certain sources, a fixed maximum amount of goods would conflict with these principles as it would
involve a discriminatory quantitative restriction. Such a commitment
would only be possible under GATT if the contracting party was, for
exceptional reasons, entitled to impose discriminatory quantitative
restrictions, for instance, under GATT's balance-of-payments exceptions. The French undertaking was, for this reason, explicitly made
subject to the application by France of the GATT provisions permitting contracting parties in payments difficulties to impose discriminatory restrictions.[45] At present, however, no industrialized country is
invoking GATT's payments exceptions.

Quantitative commitments that encounter no legal limitations
under GATT are only those providing for the non-discriminatory
purchase of minimum quantities by the state-controlled enterprises.
Such commitments are doubly unsatisfactory. First, the negotiating
partners of the country making such a commitment have no quantitative assurance that they are not being discriminated against. In this
respect the problems of the normative approach remain. Secondly,
import requirements can rarely be precisely determined in advance.
Consequently, a minimum import commitment can easily turn out to
be either superfluous or distorting; superfluous when import requirements exceed the commitments, distorting when the commitment
exceeds import requirements and the state-controlled enterprise can
dispose of its purchases only by selling them at a loss.

(C) STRUCTURAL APPROACH

This approach has been used only in the EEC Treaty and there, only with regard to state monopolies of a commercial character. The ECC Treaty requires the elimination of the exclusive trading rights of such monopolies. As we have seen in the second section of this chapter, only enterprises enjoying trade monopolies can be used for the purpose of taxing or restricting trade. With the elimination of the state monopolies of a commercial chartacter, the EEC member states have lost the possibility to use direct control over enterprises as a means to limit intra-European trade.

The drafters of the EEC treaty did not extend the structural approach to state-owned and privileged enterprises. No adjustments eliminating the possibility to use the control over such enterprises as a means to subsidize production or trade are thus required.

Would it be theoretically possible and politically feasible to extend the structural approach to state-owned and privileged enterprises?

For state-owned enterprises, structural adjustments eliminating direct state control are conceivable. State ownership can be, and in practice sometimes is, separated from state control. Thus, an enterprise may be owned by the state but the surveillance over its management and operations may be entrusted to a politically autonomous board. Changes in the institutional structure of state enterprises that remove them from the realm of daily politics can have a profound influence on their behaviour. A study by Marc J. Roberts, comparing the behaviour of three private and three public power companies in the United States and Canada, indicates that the mode of control by public authorities is more critical in explaining certain observed differences in the behaviour of these enterprises than the legal rights of ownership. Roberts suggests that a public enterprise such as the Tennessee Valley Authority, which finances its budget from retained earnings and revenue bonds and whose budget does not require anyone else's approval, may be as cost-conscious and insensitive to pressures by the public or the press as a private enterprise, while the Ontario Hydro of Canada, whose budget is routinely reviewed and approved by the Government of Ontario Province, may be more vulnerable, and as a consequence also more responsive, to political considerations.[46]

Structural changes that would eliminate the possibility of state control through grant of privilege are also conceivable. Whenever governments have broad discretionary powers to determine which enterprises are to receive favours and on which conditions, they can direct specific operations of individual enterprises. State control through grant of privilege would cease to exist, if favours were distributed only on the basis of widely applicable laws that clearly define the conditions entitling enterprises to privileged treatment. The economic constitutions of states would have to ensure that subsidies of any kind be granted in the same manner as taxes are generally levied, namely on the basis of abstract laws that make distinctions between categories of enterprises, activities, levels of income and so forth but that do not permit administrations to select individual enterprises for special tax burdens.[47] The EEC Commission had made efforts to induce Member States to take steps in this direction. It has consistently urged Member States to abandon so-called 'general' aid schemes permitting the government to grant assistance to enterprises in any sector and in any region. The Commission found that aid schemes with such vague purposes as the fostering of 'general economic growth', 'the modernization of the national economy' or 'the restructuring of firms beset by adaptation difficulties' were not in line with Community requirements, mainly because the EEC Treaty permits only aids designed to support 'certain' activities or 'certain' regions and because there was no way for the Commission and other Member States to assess the trade impact of such schemes.[48] However, while the EEC Commission has repeatedly indicated its preference for well-defined aid schemes whose impact can be determined *a priori* (by looking at the law establishing the scheme) rather than *ex post* (by looking at the administrative practices under the law) it did, in its surveillance of individual aid schemes, take into account 'that the Member States may need to possess facilities enabling them to intervene in economic activity as soon as this becomes necessary, and without being bound in advance to respect certain limits as to specific industries or to specific geographic areas'.[49]

To answer the question of the political feasibility of extending the structural approach to state-owned and privileged enterprises, one must take into account that the structural approach merely aims at making impossible what is forbidden anyway.

Under the EEC Treaty, import restrictions and taxes are in principle proscribed; the Treaty's requirement to eliminate all trade monopolies is nothing but a logical consequence of the general proscription of import controls because, in a market economy, the exclusive right of the state to import cannot serve any legitimate purpose once all import controls are forbidden. No international trade agreement exists which proscribes all subsidies. Under the GATT, the industrialized countries are committed not to grant export subsidies, but production subsidies are not forbidden. Under the EEC Treaty, the subsidization of exports is totally prohibited while subsidization of production is only partially prohibited. Governments would hardly be ready to commit themselves to restructure their relations with state-owned or privileged enterprises (with the aim of making subsidization through the direct control over these enterprises impossible) as long as, and to the extent that, they have the right to grant subsidies.

(5) TOWARDS A NEW CONCEPT OF STATE TRADING

The present tendency to expect governments to take measures to attain specific results has resulted in a spreading of laws, funds, arrangements, schemes and legal relationships under which governments have broad discretionary powers to intervene in the economy. This is particularly true in the field of government aids to industry.[50] The ways in which states intervene today in favour of individual industries have, as Goran Ohlin observed, 'contributed to the blurring of the boundary between Government and the private sector'.[51] The drafters of the international economic agreements examined in the previous sections, however, believed that this boundary can be determined. Consequently, they formulated treaty provisions that distinguished between a private sector (assumed to be subject only to general policy instruments such as import tariffs and subsidies) and a state-controlled sector (assumed to be subject also to specific governmental instructions). State-trading enterprises were seen as a separate, definable category of entities, of which each country could theoretically establish a list. To make distinctions between private and state-controlled enterprises is, however, pointless if all enterprises in the economy can be given specific governmental instructions. The following examples will illustrate and substantiate this point:

Suppose a government establishes an agency with the power to grant export credits under instructions from the ministry of trade. The agency has full discretionary power to fix the interest rates to be paid by exporters. To safeguard the commercial interests of the enterprises making use of its facilities, the agency does not disclose the rates charged in individual instances. Under instructions from the trade minister, the agency begins to give preferential rates to enterprises that would otherwise have to close down, and that are located in poor regions or that export to certain destinations. While the agency was conceived to be financially self-supporting, it turns out that it suffers losses which are then covered through budgetary allocations. Or suppose the government establishes a financial agency empowered to grant loans to private enterprises and to take over, temporarily, the capital of firms in distress. While the professed aim of the agency is to speed up the restructuring of industries, it actually aids industries to postpone adjustment and to initiate unprofitable operations in politically sensitive areas of the country. In some cases, it gives assistance to start new plants on the understanding that the additional production is sold abroad. This will avoid employment creation in the assisted enterprise being offset by an employment reduction in other domestic enterprises.

Neither of these hypothetical agencies would be considered state-trading enterprises under the present international economic agreements, because they do not purchase and sell. The enterprises to which they grant conditional privileges could, however, be considered state-trading enterprises. These two examples show that the agreements' emphasis on enterprises is misplaced. It is the broad discretionary powers of the agencies, not the enterprises influenced by them, which cause the problems that the drafters of the international economic agreements hoped to alleviate when they formulated the provisions on state trading. Through the agencies, the government can secretly take specific measures that can nullify or impair the benefits expected from the elimination of general and overt obstacles to trade. The methods with which the drafters attempted to solve the problem of state trading are also applicable to these agencies. Their practices could be subjected to rules, standards and procedures (normative approach); they could make specific commitments, for instance, on capacity adjustments in industries which they control (result-oriented approach); or they could be insulated from direct governmental interference by giving them autonomous status (structural approach).

The basic conclusion to which these considerations lead is that state trading is, in today's mixed economies, best conceived of as the target-oriented direction of specific operations of individual commercial enterprises by the government and not as trade conducted by certain categories of enterprises. The laws, funds, arrangements, schemes and legal relationships that empower governments to direct specific trading operations, not the enterprises that carry them out, should be the focus of international agreements aiming at trade liberalization.

Among the practical consequences of applying such a concept of state trading might be the following: under GATT, import monopolies are subject to certain rules as well as reporting and consultation requirements. Extending the concept of state trading, as suggested here, would mean that the operations of a government agency entitled to approve or reject the conditions of import contracts would be subject to the same rules and requirements. The contracting parties must notify the products which are exported by enterprises that have been granted special privileges; governmental agencies authorized to grant special privileges, such as favourable export credits, need not report to GATT on their operations. If state trading were understood as suggested here, the reporting requirement would not apply just to privileged enterprises but, above all, to government agencies granting privileges.

(6) CONCLUSIONS

In the western industrialized countries, governments do not only provide a legal framework for the spontaneous development of trade by enterprises pursuing their own goals, but also consider themselves more and more responsible for the specific results to which trade leads. Consequently, governments have acquired extensive discretionary powers to make enterprises serve their ends. These powers arise from ownership rights and the conditional granting of privileges or monopoly rights. With the spreading of industrial aid schemes the grant of privilege has become the most important method with which individual enterprises are made to realize specific governmental targets in the trade sphere.

The main international economic agreements aiming at trade liberalization – the GATT, the EFTA Convention and the EEC Treaty – distinguish between private and state-controlled enterprises. This distinction is based on the assumption that the private enterprises' operations can only be influenced by general rules, in particular import tariffs and similar instruments of wide applicability, while the state-controlled enterprise's operations can also be directed through specific measures. As governments acquired discretionary powers to subject all enterprises to specific measures, the distinction between private and state-controlled enterprises lost its original significance. Today, it would be more meaningful to make distinctions, in international agreements aiming at trade liberalization, between forms of government intervention (rules/measures)' rather than between

objects of governments intervention (private/state-controlled enterprises). State trading should be regarded as the target-oriented
direction of specific trading operations of individual enterprises. It
should be distinguished from state regulation of commerce, not from
private trading.

NOTES AND REFERENCES

1. GATT Secretariat. The views expressed in this paper are entirely my own.
I owe thanks to Jan Tumlir for stimulating debates on the issues raised in this
chapter.
2. On the distinction between historical and end-result principles of justice
see: Robert Nozick, *Anarchy, State, and Utopia* (New York: Basic Books,
Inc., 1974), pp. 153 ff.
3. The differences between spontaneous and planned orders have been
analysed, in great detail, most recently by Friedrich A. von Hayek, *Law,
Legislation and Liberty* (London: Routledge & Kegan Paul, 1973), Volume 1.
4. These terms have been coined by Professor Michael Oakeshott. See
Friedrich A. von Hayek, 'Recht, Gesetz und Wirtschaftsfreiheit', Paul Sie-
beck (ed.), *Freiburger Studien: Gesammelte Aufsätze* (Tubingen: S. C. B.
Mehr, 1969), p. 55.
5. The United States Suggested Charter of September 1946 contained the
following definition: 'For the purposes of this Article, a state enterprise shall
be understood to be any enterprise over whose operations a Member government exercises, directly or indirectly, a substantial measure of control'. *US
Suggested Charter*, Department of State Publication No. 2598 (Washington:
1946), p. 21.
6. GATT document L/4623/Add.15.
7. GATT document L/3653/Add.11.
8. GATT document L/4623/Add.13.
9. GATT document L/4623/Add.16.
10. Article XVII, paragraph 1 (b) and interpretative note to Articles XI, XII,
XIII, XIV and XVIII.
11. This follows from Article II, paragraph 4 discussed below. See for a
detailed discussion of the interpretative issues involved: Ivan Bernier 'Le
GATT et le problème du commerce d'état dans les pays à économie de
marché: Le cas des monopoles provinciaux des alcools au Canada', *The
Canadian Yearbook of International Law*, vol. XIII (1975), pp. 108ff.
12. See the interpretative note to Article II, paragraph 4.
13. Cf. GATT, *Consolidated Schedules of Tariff Concessions* (Geneva:
GATT, 1952), Volume 5, p. 231.
14. Ibid., p. 200.
15. See GATT Article XVII, paragraph 2.
16. See 'Public Undertakings: The Lisbon Ministerial agreement explained',
EFTA Bulletin, October 1966, p. 2 ff. For a detailed analysis of the subject
see: Peter Fuchs, *Die Liberalisierung des Handels der Offentlichen Unterneh-
mungen in der EFTA: Artikel 14 EFTA-Konvention* (Universität Zürich,
1971), pp. 41 ff.

17. Ibid., p. 4.
18. Ibid., pp. 4–5.
19. See Klaus-Dieter Huth, *Die Sonderstellung der öffentlichen Hand in den Europäischen Gemeinschaften* (Hamburg: Carl Gerber Verlag, 1965), p. 288.
20. Cf. Arved Deringer, 'Die staatlichen Handelsmonopole nach Ablauf der Ubergangszeit', *Europarecht* (July–September 1971), p. 199.
21. See Hans Würdinger, 'Probleme der Auslegung des Artikel 37 EWG-Vertrag betreffend die Handelsmonopole', *Wirtschaft und Wettberwerb* (April 1965), p. 275. On the two schools of thought see also G. van Hecke, 'Government Enterprises and National Monopolies under the EEC Treaty', *Common Market Law Review* (March 1966), pp. 459–60.
22. Aurelio Pappalardo 'Die Umformung der staatlichen Handelsmonopole (Article 37 EWG-Vertrag)', *Wirtschaft und Wettbewerb* (April 1971), p. 242.
23. See, for instance, the recommendation on the French potash monopoly in: *Journal Officiel des Communautés Européennes,* No. L6/15 of 9 January 1970. The original text reads: ' . . . il apparait à la Commission que la solution la meilleure, parce que son efficacité est dès maintenant certaine, pour atteindre l'objectif fixé par l'article 37, consiste dans la suppression des droits exclusifs. . . '.
24. *Journal officiel des Communautés européennes,* No. L6/15 of 9 January 1970.
25. Cf. *Fifth Report on Competition Policy* (April 1976), pp. 100 ff.
26. Case 59/75 (Manghera).
27. *Sixth Report on Competition Policy* (April 1977), p. 137.
28. Hans von der Groeben, Hans von Boeckh and Jochen Thiesing, *Kommentar zum EWG-Vertrag* (Baden-Baden: Nomos Verlagsgesellschaft, 1974), p. 1133.
29. Ibid, p. 1134.
30. Ibid.
31. Ibid., p. 1142.
32. *Fifth Report on Competition Policy* (April 1976), p. 105.
33. Ibid.
34. Ibid.; p. 174.
35. *Second Report on Competition Policy* (April 1973), p. 107.
36. Ibid., pp. 106 ff.
37. Ibid., p. 108.
38. Ibid., p. 109.
39. See above, pp. 267–73.
40. On enterprise types and their maximands see: P. J. D. Wiles, *Economic Institutions Compared* (Oxford: Basil Blackwell, 1977), p. 63 ff.
41. In the case of the EEC also restrictive-business practices.
42. Cf. above, p. 271.
43. Cf. Gilbert P. Verbit, *Trade Agreements for Developing Countries* (New York and London: Columbia University Press, 1969), p. 137. Verbit writes: 'In practice the "commercial considerations" clause has not been a great success. For . . . it is difficult, if not impossible, for exporters to obtain the kind of information that would enable them to determine whether the state enterprise is basing its actions on purely "commercial considerations"'.
44. GATT, *Consolidated Schedules of Tariff Concessions*, Volume 2 (Geneva: 1952), p. 200.

45. See above note 12.

46. Marc J. Roberts 'An Evolutionary and Institutional View of the Behavior of Public and Private Companies', *The American Economic Review* (May 1975), p. 424. On the importance of distinguishing between ownership and custody see also John M. Montias, *The Structure of Economic Systems* (New Haven and London: Yale University Press, 1976), pp. 127 ff.

47. In many of the industrialized countries one can observe the curious phenomenon that the government discriminates among individual enterprises through subsidies but not through taxes, despite the fact that the two policy instruments are symmetrical in their effects. For an analysis of this phenomenon in Germany see Volkmar Götz, *Recht der Wirtschaftssubventionen* (München und Berlin: C. M. Beckshe Verlagsbuchhandlung, 1966), pp. 251 ff.

48. *Second Report on Competition Policy* (April 1973), pp. 101 f.

49. Ibid., p. 102.

50. For a survey of subsidy policies in various industrial countries see Steven J. Warnecke (ed.), *International Trade and Industrial Policies: Government Intervention and an Open World Economy* (London and Basingstoke: Macmillan, 1978).

51. Ibid., pp. 28 f.

Appendixes

APPENDIX I

Agricultural state trading in the OECD area and South Africa: some quantitative estimates (1976) (million US dollars)

Commodity	X/M	Australia (1)	Austria (2)	Canada (3)	West Germany (4)	Finland (5)	France (6)	Italy (7)	Japan (8)	New Zealand (9)	Norway (10)	South Africa (11)	Spain (12)	Sweden (13)	Switzerland (14)	OECD Plus / S. Africa (15)	Ti/OECD+S.A. ×100 (%) (16)
Meat (011)	X	113.1										47.9				6028.1.	0.8
Milk and cream (022)	X									101.9		2.3			9.0	2140.2	10.2
	M											2.8				1242.8	4.4
Butter (023)	X	52.9								239.4		1.6			11.1	1332.2	22.1
	M											0.1				1224.7	3.1
Cheese (024)	X	57.6							43.2	91.8		1.2				2033.0	7.4
	M								26.6			1.6				1963.5	0.1
Eggs (025)	X	11.8										7.0				441.3	4.6
	M									1.3		0.7				420.5	0.2
Fish (031)	X			519.9												3000.4	17.3
Wheat and meslin (041)	X	1131.6	2.8	1732.7		22.8			1051.0	16.8	47.4	4.4			67.7	8543.9	33.8
	M			0.2								0.1				3087.6	38.4
Rice (042)	X								0.3							946.6	0.03
	M								7.5							481.8	1.6
Barley (043)	X		7.6	550.3		6.1			259.8		10.1	2.2			68.4	1787.3	31.3
	M			0.1												1286.6	26.9
Maize	X		8.8			0.9						276.4				6403.0	4.3
	M											2.7				4831.8	0.3
Rye (045.1)	X										10.1				3.2	60.2	22.1
	M														22.7		
Oats (045.2)	X		2.8	50.9		15.1						7.9				188.1	39.3
	M															171.5	14.9
Cereals N.E.S. (045.9)	X											2.5			5.9	872.5	0.3
	M											0.3				971.8	0.6
Flour of wheat (046)	X	50.5	0.6									2.0			0.1	798.7	6.6
	M											1.4				68 9	3.6

APPENDIX I

Agricultural state trading in the OECD area and South Africa: some quantitative estimates (1976) (million US dollars) (continued)

		Australia (1)	Austria (2)	Canada (3)	West Germany (4)	Finland (5)	France (6)	Italy (7)	Japan (8)	New Zealand (9)	Norway (10)	South Africa (11)	Spain (12)	Sweden (13)	Switzerland (14)	OECD Plus S. Africa (15)	$\frac{T_i}{\text{OECD} + \text{S.A. X}} \times 100$ (%) (16)
Citrus fruits (051.1)	X									–		61.6				992.6	6.2
	M									5.2		0.2				1433.9	0.4
Bananas (051.3)	M									3.8		0.4				1175.0	0.4
Apples (051.4)	X									22.5		61.0				525.4	15.9
	M									0.4		0.1				585.9	0.1
Grapes (051.5)	X									–		19.8				251.7	7.9
	M									0.3		–				296.6	0.1
Pears (051.92)	X									0.5		17.1				134.9	13.0
Dried fruits (052)	X											4.7(a)				313.5(a)	1.5
	M											0.9(a)				342.1(a)	0.3
Potatoes (054.1)	X											3.1				836.1	0.4
	M											0.2			2.9	1062.5	0.3
Dry Beans (054.2)	X											2.9				296.5	1.0
	M											3.1				459.5	0.7
Sugar (061.11)	X	707.3								2.1						950.0	74.5
Honey (061.6)	X	8.0														35.8	28.2
Tea (074.1)	X											0.2				120.0	0.2
	M											26.0				653.3	4.0
Feeding-stuff for animals (08)	M														101.6	4729.8	2.1
Alcoholic beverages (112.1)	X		15.9	83.8		352.9	7.9		20.4		10.1			41.5	115.1	1860.6	34.8
	M																
Beer (112.3)	X			6.5			1.7							0.8		529.8	0.5
	M						0.4							5.9		398.2	3.2
Tobacco (12)	X	4.4					186.6	232.5	338.1			9.2				3076.1	0.4
	M	29.3										191.3				3053.1	32.7

APPENDIX I

Agricultural state trading in the OECD area and South Africa: some quantitative estimates (1976) (million US dollars) (continued)

		Australia (1)	Austria (2)	Canada (3)	West Germany (4)	Finland (5)	France (6)	Italy (7)	Japan (8)	New Zealand (9)	Norway (10)	South Africa (11)	Spain (12)	Sweden (13)	Switzerland (14)	OECD Plus S. Africa (15)	T_i OECD + S.A. X / 100 (%) (16)
Oilseeds (22)	X										9.7					4107.7	0.2
	M										1.4				40.8	5056.7	0.8
Silk (261)	M								111.3							203.5	54.7
Wool (262)	X									252.5						2724.3	9.3
	M										2.3					3173.2	0.1
Salt (276.3)	X							46.3								2033.2	2.3
	M		61.2					161.5								2327.5	9.6
Oils and fat (41-42)	M														41.6	3056.2	1.4

Notes: X-export; M-imports; T_i in column 16 refers respectively to exports and imports by state-trading monopolies; Column 16 indicates respectively: exports by state-trading monopolies as percentage of total exports of the OECD countries and South Africa and imports by state-trading monopolies as percentage of total imports of the OECD countries and South Africa for a given product. (a) Referring to 1975.

Sources: (i)　FAO, *Trade Yearbook*, 1976, vol. 30, FAO Statistics Series, no. 8, (Rome, Italy: 1977).
(ii)　OECD, *Statistics of Foreign Trade OECD. Trade by commodities, country summaries* (January-December 1976).
(iii)　Government notifications on state trading to the General Agreement on Tariffs and Trade.

APPENDIX 2

Examples of agricultural STAs accounting for a significant
share of world exports and imports (1974–6)

Agricultural state trading agency	Country of origin	Products	Share in world	
			Exports (%)	Imports (%)
Australian Dairy Corporation	Australia	Butter Cheese	7.4 1.5	
Australian Wheat Board	Australia	Wheat	11.7	
Canadian Wheat Board	Canada	Wheat Barley Oats	17.2 32.2 27.5	
Citrus Board	South Africa	Citrus fruits	5.0	
Deciduous Fruit Board	South Africa	Apples Grapes Pears	6.6 3.7 3.3	
Federal Alcohol Administration	Switzerland	Wine		4.9
Food Agency	Japan	Barley Wheat		13.3 9.0
Japan Raw Silk Corporation	Japan	Cocoons and raw silk		42.3

APPENDIX 2

Examples of agricultural STAs accounting for a significant
share of world exports and imports (1974–6) (continued)

Japan Tobacco and Salt Public Corporation	Japan	Tobacco (unmanufactured)		7.5
Livestock Industry Promotion Corporation	Japan	Dry milk, other milk products		5.7 / 3.6
Maize Board	South Africa	Maize	3.4	
New Zealand Dairy Board	New Zealand	Butter / Cheese	20.6 / 7.4	
New Zealand Apple and Pear Marketing Board	New Zealand	Apples	2.8	
Seita	France	Tobacco (unmanufactured)		7.3
South African Wool Board	South African	Wool degreased / Wool greased	4.0 / 7.0	
Swiss Co-operative Society for Cereals and Feeding Stuffs	Switzerland	Barley / Rye / Oats / Olive oil		3.4 / 4.0 / 9.4 / 2.1
Sugar Board (of Queensland)	Australia	Sugar	8.9	
Tabacalera S.A.	Spain	Tobacco (unmanufactured)		6.3

APPENDIX 3

Grain trading organizations in grain importing countries

Far East

Bangladesh	Ministry of Food and Civil Supplies of the Government of the People's Republic of Bangladesh
Burma	Myanma Export & Import Corporation
Cambodia	Government of Cambodia
China	China Food (China National Cereals, Oils and Foodstuffs Import & Export Corporation)
India	Food Corporation of India and Department of Food (Ministry of Agriculture and Irrigation)
Indonesia BULOG	Bureau of Logistic Affairs
Japan	Food Agency (wheat and barley)
North Korea	Korea Cereals & Foodstuffs Export & Import Corporation
South Korea	Korea Flour Mills Industrial Association (wheat) (private organization subject to government control)
	National Agricultural Co-operative Federation (barley, sorghum and millet, and corn; quasi-government organization)
	Office of Supply of the Republic of Korea (rice)
Malaysia	National Padi and Rice Authority (rice)
Pakistan	Ministry of Food and Agriculture, Government of Pakistan.
Philippines	National Grain Authority
Sri Lanka	Food Commission (flour)
	Sri Lanka State Flour Milling Corporation under authorization from the Food Commission (wheat)

APPENDIX 3

Grain trading organizations in grain importing countries (continued)

Taiwan		Taiwan Supply Bureau
		China Trade and Development Corporation Central Trust of China
North Vietnam		Agrexport, Hanoi
South Vietnam		

Latin America

Cuba	ALIMPORT	
Mexico	CONASUPO	Compania Nacional de Subsistancias Populares
Colombia	IDEMA	Instituto de Mercadeo Agropecuario
Venezuela	CORPOMERCADEO	Corporacion de Mercadeo
Chile	ECA	Empresa de Comercio Agricola
Brazil	SUNAB	Superintendencia Nacional do Abastecimento

Middle East and Africa

Algeria	OAIC	Office Algerien Interprofessionnel des Cereales
ARE (Egypt)		General Authority for Supply Commodities
Iran	FTC	Foreign Transactions Corporation
Iraq		Grain Board of Iraq
Lebanon		Cereals and Sugarbeets Office – Ministry of National Economy
Libya	NSC	National Supply Corporation
Morocco	ONICL	Office National Interprofessionel des Cereales et des Legumineuses
Saudi Arabia		Grain Silos and Flour Mills Organization
Syria		General Establishment for Cereals Processing and Trade

APPENDIX 3

Grain trading organizations in grain importing countries (continued)

Tunisia	ODC	Office des Cereales
Turkey	TMO	Toprak Mahsulleri Ofisi
Angola	ICA	Instituto dos Cereais de Angola
Nigeria	NNSC	Nigerian National Supply Company
Zambia	INDECO	Industrial Development Corporation
Europe		
Finland		Finnish State Granary
Portugal		Institute of Cereals
Spain	SENPA	Spanish Grain Service
Sweden		Swedish Agricultural Marketing Board
Norway		Norwegian Grain Corporation (Statens Kornforretning)
Switzerland		Swiss Cereals Administration
USSR		Exportkhleb
Poland		Rolimpex
Rumania		Agroexport
Czechoslavakia		Koospol
Bulgaria		Hranexport
East Germany		Dianahrung
Yugoslavia		Granexport
Hungary		Agrimpex

Source: Correspondence with J. Leibfried, Commissioner, Canadian Wheat Board, Winnipeg, Manitoba.

FRAMEWORK FOR ANALYZING PRICE FORMATION

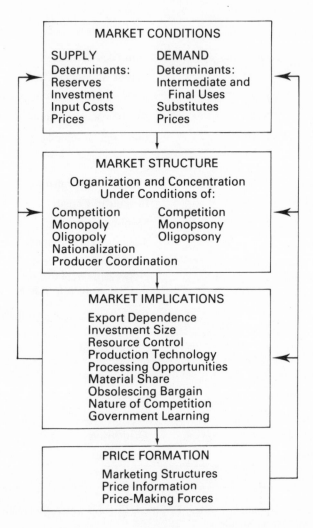

APPENDIX 4
Framework for analyzing price formation

Source: W. C. Labys, *Market Structure, Bargaining Power and Resource Price Formation* (Lexington Mass.: Heath Lexington Books, 1979), p. 2–2.

Select Bibliography on State Trading

BOOKS

J. C. ABBOTT, H. C. CREUPELANDT, *Agricultural Marketing Boards: Their Establishment and Operation*, FAO Marketing Guide, no. 5 (Rome: FAO, 1974).

R. E. BALDWIN, *Non-tariff Distortions of International Trade* (Washington, DC: Brookings Institution, 1970).

D. F. CAMBELL, 'Control of Agricultural Marketing in New Zealand', in M. J. Moriarty (ed.), *New Zealand Farm Production and Marketing*, (London: Oxford University Press, 1963).

R. E. CAVES and R. W. JONES, *World Trade and Payments: An Introduction* (Boston: Little, Brown, 1973).

W. M. CORDEN, *The Theory of Protection* (Oxford: Clarendon Press, 1971).

W. M. CORDEN, *Trade Policy and Economic Welfare* (Oxford: Clarendon Press, 1974).

KENNETH W. DAM, *The GATT* (University of Chicago Press, 1977).

JOHN FREVALS, *Grain Trade: The Key to World Power and Human Survival* (New York: Stein and Day, 1976).

DHARAM P. GHAI, *Current Problems of Economic Integration; State Trading and Regional Economic Intergration Among Developing Countries* (New York: United Nations, 1973).

BRIAN HINDLEY, *Britain's Position on Non-Tariff Protection*, Thames Essay no. 4 (London: Trade Policy Research Centre, 1972).

SIDNEY HOOS(ed.), *Agricultural Marketing Boards – An International Perspective* (Cambridge, Mass.: Ballinger, 1979).

KLAUS DIETER HUTH, *Die Sonderstellung der Offentlichen Hand in den Europaischen Gemeinschaften* (Hamburg: Claus Gerber Verlag, 1965).

J. H. JACKSON, *World Trade and the Law of GATT* (New York: Bobbs-Merrill, 1969).

D. GALE JOHNSON, *The Soviet Impact on World Grain Trade* (Montreal: British North American Committee, 1977).

HARRY G. JOHNSON, *Aspects of the Theory of Tariffs* (Cambridge, Mass.: Harvard University Press, 1972).

WILLIAM KEYSER, *Public Enterprise in the EEC* (Alphen: Sifthoff and Nordhoff, 1978).

M. M. KOSTECKI, *East-West Trade and the GATT System* (London: Macmillan for Trade Policy Research Centre, 1979).

WALTER C. LABYS, *Market Structure, Bargaining Power and Resource Price Formation* (Lexington, Mass.: Heath Lexington Books, 1979).

P. J. LLOYD, *Non-Tariff Distortions of Australian Trade* (Canberra: Australian National University Press, 1973).

PETER LLOYD, *Antidumping and the GATT System*, Thames Essay no. 9 (London: Trade Policy Research Centre, 1977).

HARRIET MATEJKA, *Trade Control in East Europe*, Thèse no. 265, Université de Genève (1973) (Genève: Médecine et Hygiène, 1978).

JAMES E. MEADE, *The Theory of International Economic Policy*, volume 2, *Trade and Welfare* (London: Oxford University Press, 1955).

J. PANGLAYKIM and I. PALMER, *State-Trading Corporations in Developing Countries with Special Reference to Indonesia and Selected Asian Countries* (Rotterdam University Press 1969).

M. RADETZKI, *Market Structure and Bargaining Power – A Study of Three International Mineral Markets* (Stockholm: Institute of International Economic Studies, 1972).

KLAUS STEGEMANN, *Canadian Non-Tariff Barriers to Trade* (Montreal: The Private Planning Association of Canada, 1973).

I. J. TETHER, *Government Procurement and Operations* (Cambridge, Mass.: Ballinger, 1975).

CHRISTOPHER TUGENDHAT and ADRIAN HAMILTON, *Oil – the Biggest Business* (London: Eyre Methuen, 1965).

JACOB VINER, *International Economics* (Glencoe, Illinois: The Free Press, 1951).

STEVEN J. WARNECKE (ed.), *International Trade and Industrial Policies: Government Intervention and an Open World Economy* (London and Basingstoke: Macmillan, 1978).

E. H. WHITHAM, *Agricultural Marketing in Africa* (London: Oxford University Press, 1972).

CHAPTERS AND ARTICLES

J. C. ABBOTT, 'The Efficiency of Marketing Board Operations', in *The marketing Board System*, (February 1974).

J. C. ABBOTT and H. CREUPELANDT, 'Les offices de commercialisation agricole dans les pays en voie de développement: Problèmes d'évaluation du degré d'éfficacité', *Bulletin mensuel, économie et statistique agricoles* (September 1967).

KEITH ACHESON, 'Revenue versus Protection: the Pricing of Wine by the Liquor Control Board of Ontario', *Canadian Journal of Economics* (May 1977).

E. L. BANKS and R. G. MAULDON, 'Effects of Pricing Decisions of a Statutory Marketing Board: A Case Study', *The Australian Journal of Agricultural Economcis* (June 1966).

ROY BEBAN, 'State Trading and the GATT', *Journal of World Trade Law* (July/August 1977).

BELA BELASSA, 'Export Incentives and Export Performance in Developing Countries: A World Comparative Analysis' The World Bank, Bank Staff Working Paper no. 248, (Washington, DC: January, 1977).

IVAN BERNIER, 'Le GATT et le problème du commerce d'état dans les pays à économie de marche: Le cas des monopoles provinciaux des alcools au Canada', *The Canadian Yearbook of International Law*, vol. XIII (1975).

J. BHAGWATI, 'On the Equivalence of Tariffs and Quotas', in R. E. Baldwin et al., *Trade, Growth and the Balance of Payments: Essays in Honor of Gottfried Haberler* (Amsterdam: North-Holland, 1965).

J. BHAGWATI, 'The Generalized Theory of Distortions and Welfare', in J. Bhagwati et al. (eds), *Trade, Balance of Payments and Growth: Papers in International Economics in Honor of P. Kindleberger* (Amsterdam: North-Holland, 1971).

J. BIERI and A. SCHMITZ, 'Market Intermediaries and Price Instability: Some Welfare Implications', *American Journal of Agricultural Economics*, vol. 56, no. 2 (May 1974).

R. N. BRITZ, 'The Marketing of South African Maize', *South African Journal of Economics* (September 1969).

KEITH CAMPBELL, 'The State Marketing Board – Relic of Prototype', *The Australian Journal of Agricultural Economics* (December 1973).

RICHARD CAVES, 'Economic Models of Political Choice: Canada's Tariff Structure', *Canadian Journal of Economics*, no. 2 (1977).

RUTH L. COHEN, 'Further Reflections on Agricultural Marketing', *Journal of Agricultural Economic* (December 1961).

STEPHEN ENKE, 'The Monopsony Case for Tariffs', *Quarterly Journal of Economics* (February 1944).

J. E. S. FAWCETT, 'State Trading and International Organization', *Law and Contemporary Problems* (Spring 1959).

GOTTFRIED HABERLER, 'Some Problems in the Pure Theory of International Trade', originally *Economic Journal* (June 1950), re-printed in R. E. Caves and H. G. Johnson (eds.), *Readings in International Economics* (Homewood, Illinois: Irwin, 1968).

ALBERT H. HANSON, 'Organization and Administration of Public Enterprises', (New York: United Nations Economic and Social Council 1968).

J. N. HAZARD, 'State Trading in History and Theory, *Law and Contemporary Problems* (Spring 1959).

A. HAZELWOOD, 'State Trading and the East African Customs Union', *Oxford Bulletin of Economics and Statistics* (May 1973).

G. VAN HECKE, 'Government Enterprises and National Monopolies under the EEC Treaty', *Common Market Law Review* (March 1966).

G. K. HELLEINER, 'The Fiscal Role of the Marketing Boards in Nigerian Economic Development, 1947–1961', *Economic Journal* (September 1964).

G. K. HELLEINER, 'The Political Economy of Canada's Tariff, Structure: An Alternative Model', *Canadian Journal of Economics*, no. 2 (1977).

E. P. HIBBERT, 'Statutory Marketing in a Developing Economy', *European Journal of Marketing* (Autumn 1972).

D. D. HUMPHREY, 'The Economic Consequences of State Trading', *Law and Contemporary Problems* (Spring 1959).

TIM JOSLING, 'Government Price Policies and the Structure of International Agricultural Trade', *Journal of Agricultural Economics* (September 1977).

R. E. JUST, A. SCHMITZ and D. ZILBERMAN, 'Price Controls and Optimal Export Policies Under Alternative Market Structures', *American Economic Review*, forthcoming.

M. M. KOSTECKI, 'State Trading in Industrialized and Developing Countries', *Journal of World Trade Law* (May–June 1978).

M. M. KOSTECKI, 'International Implications of State Trading by the Advanced Countries' (Boston: Harvard Business School for State Owned Enterprises Conference, March 1979).

J. N. LEWIS, 'Organized Marketing of Agricultural Products in Australia', *The Australian Journal of Agricultural Economics* (September 1961).

H. MATEJKA, 'State Trading: Instrument or Object of Trade Control', *Journal of World Trade Law* (March/April 1974).

ALEX F. MCCALLA, 'A Duopoly Model of World Wheat Pricing', *Journal of Farm Economics* (August 1966).

ALEX F. MCCALLA, 'Strategies in International Agricultural Marketing: Public vs. Private Sector', in Jimmeye S. Hillman and Andrew Schmitz (eds.), *International Trade and Agriculture: Theory and Policy* (Boulder, Colorado: Westview Press, 1979).

ALEX F. MCCALLA and ANDREW SCHMITZ, 'Grain Marketing Systems: The Case of the United States vs. Canada', *American Journal of Agricultural Economics* (May 1979).

E. MESTMÄCTER, 'State-Trading Monopolies in the European Economic Community', *Vanderbilt Law Journal*, vol. 20 (1967).

F. V. MEYER, 'Bulk Purchases', *Economica*, New Series, vol. XV (1948).

MOHAMED E. MOUSTAFA, 'Pricing Strategy for Export Activity in Develping Nations', *Journal of International Business Studies* (Spring–Summer 1979).

AURELIA PAPPALARDO, 'Die Umformung der Staatlichen Handelsmonopole (Article 37 EWG-Vertrag)', *Wirtschaft und Wettbewerb* (April 1971).

R. M. PARISH, 'The Costs of Protecting the Dairying Industry', *The Economic Record* (June 1962).

M. D. PELCOVIST, 'Quotas versus Tariffs', *Journal of International Economics* (November 1976).

J. M. REULAND, 'GATT and State-Trading Countries', *Journal of World Trade Law*, no. 9 (1975).

J. DAVID RICHARDSON, 'The Subsidy Aspects of a 'Buy American' Policy in Government Purchasing', *The Economics of Federal Subsidy Programs* (Washington: US Government Printing Office, for the Joint Economic Committee, US Congress, 1972).

MARC J. ROBERTS, 'An Evolutionary and Institutional View of the Behavior of Public and Private Companies', *The American Economic Review* (May 1975).

L. H. SAMUELS, 'Aspects of Controlled Marketing in the Union', *South African Journal of Economics* (March 1947).

ANDREW SCHMITZ AND ALEX MCCALLA, 'The Canadian Wheat Board', in Sidney Hoos (ed.) *Agricultural Marketing Boards – An*

International Perspective, (Cambridge, Mass.: Ballinger, 1979).

J. B. SHEAHAN, 'Public Enterprise in Developing Countries', in W. G. Shepherd (ed.) *Public Enterprise: Economic Analysis of Theory and Practice*, (Lexington, Mass.: Heath Lexington Books, 1976).

WILLIAM G. SHEPHERD, 'Objectives, Types and Accountability', in William G. Shepherd (ed.) *Public Enterpries: Economic Analysis of Theory and Practice*, (Lexington, Mass.: Heath Lexington Books, 1976).

KLAUS STEGEMANN, 'The Rationale of Antidumping Protection for Purchasing Policy', *Journal of World Trade Law*, vol. 6 (1972).

KLAUS STEGEMANN, 'The Rationale of Antidumping Protection for the Steel Industry', Discussion Paper no. 321, Institute for Economic Research, Queen's University, Kingston, Ontario (1978).

GIUSSEPINE TREVES, 'Public and Private Enterprise in Italy', in Wolfgang G. Friedmann (ed.) *Public and Private Enterprise in Mixed Economies*, (New York: Columbia University Press, 1974).

MICHELE DAWE VEEMAN, 'New Zealand Marketing Boards', in Sidney Hoos (ed.) *Agricultural Marketing Boards: An International Perspective*, (Cambridge, Mass.: Ballinger, 1979).

R. VERNON, 'Foreign Enterprises and Developing Nations in the Raw Materials Industries', *American Economic Review, Proceedings* (1970).

J. VINER, 'International Relations between State-Controlled National Economies', *American Economic Review, Supplement* (March 1944).

T. K. WARLEY, 'The Future Role of Marketing Organizations', *Journal of Agricultural Economics* (December 1963).

LESLIE A. WHEELER, 'The New Agricultural Protectionism and Its Effects on Trade Policy', in Robert L. Tontz (ed.) *Foreign Agricultural Trade, Selected Readings*, (Ames: The Iowa State University Press, 1966).

O. E. WILLIAMSON, 'Peak-Load Pricing and Optimal Capacity under Individuality Constraints', *American Economic Review*, vol. 56 (1966).

LARRY J. WIPT, 'Tariffs, Non-Tariff Distortions, and Effective Protection in US Agriculture', *American Journal of Agricultural Economics* (August 1971).

Index